WOUNDS THAT HEAL

WOUNDS THAT HEAL

Theology, Imagination and Health

Edited by Jonathan Baxter

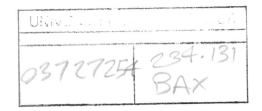

First published in Great Britain in 2007
Society for Promoting Christian Knowledge
36 Causton Street
London SW1P 4ST

British Library Cataloguing-in-Publication Data
A catalogue record for this book is available from the British Library

ISBN: 978-0-281-05830-3

1   3   5   7   9   10   8   6   4   2

Typeset 10.5/12.5pt Minion by Graphicraft Limited, Hong Kong
Printed in Great Britain by Ashford Colour Press

Contents

Contents

Contributors

Paul Avis is General Secretary of the Church of England's Council for Christian Unity. His recent books include: *God and the Creative Imagination* (Routledge, 1999); *The Anglican Understanding of the Church* (SPCK, 2000); *Anglicanism and the Christian Church* (T&T Clark, 2002), *A Church Drawing Near: Spirituality and Mission in a Post-Christian Culture* (T&T Clark, 2003) and *A Ministry Shaped by Mission* (T&T Clark, 2005). He edited *The Christian Church: An Introduction to the Major Traditions* (SPCK, 2002) and *Public Faith? The State of Religious Belief and Practice in Britain* (SPCK, 2003) and *Seeking the Truth of Change in the Church: Reception, Communion and the Ordination of Women* (T&T Clark, 2004). He is Convening Editor of *Ecclesiology*.

Clive Barrett is Priest in Charge of a deprived urban parish in Leeds, West Yorkshire. A former Chair of the Anglican Pacifist Fellowship, he is a trustee and director of The Peace Museum, the Centre for the Study of Theology and Health and the Centre for Health and Pastoral Care, Thirsk. With a doctorate in Christian peace movement history, he is a Visiting Fellow in the School of Applied Global Ethics at Leeds Metropolitan University, specializing in the history, imagery and spirituality of peacemaking, nonviolence and war-resistance.

Elizabeth Baxter began work in East London among the elderly poor. Trained in youth and community work she developed projects on housing estates in Bexhill and Corby. Working as a Deaconess from 1984 led her to become one of the first women priests, after a decade of campaigning. Following inner-city ministry and school chaplaincy in Leeds, she was invited with her husband, Stanley, to set up Holy Rood House in 1993. She has been enriched and inspired by the love of her family and continues her own research while delighting in accompanying people on their therapeutic and spiritual journeys.

Contributors

Jonathan Baxter is an artist and poet, formerly coordinator of the Centre Study for Theology and Health (2003–5) and project coordinator and lead artist for the Sheffield Care Trust Mental Health Chaplaincy Art Project (CAP) (2005–7).

June Boyce-Tillman read Music at Oxford University. Her research into children's composing has been translated into five languages. She is a composer specializing in religious music. Her work is widely sung in the English speaking world and has recently been published in a collection entitled *A Rainbow to Heaven* (Stainer & Bell, 2006). She has written widely, performed and run workshops internationally on the association between music and education, peacemaking, gender, healing, spirituality, working particularly on Hildegard of Bingen. She is Professor of Applied Music at the University of Winchester, UK, and has been a Scholar in residence in Indiana and Cambridge, USA.

Elaine Graham is currently Samuel Ferguson Professor of Social and Pastoral Theology at The University of Manchester. Her research interests include: religion, culture and gender; contemporary Christian social thought, especially urban theology; method and theory in practical theology; ethical implications of digital and biomedical technologies. Her publications include *Life-Cycles: Women and Pastoral Care* (SPCK, 1993, co-edited with Margaret Halsey), *Making the Difference: Gender, Personhood and Theology* (Mowbray, 1995), *Transforming Practice* 2nd edn (Wipf & Stock, 2002), *Representations of the Post/human* (Manchester University Press, 2002) and numerous articles and reviews. She has recently served on the Church of England's Commission on Urban Life and Faith, and contributed to its report, *Faithful Cities: a call for celebration, vision and justice* (Methodist Publishing House, 2006). She has also recently completed a volume entitled *Theological Reflection: Methods* (SCM Press, 2005, with Heather Walton and Frances Ward), and she is working on a book on the theology of technology.

Roger Grainger worked as Chaplain of a large psychiatric hospital in the north of England from 1973 to 1990. Before – and also during this time – he was a professional actor, becoming a dramatherapist in 1985. He has written a succession of books about dramatherapy, including *Drama and Healing* (Jessica Kingsley, 1990), *The Glass of Heaven* (Jessica Kingsley, 1995) and

Researching the Arts Therapies (Jessica Kingsley, 1999), and received a PhD in Dramatherapy Research (LMU, 2001). His latest book, which appeared in 2006, is entitled *Healing Theatre: How Plays Change Lives* (Trafford Publishing, 2006). For quite a few years now he has been running dramatherapy groups at Holy Rood House, Centre for Health and Pastoral Care.

Mary Grey is Professorial Research Fellow at St Mary's University College, Twickenham UK, and D. J. James Professor Emerita of the University of Wales, Lampeter. She is also Founder trustee of the NGO 'Wells for India', Patron of 'Friends of Sabeel', UK and Vice-Patron of the Centre for the Study of Theology and Health, Thirsk. Recent works include: *Sacred Longings: Ecofeminist Theology and Globalisation* (SCM, 2003), *The Unheard Scream: The Struggles of Dalit Women in India* (New Delhi, 2004), with Rabbi Dan Cohn Sherbok, *Pursuing the Dream: A Jewish Christian Conversation*, (Darton, Longman & Todd, 2005), and forthcoming, *Struggling with a Reconciling Heart: A Christian Feminist Spirituality of Reconciliation* (Darton, Longman & Todd, 2007).

Grace M. Jantzen was Professor of Religion, Culture and Gender at Manchester University from 1996 until her death from cancer in 2006. Her publications include *God's World, God's Body* (Darton, Longman & Todd, 1984), *Julian of Norwich: Mystic and Theologian* (SPCK, 1987), *Power, Gender and Christian Mysticism* (Cambridge University Press, 1995), *Becoming Divine: Towards a Feminist Philosophy of Religion* (Manchester University Press, 1998) and the first volume of an intended six-volume study on 'Death and the Displacement of Beauty in Western Philosophy' entitled *Foundations of Violence* (Routledge, 2004).

Elizabeth Stuart is Professor of Christian Theology and Director of Research and Knowledge Transfer at the University of Winchester. She edits the journal *Theology and Sexuality* and has written a number of books on contemporary Christian theology. She is a bishop of the Liberal Catholic Church International.

Brian Thorne is Emeritus Professor of Counselling at the University of East Anglia, Norwich, co-founder of the Norwich Centre and a lay canon of Norwich Cathedral. He is an international figure in the world of person-centred therapy and has made substantial contributions to the professional literature. His latest publications include *The Mystical Power of Person-Centred Therapy* (Whurr Publishers, 2002) and his autobiography *Love's Embrace* (PCCS Books Ltd, 2005). His meditation on the passion and crucifixion of Christ, *Behold The Man*, was republished in November 2006 by Darton, Longman & Todd.

Andrew Shanks is Canon Theologian at Manchester Cathedral. He has previously worked as an academic at the universities of Leeds and Lancaster; and as a parish priest, most recently in North Yorkshire, not far from Thirsk. Among his publications are *'What Is Truth?' Towards a Theological Poetics* (Routledge, 2001), *Faith in Honesty: The Essential Nature of Theology* (Ashgate, 2005) and *The Other Calling: Theology, Intellectual Vocation and Truth* (Blackwell, 2006).

Rowan Williams, born in Swansea in 1950, studied theology in Cambridge, did research in Russian religious thought and has spent many years in university teaching. He was Bishop of Monmouth from 1992 to 2002; Archbishop of Wales from 1999; he has been Archbishop of Canterbury since 2002. He has published several books on theology and Christian life and three collections of poetry. He is also Patron of the Centre for the Study of Theology and Health and the Centre for Health and Pastoral Care, Thirsk.

Haddon Willmer, jack of too many theological trades, so master of very little, taught mostly with pleasure at the University of Leeds 1966–98. Ramshackle interests include the Bible, Barth and Bonhoeffer, the futures of Christianity, of the globe and of God, Evangelicalism in England, forgiveness and politics, child theology, the Coalition for the Removal of Pimping, painting, poetic scribbling and friends, especially Hilary (married 1966) and Nathaniel.

Acknowledgements

This book owes its existence to the love and perspicacity of Elizabeth and Stanley Baxter, Executive Directors of Holy Rood House, Centre for Health and Pastoral Care. Holy Rood House was established in 1993 as a Residential Therapeutic Centre in Thirsk, North Yorkshire, and has grown to include the Centre for the Study of Theology and Health (2001) and Hexthorpe Manor in Doncaster, South Yorkshire (2005). The roots of Holy Rood House were established in 1981 under the Trust's original name, The North of England Christian Healing Trust, a Healing and Retreat House in Spennithorne, Leyburn, an initiative of the Healing Prayer Fellowship started by the Rt Rev Morris Maddocks, the then Bishop of Selby. The book is indebted to all involved in the running and management of the Trust since the time of its inception, including community members, staff members, trustees, and all manner of volunteers. A particular *salute!* to Juliet Ramsden for her indefatigable support as trustee-guide throughout the years. I would also like to acknowledge the generosity of the contributors, all of whom have given of their time freely. I am also mindful of Grace Jantzen, whose death occurred during the final edit of this book, and I would like to acknowledge her vital contribution to the fields of feminism, philosophy and theology. Heidi Walter also deserves a personal mention here, for being, among other things, both loving and irascible. Finally, I would like to acknowledge all the guests, past and present, who continue to shape the life of Holy Rood House. It is to their journey and spirit that this book is dedicated.

Introduction

JONATHAN BAXTER

———•◆•———

The essays brought together in this volume constitute part of an ongoing dialogue taking place at Holy Rood House, Centre for Health and Pastoral Care, and its educational component, the Centre for the Study of Theology and Health. Each contributor has played a vital role in defining how Holy Rood House reflects upon and engages with the Christian healing ministry, and it is a particular pleasure to bring their contribution into print.

Three of the chapters included here were first delivered as part of the annual Hildegard Lecture series (Rowan Williams, 2003, Grace Jantzen, 2004, and Elaine Graham, 2005) and the remaining chapters were either written specifically for inclusion here, or offered as representative of a contributor's ongoing dialogue with the Centre (see Brian Thorne's chapter).

As is to be expected from the dialogic nature of this volume, each contributor brings his or her own interpretation to the material at hand. Often that makes for fascinating reading, when, for example, one chapter rubs creatively against another, sparking complementary or sometimes challenging interpretations.

The diversity of voices also reflects the ecological model practised by the Centre, where the biomedical, environmental, personal, socio-political and spiritual components of health are all equally valued. Therefore the absence of specific chapters on the biomedical or economic components of health, for example, should be noted as a short-coming, as a constraint upon the present volume, and not as an intentional eclipse. That said, the emphasis upon the imagination as a reoccurring theme within this volume is an aspect of health often under-represented in the Christian healing ministry, and it is to this imaginative dimension that the present volume speaks.

1

A theology of health for today

ROWAN WILLIAMS

Archbishop of Canterbury

———◆◆◆———

First delivered in 2003 as the inaugural Hildegard Lecture, Rowan Williams' contribution sets the context for discussing a theology of health for today. Theology, he suggests, tells the story of how the world becomes inhabited by God, 'how God transforms flesh . . . by creating living relationships with himself'. Specifically, Williams argues, it is through our experience of healing that this transformation takes place. Consequently this poses a question to theology: do our theologies tell a story about healing, and if not, in what sense can they be re-imagined to do so?

* * *

> When the unclean spirit has gone out of a man he passes through waterless places seeking rest, but he finds none. Then he says, 'I will return to my house from which I came.' And when he comes he finds it empty, swept and put in order. Then he goes and brings with him seven other spirits more evil than himself, and they enter and dwell there; and the last state of that man becomes worse than the first. (Matthew 12.43–45)

One of Jesus' most powerful and memorable images is that picture of an untenanted space, an uninhabited space into which flow the forces of destruction. My argument here will be that, in thinking about the theology of health, we are thinking about how the world comes to be inhabited. Let me explain a bit further.

You'll be familiar with the way in which St Paul, in more than one letter, speaks about the flesh, that system of destructive reactions and instincts that keeps us prisoner to sin. You'll

3

remember his catalogue in Galatians, chapter 5, of the works of the flesh, beginning, you might say predictably, with more obvious physical disorders – debauchery, sexual immorality – and then proceeding to party spirit and envy and things which don't seem quite so obviously physical. And then returning, just to round it all up, with drunkenness.

The flesh, as St Paul uses that term, is, you might say, a word that describes human life minus relationship. Or perhaps human life that is not inhabited. What St Paul seems to mean by flesh is precisely the kind of thing that Jesus describes in that image of the untenanted space; flesh is human life that is not properly inhabited. Flesh is human life somehow alienated, cut off from its environment, cut off from that life of spirit which in St Paul's usage is always about relation. And if salvation is, in its widest sense, seen as the bringing together of flesh and spirit in body, then perhaps we can see how all this has some pertinence to what we mean by health.

The gift of the spirit in St Paul's theology is a gift that always brings relation. And the life of the spirit, as opposed to the life of the flesh, is life in free relation to God and generous relation to one another. Flesh, as the opposite of that, is the system of empty, untenanted life, where there is no spark to relate. So that the process of our salvation can be described as how flesh becomes something fuller, becomes body, part of the body of Christ, a temple of God's Holy Spirit. Because the Bible assumes, from beginning to end, that this material flesh is made to be inhabited and that the whole material world is made to be inhabited by the action of God.

God's grace makes people fully human, says the Church of England report *A Time to Heal: A Contribution Towards the Ministry of Healing* (2000). God's grace makes people fully human. If what I've said so far makes any sense then, what we might say is that God's grace makes flesh to be inhabited by spirit: that is, makes flesh something more than the dead lump of untenanted material which lies around for other people to fall over. It becomes a language, a system, a means of connection. And it seems to me that this is not just something we need to say about the theology of health, as if that were a little part of the map, it's something we need to say about theology as a whole.

I want to move on from that initial point about flesh and spirit to suggest that the whole business of theology is, in one sense, to trace how God transforms flesh, how God makes flesh inhabited, by creating living relationship with himself.

It's an awkward set of words, because when we speak of flesh being inhabited we can run away with the idea that something is being injected into this lump of flesh from outside, rather than what the Bible much more readily tends to assume – that the life of the body is the flowering of everything that God has made there and that the spirit and soul are bound up with that. But bear with me as I use that imagery because it helps in some other areas.

Theology is the art of tracing how God transforms the flesh by creating living relationship with God, and through that living relationship with the rest of what God has made. We could say that there is a sense in which every good human story is about how flesh is inhabited, how flesh is filled with meaning. How do you tell the story of your own life? Not simply as a record of what happened to this particular lump of fat and bone. You can tell your story as a story of how you learned to speak and to relate, to respond and to interact. In other words, you tell your story as the story of how your life, how your flesh, became inhabited.

A novel about the growth of a human self is that kind of model. The *Bildungsroman*, as the Germans call it, that evolution of the sense of self, flesh becoming inhabited. And a good life is supremely, superlatively a story about how flesh comes to be inhabited and comes to mean what had never been dreamed of.

And so for the theologian the story being told is about how flesh comes to signify God, how flesh is inhabited by the life of God so that, in relation to God, it becomes transfigured and transfiguring. 'The Word became flesh and dwelt among us', says the fourth Gospel. God inhabits flesh with the divine communication and the divine freedom itself. And that most fully inhabited, most fully, can I say, *saturated* flesh, which is the humanity of Jesus Christ, becomes the supreme instance of health, flesh and spirit in one life; the world inhabited by life. The presence of God's word, God's freedom to love and to communicate, so soaked through that piece of the human world which is Jesus of Nazareth, that the fullest possible meanings of God are communicated there

5

and the very freedom of God is acted out in that life to make us free. And once again, to refer to the Church of England report, Christ's body, says that report, is an instrument of grace. Christ's body, in the incarnate life of Jesus, is an instrument of grace.

So the story which theology tells, which theology reflects on, is, you might say, the most comprehensive version of a story we're telling ourselves and one another all the time; our own stories of how our flesh came to mean something, came to say something. As I have said, we can tell it simply in terms of the story of our lives. We can tell it in terms of a love story. We can tell it, sometimes, in terms of a therapeutic relationship. We can tell it in terms of, and through the medium of, artistic creation. The world is no longer an empty space as the story is told.

One of the most incisive records I've read in recent years relevant to this, is a book on music therapy as exercised with children and adults who have Asperger's Syndrome, and how communication is established in such situations; through long, arduous, stretching work. The filling of a kind of space, or perhaps rather the recognition that a space is already inhabited and is only waiting for that which will draw it out in freedom to communicate. Perhaps I can mention here the extraordinary series of books on Asperger's Syndrome published by Jessica Kingsley over the last five or six years. Jessica, who is an independent publisher, has made, I think, a unique contribution to the understanding of autism by publishing this wide range of studies and selected essays and testimonies on this subject.

I have already hinted, then, what sort of model of health is around here. Health is something to do with the bridging of a gulf between flesh and spirit. And often as we look at the Gospel stories of healing, as we look at them hard and carefully, we will see how healing there emerges in a situation, where as we look more closely at it, there is some sort of concealed alienation, some sort of bruised relationship. Much too simple to say, 'Jesus comes and heals sick people and that's wonderful and everyone is very glad.' That is very much the bottom line of the Gospel stories. But look harder and you can see how the act of healing in these contexts is, again and again, subtly connected with different kinds of isolation, different kinds of alienation.

If you look at the first four stories of healing in St Mark's Gospel, this comes over rather clearly. The first dramatic story is about the demoniac in the synagogue. 'What have we to do with you? Have you come to destroy us?' The empty, fleshly life, is one which lives in fear of being destroyed, and in that fear destroys itself more and more deeply, inviting in destructive forces and colluding with them. And not surprisingly when fullness appears, in the shape here of God's word in flesh, the reaction is terror.

The next story of healing is about Simon Peter's mother-in-law. Not nearly such an obvious one, you might think, and yet there, what we see is how relationship with Jesus flows over into a healing relationship with those around those related to Jesus; how the work of Jesus creates a network, a set of connections.

With that in mind, moving forward to the next story of the healing of the leper, we have most painfully obviously the case of someone whose sickness is utterly bound up with exclusion, who is not permitted to be part of a worshipping and thanking community. His healing, therefore, is very much a matter of integration into the life of a community that praises God. And when, in the last of this quartet, the paralytic is let down through the roof by his friends, Jesus' first response is a word of forgiveness; as a recognizing that what is there on the surface is somehow bound up with an inner alienation, fear or guilt.

In all these stories and in many, many more, what we have in Jesus' healings seems to be restoration of relation, inclusion in community, the bridging of a gulf between spirit and empty or alienated flesh. These people, as they are healed or exorcised, come to be places inhabited by love, by thanksgiving, by peace, by the sense of absolution. So healing, in these stories is, as I've suggested, more than simply the act that brings physical health to the midst of physical sickness. It's a point that the Gospel narratives make, in various ways, again and again. Somewhere in the background is a brokenness, an emptiness that needs to be addressed. And the act of healing frees the person to express what they are made and called to be, which is members of a community that lives in gratitude and in praise; members of a community in which flesh gives voice to spirit and, in so doing, creates further networks of healing, integrating relation.

Two other stories give some extra perspectives which just fill that out a little further. One is St Luke's story of the ten lepers who were healed and the one who returns to give thanks. He is told that his faith has made him whole because the act of thanksgiving is the end of the story of healing. That person is again a part of a community which gives thanks, which utters praise, which celebrates and which therefore fulfils what human beings are made to be.

And the other, darker story, is the one which appears after the narrative of the Transfiguration in the Synoptic Gospels; the man with the epileptic son who waits at the foot of the mountain while the disciples try, without success, to cast out the demon. A demon which, says the father, casts the boy into fire and water, as if the inner emptiness of diabolical action is a kind of anger with the body, the deepest rupture of all when spirit is angry with body and has to be reconciled.

Now those are the principles on which I think we can proceed to think through a little further, not only what a theology of health is about but perhaps, as I've already hinted, what theology itself is about. Let's stay just for a moment with what health and healing are about.

This vision of health as some kind of reconciliation of flesh and spirit, the making of flesh to be inhabited by spirit in life-giving relationship with God and others, that sense of health can, of course, take us in two directions as we think about healing.

Of course it has to do with physical healing and there's no way around that in the Gospels, nor should there be. Jesus did actually make sick people better in a perfectly simple and straightforward sense according to the Gospel narratives. And let's not get too complicated about that because the reconciliation of flesh and spirit is, as in those stories that I've mentioned, very deeply bound up with restoring a person's suffering from different kinds of alienation to that place where they are free in their flesh to praise God in community. And that, in these cases, requires them to be made whole in a simple, physical sense. But as we understand this theologically we also see the possibility of understanding healing in different ways.

Reconciliation with the body can take many forms and I don't think it is at all an evasive way of looking at this to say that healing, therefore, is potentially about reconciliation with a body that is not going to 'get better'. There are reconciliations and liberations, as we know, to be made within a situation which, physically, may not change much. And that's what people learn when they minister with the terminally ill. It's what people learn when they minister with those who live with long-standing, continuing disabilities, as we call them. We know that there is a healing there that has to do with an inhabiting of the body, a freedom within the body which may be dying, mortal, limited, pained, in all kinds of ways.

What is common, both to the more obvious kind of physical healing and to that kind of reconciliation with the conditions of the body, is that, again and again, healing is what makes it possible for an embodied spirit to praise God in community with other embodied spirits. That may equally be material healing or simply a sense of how to inhabit a body which is dying, limited and suffering.

It's impossible to generalize beyond that, I believe, and woe betide us if we do; woe betide us if we try to say every real healing is really a physical transformation or every real healing is some kind of inner transformation. I don't think either of those will do. I don't think that the New Testament lets us get away with either of those reductions because of the way the stories of healing are told; never just the solution of the physical problem, but bound up without addressing bruised, limited or damaged relationship, and bound up with the inhabiting of what could be a dangerously empty space. It also shows us how the imagery of healing can relate to the whole agenda of how we grow and develop and become *holy* (a related word of course) as persons.

Sin, as St Paul seems to see it, certainly in Galatians 5 but in other places too, seems very much to be about uninhabited flesh, the flesh used in a meaningless, a destructive or an isolating way, and our simple habits, things that keep us prisoner in our relation with God, the things that set a ceiling on our growth towards God; these have a great deal to do, I believe, with that sense of uninhabited flesh.

I can't remember who it was who first said, alarmingly, that by the age of 40 you have the face you deserve – a very sobering thought, as you look in the mirror. But that half-serious observation reflects something, in fact, very profound about how we are with one another and the difference between inhabited and uninhabited faces. The poet, W. H. Auden's remark, about private faces in public places being wiser and nicer than public faces in private places, bears on this also! When you're with someone, are you seeing in them an inhabited face? Those of us who habitually have to speak in public may very well ask ourselves awkward questions about this. Faces can look uninhabited because they are working at a shallow level, at a protected level, even at a destructive level. And we learn a great deal simply from looking at faces – the instinct of the Eastern Orthodox Church that our own holiness is enriched by looking at the faces of the holy is a very sound instinct. When I think of those people that I've known who are most obviously holy throughout my life I think of faces that look, in the best sense, lived in.

So I don't think it's necessarily some kind of evasion to suggest that there is more to this business of theology and health than simply treating healing as a demonstration of divine power in solving physical problems. It's not how the Gospels tell the story, it's not the picture of humanity that the New Testament and, indeed, the Old Testament as a whole would give us.

I see this as leading us towards a whole way of looking at theology itself – the art of tracing how God transforms flesh by creating living relationship; theology, therefore, as a discipline that traces the process of how the world gets to be inhabited. After all, the biblical story itself begins with a situation in which the world is empty, waste and void. God, mythologically speaking, rubs his hands and says, 'This void will be inhabited.' History begins and the world comes to be a system of relationships and of means. Theology traces how the world in general, and human history in particular, and your human body and mine in even more particular, come to be inhabited. And we can speak of healing as the means of this, just as we can speak of repentance as a means for this to happen, or of conversion as a means for this to happen and of transfiguration as that which holds it all together. So that healing aims at what theology deals with: a spirit-inhabited body or a body becoming spirit, inhabiting a world and so transfiguring the world in and through Jesus Christ. Because Jesus Christ's inhabiting of the world and the body for the sake of healing in the broadest sense has made that possible for us.

Ultimately it's not just that God has made a world to be inhabited, but that God has made a world which *God* purposes to inhabit and which in some sense God does already inhabit in that wisdom, that beauty, that order, that alluring wonder which is there in our environment. God is already inhabiting what has been made but the task that God undertakes in our human history is, you might say, the harder one of inhabiting the thoughts, the feelings, the reactions, the passions, the grief and the exhilaration of very contingent and messy human beings like you and me. And the pivotal moment is when God fully and unequivocally inhabits that life which is Jesus of Nazareth, that death and that resurrection which belong to Jesus of Nazareth and which make all the difference to your body and mine so that our own inhabiting of the world changes.

So this is where we move on to how important it is to link healing, in what can sometimes seem a rather narrowly focused sense, with everything we want to say about the gospel. I've been suggesting, in effect, that the Good News the gospel tells us is that, first of all, the world is inhabited by its maker; second, that the maker of the world has made it possible for us to inhabit the world more fully, more deeply, more joyfully than we could ever have possibly imagined. That's one way of expressing the gospel. But that inhabiting of the world involves something more than simply healing in the narrower sense, it involves our self-knowledge, it involves our art and our science, it involves our labours for justice, because all of these are about inhabiting the world. A world in which there is no hunger and thirst for justice would be a world of flesh. We would, so to speak, be sitting next to one another 'uninhabited'. We would have no passion, no spark of relation with one another which made us hungry and thirsty for justice. A world without art would be, again, a world in which flesh sat on its depressing own, one in which we would feel no passion to discover how the environment is inhabited by God's glory and reflected in word and in image.

I mention self-knowledge as well, which sounds a strange thing to bring in here. But I believe it's really quite an important dimension of this. The gospel tells us that we can inhabit our own lives and our memories – come to terms with, be at peace with ourselves, remember who we are without pain and alienation – because we trust a forgiving God. That, too, is part of the gospel, that, too, is part of inhabiting the world. And of course, above all, that has to do with the way in which we learn to inhabit the world in prayer – prayer which is not, in spite of quite a lot of encouragement to think otherwise, an activity of something that goes on outside the body but prayer which is, essentially, the action of an embodied spirit. Remember the phrase I used earlier on about embodied spirits praising God in community with other embodied spirits. That's where prayer begins and ends. We are slowly becoming aware of the way in which we learn to 'be' our bodies as we pray, to attend to our bodies as we pray and to be conscious of how they inform the desire and the openness of prayer. It is good to know that the tradition represented by Hildegard and others has helped us recover that in these last couple of decades.

Lest you think this is just some kind of eccentric aspect of Christian piety or Christian theology – and some do – remember what St Teresa of Avila, a standard orthodox Catholic mystic after all, has to say about this. She describes the process by which at the beginning of your life of prayer, you are mostly aware of disorientation. You don't know quite what's going on and strange things may happen in your body and you may feel that you're not in control or you're out of it. But as you become accustomed to God, as you become more deeply at home with God, prayer is something that happens from where you are. Teresa, with typical acidity and humour, describes her memory of the day when she decided she no longer wanted to be dead (the feast of St Mary Magdalene in 1560), when she realized that some kind of breakthrough had occurred in her life of prayer which made it possible for her to say, 'It's here and now that I need God. It is in this body and in this place.' So she speaks about walking with God among the pots and pans in the kitchen and she realizes that the vocations of Mary and Martha are not quite as far away as she once thought; 'As this body, speaking, moving and acting, I am praying, and the journey has been back to that starting point here in the present moment.' And that too, I suggest, is part of the story that theology tells and which a theology of health, in particular, will bring to the fore.

So in this brief reflection I've tried to express the sense that I have of the work that's been done at Holy Rood, which goes on being done, and how it asks questions, both of what we think of health and what we think of theology. It asks questions of a view of health that is narrowly functional, it asks questions of a view of healing that is simply about making things better for individuals. It is in that sense very closely bound up with the theological content of this Church of England report which I've mentioned once or twice. The work done here at Holy Rood House makes those connections that I have mentioned – with the arts, with therapy, with the labour for justice; and, in so doing, puts the question to theology itself: Is theology a story of healing? In what sense can theology be re-imagined as a story about how peace is made between flesh and spirit, a story of how God's inhabiting of the world in creation, redemption and sanctification bridges that gulf which opens up when we're not looking between flesh and spirit? It's often quoted, and I make no apology for quoting it again: the Russian theologian Vladimir Lossky said, 'What do you say if you're asked what the Holy Spirit looks like?' His reply was, 'You look at holy people.' That's to say, you look at inhabited faces, faces that have stopped being flesh in that negative sense with which we began, the untenanted, the empty space, where relation doesn't happen, the spark doesn't kindle, where there is a kind of deadness and a kind of isolation which makes us less than human.

God has made us to live as material beings in a material world and has made us, therefore, as creatures who have to learn how to live in our world. Because we have intelligence and love and imagination, our living in our environment is a story, not just a given fact. The story of our salvation is the story of that learning and that teaching by the God who brings the very divine life itself to inhabit our world – to touch, to heal, to promise and to transfigure. So, with I hope all of you here, I want to wish every blessing in the years to come for Holy Rood House and for that work which the Church (not just the Anglican Church) needs desperately to recover. A sense that the gospel is about healing, about telling effectively, powerfully, transformingly the story of how God inhabits this world, telling it in words and thoughts and theology, telling it also in what we do in our work for justice, in our arts, in our care and our pastoring. Remembering that one of the greatest paradoxes of the Christian faith is that we only learn to live in heaven in the presence of our maker, saviour and lover when we learn to live on earth in the here and now, inhabiting the space in which God has placed us.

13

References

A Time to Heal: A Contribution Towards the Ministry of Healing. Church House Publishing, London, 2000.

For books on autism and Asperger's Syndrome published by Jessica Kingsley, see <www.jkp.com/catalogue/index.php/cat/autism>.

2

Beloved community: a glimpse into the life of Holy Rood House

ELIZABETH BAXTER

———◄•◆•►———

Developing what she calls a 'threshold theology', Elizabeth Baxter reflects upon the healing journey as undertaken at Holy Rood House, Centre for Health and Pastoral Care. Emphasizing, in particular, community accompaniment, rites of passage and the indwelling of the divine, Baxter weaves together the healing stories of both guests and staff with the socio-political challenges that shape and reshape the community's therapeutic and theological practice. A particular emphasis upon the 'wounded healer' is central to Baxter's vision.

* * *

> Joy is peace dancing,
> Peace is joy resting
> (January 2001)

In this chapter I shall be referring to what I call a 'threshold theology' arising from the praxis of Holy Rood House.[1] The indented quotations are from pieces written by guests who have shared their lives in the shaping of the life of the house,[2] and prayers written for the liturgy[3] that have sprung from the therapeutic work. As Philip Sheldrake argues, 'the building is a doorway or access point and its harmony is represented . . . by the degree to which it fulfils this [worship] function – that is its beauty, its harmonia' (Sheldrake, 2001, p. 54).

The porch

Come and journey with me to this community where we tread boldly with anticipation towards our own harmonia, our own wholeness, our healing within community. We begin by stepping through and over the porch, which holds significant symbolic resonance for this threshold theology. R. S. Thomas's poem, 'The Porch', stands as poetic witness, speaking of transitional space; a place for the traveller who 'kept his place there for an hour on that lean threshold, neither outside nor in' (Thomas, 1995, p. 326). I see the porch of Holy Rood House acting as a metaphor not only for the work of the community but also for the work and movement of the divine. Here is transitional space where vulnerabilities meet and embrace. Here hope is realized and the interface of safety and risk takes place. Here is a liminal place, the state of 'betwixt and between' (Ward and Wild, 1995, pp. 2–3). It is this threshold of liminality, this boundary place of wounded healing, where the Wounded Healer is not only present, but in process, and at a place of becoming. For individuals the experience of this in-between place is usually present before arriving at Holy Rood House. It is sharpened by the literal crossing of the threshold as people find courage to address issues in their lives preventing them from moving on in their well-being. There is a sense of anticipation for new beginnings. People find themselves stepping into hope and discovering the hopefulness abiding within them, leading them towards radical action. Dwelling on such a threshold can be threatening and risky, yet creates new energy, making connections for change and justice. Mary Grey refers to a 'spirituality of epiphanies of connectedness', a way of healing fragmentation and brokenness, referring to God as 'the power of crossing over' (Grey, 1997, p. 20).

This 'crossing over' is very important in the work of the community, for it is here that we meet the threshold once more where God is discovered as the very action itself, the movement from one place to another. In and through this crossing over we find ourselves empowered for love in action for our own journeys and the journeys of others made possible through relationship. The relational dynamic between all who share the life of the community is held within an environment of natural beauty and changing seasons. Life-giving thresholds of becoming and the realization of hopeful dreams begin to flourish. Such 'power in relation' (Heyward, 1982, p. 41) is enabled through something quite profound happening within the very building itself. We therefore tread gently because 'the house serves as much to reveal

16

and display as it does to hide and protect . . . as [h]ouse, body and mind are in continuous interaction' (Carston and Hugh-Jones, 1995, p. 2).

That which is held safely within bricks and mortar also helps us to give ourselves permission to feel unsafe as we dare to drop our defences, touching a deeper inner threshold, knowing we are held, accepted and beloved. Those of us who have committed part of our lives to this community, experience the joy and wonder of seeing life transformations happening before us and even despite of us. This experience enriches and transforms our own lives and faith journeys. There is something here to do with 'place' becoming 'home', and hospitality being the key to this.

Home and hospitality

I will never forget walking in through the front door and the feeling of a blanket of peace, love and calm completely enveloping me.

(July 1997)

Entering Holy Rood House we find ourselves in a home, previously home to a community of sisters[4] and presently home to a small residential community welcoming residential and day guests. Creating home lies at the heart of the work of Holy Rood House in Thirsk and Hexthorpe Manor in Doncaster.

In his essay, 'The homecomer', written in 1945, the social theorist, Alfred Schutz, wrote that the idea of home is central to human experience, not simply as a place, but as a state of being where issues of identity, belonging and origin coalesce (Schutz, 1964, pp. 106–119; cf. Richard, 2000). I would argue that the movement towards this state of being is an integral process and journey wherein lies the discovery of God, who is our home. As a community, we engage with this process on different stages of our journey, learning from one another. Inclusion and safe space are essential to this but may require tough decisions. The welcoming of strangers across the threshold is sometimes a painful and threatening experience as it 'may lay bare both the pain and inadequacies of our own lives' (Pohl, 1999, p. 118). For example, we are not able to provide nursing care or hospitality for someone who is going to create an unsafe space for others, or be too unsafe themselves. Seeking to be a welcoming community is challenging as we try to break away from concepts of them and us, or outsiders and insiders, or community members and non-community members. I find it helpful to imagine a pond where a stone is thrown into the centre, sending out ripples, where I may choose or find myself at any place on any circle at any time, in the centre or on the margins, looking inwards or outwards. I feel held within these moving threshold spaces of well-being, home and belonging. I can learn to 'be' and 'become' and can express my 'longing' for others to find their belonging too.

The community is shaped by the varied and rich experiences of people who share its inclusive witness and celebration of difference. The phrase 'I was a stranger and you welcomed me' (Matthew 25.35) raises questions of human identity, as hospitality means 'valuing the strangeness of the stranger' (Palmer, 1981, p. 12). The community is enriched and the common life enhanced as we live within a framework of mutuality and friendship while moving across new thresholds within therapeutic boundaries. Support systems, including professional supervision and prayer, become part of this framework. It is through the stranger that we view ourselves, our world and the divine. Compassionate accompaniment needs to be experienced as genuine, empowering and life-enhancing, and not patronizing or controlling, for 'hospitality is not a subtle invitation to adopt the lifestyle of the host, but the gift of a chance for the guest to find his [sic] own' (Nouwen, 1987, p. 51). This process sometimes leads to a role reversal, particularly at Hexthorpe Manor, as previous guests become the hosts, welcoming others to their new home. This is reflected in our liturgy.

> In Christ
> you sit as the guest
> at the table of the stranger.
> In Christ
> you stand among us as host and guest
> at the heart of this community.[5]

A mutual process of acceptance presents a challenge, not least for those who find themselves having to accept those who welcome and accompany them on their journeys! However, we recognize, as one guest wrote, how 'the unconditional acceptance has been a life-saver' (November 1998). Such acceptance lies at the heart of the thresholds we cross together. But it is also acknowledged that acceptance to live together in a community cannot always be unconditional, as any of us may become too unwell and unsafe. Nevertheless, a compassionate response is always called for and may be part of an ongoing and painful process. I would advocate the need for tender and attentive care, for in such vulnerable moments we may come close to where the divine is to be found.

Being part of a community becomes important as a way of offering the support, compassion and listening to each other that is required for growth. This enables us to find our own value, leading to a sense of belonging and homecoming, that sense of home converging into a sense of God who is 'at home among us' (Heyward, 1989, p. 33). This is especially important to those who have felt themselves to be, or have been told they are, 'out of place'. Individuals or groups who do not fit into the accepted norms of present-day society or within the Church become displaced persons, and welcome, acceptance and belonging, and a reassurance of solidarity and work towards justice, are all crucial to their well-being and the possibility of knowing them-selves beloved.

> God of the displaced
> you weep with those who long for home,
> you laugh with those who are united.
> Through tears and laughter
> help us to hear your voice.
> Through the dreams of children
> teach us your ways of justice.[6]

Beloved community

> I came desolate and bereft
> I found safety and peace
> A place where I could be me
> Where there is no judgement or condemnation . . .
> I have found hope where I thought there was none . . .
> (February 2001)

The community expresses its life within a healing story, that of the Christian narrative, engaging with the questions: What is Christian healing? How is the Christian healing ministry expressed today? And how may Holy Rood House support this ministry? Discovering the presence of Love among and between us is crucial to this engagement and is discovered through vulnerability. We have to be prepared to work with the 'edgeless love' Gillian Rose wrote about, commanding 'the complete unveiling of the eyes, the transparency of the body' (Rose, 1997, p. 98). Such an embodied process challenges boundaries and touches deep places of human anguish. Ideas of love may have been distorted through abuse, neglect and violence. Love may seem to have vanished for someone tumbling into a world of losses and bereavements. Religious systems may have led to guilt, fear and an underlying sense of inadequacy, internalized self-loathing and evil. It continually amazes me how people so wounded and broken-hearted are still able to find within themselves the possibilities for change. The courage found to step over the threshold is a constant reminder of the inner strength, wisdom and capability of the human being. The community encourages people to build on the glints and glimpses they discover within themselves which drive them forward towards hope and their own well-being. And the community, in turn, has the privilege of being part of that movement, re-affirming the community as beloved. The tender threshold experiences that guests and hosts share together can create a space of divine presence that brings hope and healing to the most fragile of situations: 'We have been on holy ground . . . we have felt loved' (n.d.).

Martin Luther King Junior used the term 'beloved community', calling it 'an experiment of love' (*A Testament of Hope*, p. 18, cited Welch, 2000, p. 81), and this idea is developed by Sharon Welch as 'the matrix of communal resistance against the injustice of structural evil' (Welch, 2000, p. 160). In order to be a beloved community and to resist injustice, we seek to be a listening community, in the counselling process, around the meal table, in solitude, or within more formal structures such as the research and conference work where making connections is paramount. The community becomes a place of storytelling where each person's story is valued and nurtured as a story of the beloved.

The work of the community helps to create an environment where we may find our voice and name ourselves, our pain and our hope. This takes time, courage and risk, and even the process towards that path of communication is unique and sacred. Here is an inner space experienced by the beloved and respected by the community. The non-verbal naming of pain and hope is often expressed through the therapeutic arts, where, in the company of trained and compassionate therapists, individuals are able to release inner emotions and suppressed memories through the use of materials, space and movement, or through ritual in the Chapel or gardens. These are deeply embodied, fleshed out threshold actions, when the body speaks and the senses become acute.

Therapeutic community

I am still on the journey,
thank you for accompanying me and allowing the 'me' to emerge.
(October 2001)

The creation of safe or safer space is the key to commencing or continuing a therapeutic journey, and as the journey progresses a moving and flexible space of response and empowerment is needed where pain is not denied and where healing is located in brokenness. Working within and through pain challenges contemporary culture and quick-fix definitions of healing that many visitors may have already experienced.

The rejection of and projection on to whole groups of people by society and often by the Church is the cause of much stress and distress presented by people coming to Holy Rood House. The community needs to be inclusively embodied at its heart, therefore always theologically reflecting on the implications of diverse human experience. It then becomes more available for people from differing cultures and circumstances to find their way and to share in and shape the life of the community with sensitivity and openness towards the diversity of human living.

While some boundaries are being broken down in the community to create more porous and life-giving thresholds, other boundaries need to be maintained for a creative and safe space where therapeutic work becomes an integral part of the whole; making connections with spirituality and creating the life-giving thresholds within which guests and staff may flourish. One guest wrote 'I came in need of peace and tranquillity. It has been a revelation I cannot express in words of gratitude I feel for the love and care, and the spirituality I have received' (September 2001).

Many people crossing the porch seek to put the responsibility for their healing on to a God they understand to be all powerful, whereas within this therapeutic community[7] people are encouraged to find their own wisdom and discover Christ the wisdom of God (1 Corinthians 1.24) accompanying their healing process. The discovery of their own resources for healing is often cause for great relief and freedom from systems that have kept them caught in their ill-health and disempowerment.

The biblical image of Wisdom/Sophia at the crossroads is particularly helpful and inspiring for women, who discover a threshold image with which they may identify: 'Does not wisdom call, and does not understanding raise her voice? On the heights, beside the way, at the crossroads she takes her stand' (Proverbs 8.1–2).

For women and men whose images of God may have been the cause of guilt, fear or disempowerment, a safe enough space to re-image God may be found through art, creative writing or quiet meditation and prayer. The community takes care of language and symbol, providing creative possibilities within which people may find their own way into prayerful journeying. The spirituality of the community gently encompasses all areas of the house and an open approach enables people to maintain their own integrity, to continue their search for spiritual identity, to question and struggle with issues of belief and to find their faith nurtured and strengthened.

As the community provides space for the spiritual and therapeutic process to become a natural part of mutual relationships, the listening process, listening to oneself, the other, the earth, and being listened to, helps enable people to travel across the threshold from containment into places of loss. For this to happen we need to know how compassion and passion are felt in the body and to experience a 'shiver of solidarity' (Mollenkott, 1993, p. 162) leading towards compassionate action in the midst of loss and pain.

June Boyce Tillman suggests that Hildegard of Bingen's image of God as a counsellor of all souls (Opening antiphon: 'O pastor animarum', cited Boyce-Tillman, 2000, p. 43) may have been a response to her lost childhood. Similar losses have been experienced by many who find their way to the house and the idea of God as counsellor becomes a valuable notion to work with. Hildegard's journey took place within a praying and creative community and was expressed for her through music, art, nature and theology, all of which find their echo within our therapeutic journeys. The Centre for The Study of Theology and Health's Annual Lecture is named The Hildegard Lecture for this very reason.

Paradoxically, then, the strength of Holy Rood House is its daily engagement with weakness and vulnerability of all who live and work there, identifying with a vulnerable God in process with the community, accompanying therapeutic journeys towards well-being as wounded healers (cf. Nouwen, 1994). Lisa Isherwood's reflection on Rita Brock's notion of 'broken-heartedness' develops the theme of wounded healer and she argues that 'divinity is found lying in the heart's fragility – we are vulnerable . . . we are, as Jesus was, broken-hearted healers. The only way to heal both others and ourselves is in and through our redeeming vulnerability' (Isherwood, 2001, p. 55). We recognize vulnerability as a process through which we find our healing, rather than a place of victimization that holds people into their place of pain. I see this as an important threshold experience to engage with, as Jesus did on so many occasions, culminating with his Gethsemane experience and abandonment on the cross. The deeply embodied threshold experiences of Jesus were expressed through homelessness, hunger, tears, sweat and torture, and many guests identify with such embodied realities and thus with the vulnerability of Jesus and a disabled God (cf. Eiesland, 1994). Rather than causing hopelessness, this gives cause for hope as the Christian promise of new life and justice is expressed through the love, liturgy and liberation of the community.

This theme of liberation is taken up in the community's Christology. Here we witness incarnation, crucifixion and resurrection played out in the community at large: in the chapel, therapy rooms, and privacy of a person's room and heart. For brokenness and loss of innocence is part of the experience of therapeutic community. A metaphorical threshold experience for many guests can be seen within the Easter Saturday imaginal. The waiting time both within and around the symbolic enclosure of the tomb, where much inner work is taking place and the grief process is being realized and travelled, may be an integral and embodied transitional performance experienced before the liberation promise of Easter Sunday. The therapeutic community acts as a witness to this process, also played out in the gardens through the changing seasons, as the barrenness and harshness of winter leads into signs of spring and new life. The therapeutic process may include engagement with the Christian story and stories of the earth. This leads to hope and empowerment for change following feelings of fear, abandonment and absence, both of self and of God. Grieving for this loss is an essential part of this transition.

Extreme loss and trauma leading to feelings of guilt and power-lessness, lowering self-esteem, confidence and hatred of oneself may lead to self-harm. The community will act as witness to the story and the story-teller, who may indeed have lost all sense of feeling, and for whom beauty and love are reproaches to their place of pain. I recall a person living with such pain who shaded his eyes from any form of light because he was unable to con-template or enter into the possibility of hope. Witnessing his pain was through silent presence and occasional touch. I may be a witness to a person's process as we spend time together with images or journal writing, and occasionally it may be necessary to witness self-harm and to be alongside someone as emotional pain is released. Part of the witness in such situations may be to act differently from those who did not listen previously to their anguish, or from the abusive adult in the person's memory who used power to control, leading to secrecy and denial. It is essential to provide safe enough space for a person to get in touch with repressed feelings. Such situations challenge the meaning of the call to be witnesses for Christ. These are fragile thresholds as we become witnesses to Christ's pain and are called to accompany Christ through this process into liberation.

Sexual abuse is a particular area where there may be repression of all feeling. A person will have learned ways to split off from reality, becoming detached from the pain and abuse. Dissociation may have been learned at a young age in order to survive, and some of our guests take a long time to touch the threshold of pain and only do so when they feel safe enough to go to painful places. Therefore an important role for the therapeutic community is one of holding and being held. However, through the healing process there is often an awakening to one's own presence and a reclaiming and celebration of the self that had been lost. As one guest wrote: 'I feel as if I'm waking up!' (October 2002). My under-standing and experience in community leads me to view these threshold moments as a merging of self and divine presence.

The embodied therapeutic process takes into account the powerful effects of touch. The bodyself is essential to well-being because 'bodies are the nature and destiny of God' (Heyward, 1989, p. 71). The community sees this as part of the Christian narrative of incarnation as we seek to accompany people who are reconnecting with their own personhood through a variety of counselling and psychotherapeutic models, creative art therapies, body therapies and liturgical frameworks.

Personal identity is an integral part of the healing process for many who find a safer space to push out boundaries and encompass new ways of thinking and connecting. This requires huge risk, especially for those who have become disassociated from their personhood due to inappropriate touch or extreme trauma. Work in the garden or use of the creative arts becomes part of the healing process. It is as if there is a need to redeem this gift of touch through the touch of natural material, clay, earth, water or wool, or to touch the pony, goat or cat, or be touched by them. This touch has a contemplative and healing role and often solicits thanks from our guests: '. . . the right place "to be" and to feel touched . . .' (July 1995). Or: 'Thank you for . . . the colour, texture and taste you have added to our lives' (April 1997).

Feelings of vulnerability may also arise from a realistic fear of the wider world, not least for those who find themselves marginalized by society and the Church. Thus Carter Heyward's description of 'keeping the lid on, lest we simply disintegrate in the midst of a culture hostile already to who we are' (Heyward, 1989, p. 32), expresses something of our therapeutic approach. It may be necessary to 'keep the lid on' until we feel safe enough with the support of the community to lift it, and even then to take that process gently!

Sharing in, and acting as a witness to the unfolding threshold experiences of healing through participation and compassionate relationship becomes a journey of solidarity travelled in community. I find that the accompaniment of people is both a privilege and a constant learning curve as together we discover the inter-relatedness of this therapeutic and divine process at the threshold of our lives at Holy Rood House.

> I came unable to
> find peace within myself
>
> I leave with the stirrings of
> stillness gradually dawning
>
> I needed love
> you loved me

I needed to be held
you held me

I needed to be surrounded by
warmth, softness and gentleness
you enfolded me

I was frightened
your calm strength
gave me some peace

(2002)

Liturgy and ritual

Rediscovery – prayer, paint, rhythm, rest, music, love – of self
in God.   (May 2002)

A house full of the rustlings of a new energy and renewal.
                                                            (May 1993)

I hope I am showing you that the ministry of healing at Holy
Rood House is a celebration of integration, connectedness and
relational power, a 'fresh expression'[8] of 'being church' that includes the power of the senses to bring healing through simple
and ordinary things like baking, breaking and sharing bread
together, listening to the sound of chimes in the garden, and witnessing the simple self-acceptance of the animals in the paddock.

Playful Spirit,
hues of colour
evoke our senses,
Pentecost poppies
burst with pride
calling us to dance.
As water cascades over rocks
tumbling onto lily pads,
God's spirit becomes our wellspring,
our bubbling inspiration for vision,
our energizing of discovery,
our engagement with opportunity.[9]

For many people, especially those who have experienced abuse,
the life-enhancement of the senses has been curtailed or distorted
and people have to work hard to reclaim their embodied integrity.

26

The liturgy aids this process especially through the sacraments – water, bread, wine, oil, touch and incense. This offers an expressive and holistic way into possibilities of sensing and reflecting the presence of Christ in embodied living. It leads to a sacramental embrace of all the community celebrates and engages with. This sacramental sensibility provides the encompassing framework within which people are able to glimpse their own loveliness, their wholeness and their holiness. This discovery of our own sacrality moves us into the place of 'godding' (Heyward, 1989, p. 34), giving authority to the community to continue its mission towards justice, health and well-being.

To this end inclusive, creative language and symbol affirms and encourages hope for change and justice-making, while creating a framework in which people are able to reclaim the joy of the senses, opening them up to new vistas of hope. This is especially important for people who have experienced ritual as abusive, whether in the church or other ritualistic settings.[10] The use of ritual and liturgy has to be sensitive and life-giving, encompassing all the spaces. The gardens where pets have been laid to rest, ashes have been scattered, bulbs and shrubs have been planted, names spoken, treasures buried and letters burned, the labyrinth, where people meditate to the accompaniment of bird song, squirrels and the sound of the wind, and the herb garden and pond where prayers are said and tears can flow. Opening the door into the Secret Garden and the Chapel of Sophia offers another threshold where wisdom may be found as people discover spaces and places that are right for them.

The daily rhythm of prayer forms the backbone of community life. It becomes a threshold place of encounter and transition springing from the Eucharist at its heart. As an Ecumenical Trust we seek to provide a space for people of all denominations and of none to find a place where they may feel at home within the liturgy. To this end it is important to have a male and female priest and other ministers providing a chaplaincy role. Liturgy is written and developed out of community life and experience and the therapeutic process is expressed through word and symbol. The community enters into a liturgy born from tradition and experience, especially recently as we are creatively challenged by the presence of other faith traditions in the community surrounding Hexthorpe Manor. I see the liturgical journey unfolding and travelled by the divine as both host and guest in process of becoming.

> Come,
> make your home in us!

> In this humble meal
> we receive you,
> in our embodied hospitality
> you take your refuge,
> when your wings are broken,
> and your fire
> quenched.

> Come Spirit
> yearn for us
> as we yearn for you.
> Together we shall burst the bars of fear,
> flying freely,
> bringing warmth to the earth
> and winds of justice to those who cry 'Peace'.[11]

Within the liturgy and therapeutic work care is taken in relation to issues of forgiveness. This may or may not become part of the healing process. Through the painful processes of breaking down in order to break through, guilt and fear may be laid down and one's own voice may be recovered. At the right time this may lead to words of forgiveness for those who have been responsible for the wounded parts of ourselves. At other times forgiveness may not be possible. The pain may be too entrenched even for the transformative gift of rage to emerge. Often such pain has created enormous embodied damage and there may be a little energy for survival, but certainly not enough to consider the forgiveness of another. Forgiveness is a process and the community holds the pain. The Eucharist becomes the catalyst for possibilities of hope towards a just future as we are held together within the forgiveness and embrace of the divine.

> Risen One
> stand among us
> speak your words of peace
> release us from our fears
> heal us from our wounds

forgive our betrayals
our denials of your love
that we may participate
in your just living.[12]

Through the support and creativity of this liturgical community we find ourselves reawakened to a prayerful way of being. Prayer includes the sharing of meals in the dining-room as well as the meal shared around the altar. Each area informs the other, dovetailing together with the prayer, process, hopes, dreams and journeys of those who have shared the community previously and who have helped to shape the sense of presence and ethos.

As a Christ-centred community there is ongoing theological reflection of all that takes place and a process of re-visioning, enabling us to move on from the threshold of the Eucharist where what is broken is re-membered and liberated. This liberation is something people take with them to their own communities and that lies at the threshold of mission.

A prophetic and embodied community

Welcoming friends and flowers and hearts.
On a day of worldly strife and disaster pray that others may know
the peace that *is* to be found when love is more than anger.
(September 11th, 2001)

Holy Rood House seeks to engage more meaningfully in the dance of life and understand afresh the creative energy at its heart. Such a dance, at the cutting edge of a hostile world, inspires a longing for hope, springing from both pain and passion, leading the community towards compassion for embodied justice. This requires making connections between all aspects of human living and earth's evolving. This is a challenge to a community seeking to bring healing to people who are broken by the world's injustice while speaking out for liberation and justice for individuals, marginalized groups, communities and international concerns. The Centre for the Study of Theology and Health provides an important place of dialogue in the making of such connections, creating safe spaces for engagement and discourse.[13]

Justice calls for solidarity and compassionate community. We stand in solidarity with individuals and groups who experience oppression, working within a theological framework leading to liberation. Such solidarity and theological praxis cannot be a disembodied experience, for there are profound bodily implications for both individuals and community. Experiences of oppression are often expressed in the sexual stories of individuals and communities, and such stories have a profound implication for the work and witness of the community. Primarily it needs to be a place where individuals and groups can feel assured that they are not only welcome but that the stories they bring will enrich and help the continued reshaping of the community. Diversity and solidarity should not only become the norm, but also the political outcome of welcoming the stranger, involving the community in prophetic and embodied justice. This we do on a personal level, through the therapeutic work undertaken with guests and within our own lives, and on a political level, by stating where we encounter injustice and taking individual or community action when and where possible.

The years between 1993 and 2006 brought shock, distress and rapid changes to the world, and the community has accompanied many people, far from their homes, through traumatic times, including, the Dunblane Massacre, Kosovo, the destruction of the twin towers of 9/11, the war on Iraq, the Tsunami and the London bombings, as well as national events such as the death of Diana, and local tragedies including flooding. Such times have often connected with our own painful memories and become a part of the therapeutic journeys we find ourselves travelling. Many have found their way to Holy Rood House whose families have been directly touched by these and other events, and the community is learning therapeutic responses to such traumas and seeking to express that response liturgically.

The community seeks to respond to the changing social and political climate as a justice-making community. In recent years, welcoming young people from other countries has enhanced the life and work of the community through the challenge of different cultures, ways of thinking and expressions of life and faith, sharpening our awareness of being part of a global community.

New areas for training were recognized when refugees from Kosovo were coming to settle near York, and the war on Iraq challenged the community to be more equipped to respond to future needs as well as offering a more informed critique of the political times in which we live. The development of Hexthorpe Manor, in an area of Doncaster home to many asylum seekers, re-affirmed this. We know from our work with survivors of ritualistic sexual abuse and torture the painful process of reintegration, and the community needs to provide safe space and professional expertise to respond to times of political change. To this end staff training in 2006 included work by The Medical Foundation, working with victims of torture. The map of the world hanging in the chapels at Thirsk and Doncaster are a constant reminder of the important place of justice and peacemaking.

Time to move on

> I feel affirmed and special as a person thro' being here.
> I hope to take away some of the peace from here and try to introduce it into the chaotic lives of those we try to help.
> (November 1995)

The process of time plays an important part in the life of the community. St Paul, quoting from Isaiah, reminds his readers that 'now is the acceptable time; see, now is the day of salvation!' (2 Corinthians 6.2). We seek to work together in community within that sense of urgency, promise and presence, and this is understood and realized through time given for journeys to unfold, giving due attentiveness to each moment. Reading this book you have become part of that process as time opens to us, 'bringing us into a deeper presence, that of coming into our own' (Ulanov, 1987, p. 285). This shared experience is made possible through faith in God, ourselves and one another, and above all, belief in God's faith in the community, and those who at any one time share in it, to move on: 'Thanks for believing in me, when I could not believe in myself' (August 1997).

I see the development of Holy Rood House, The Centre for the Study of Theology and Health and the unfolding work of Hexthorpe Manor as a process and an adventure, and it is encouraging to see how many people, during their visit, catch this spirit of adventure for themselves. One of the community members was heard to say, 'I like working here because every day is different!' Another guest wrote, in reference to Wisdom-Sophia, and the care she had encountered,

> She paints the sky purple
> roses sky blue
> trees lemon yellow.
>
> All is strange, changed.
> 'Go on,' she says,
> 'enjoy the adventure.'
> (Jean Barker, 1995)

A person's visit to Holy Rood House may be a profound moment on their journey. There may have been a pivotal change towards well-being. The threshold of the porch becomes important again as courage is found to leave, decisions may be made to return, and farewells are made between friends and the adventure is continued elsewhere.

The challenge of engagement with the world, and in particular the Church, is an integral part of the process of the Christian ministry of healing. There cannot be health without justice. Healing has to embrace all aspects of human living as we move towards a future that not only belongs to God but is also part of God's becoming. Experience has a vital role to play in the shaping of the future of the community. We are challenged by questions arising out of personal stories and the larger cultural and religious narratives of which they are a part. Such narratives demand therapeutic and theological responses to a rapidly changing world and Church, inspired by the hopes and dreams of those who have shaped the community over the years. As a guest wrote: 'Somehow, deep in Holy Rood House, there seems an Echo, a repeat of those hopes and dreams of yesterday' (May 1998).

> God of grace
> you seek us out
> when we hide from you,
> you call our name
> when we least expect to hear,
> you believe in us
> when we live in doubt.
> Lay hold of our hearts,
> our minds, our lives,

as we commit ourselves
afresh to this healing ministry,
of loving one another,
accepting ourselves
and proclaiming your justice
in the world.[14]

Notes

1 Holy Rood House Centre for Health and Pastoral Care was set up in 1993 as a Residential Therapeutic Centre in Thirsk, North Yorkshire. Previously, the Charitable Trust worked under the name of The North of England Christian Healing Trust in Spennithorne, Leyburn, from 1981 through the Healing Prayer Fellowship started by the Rt Revd Morris Maddocks, the Bishop of Selby. In 1996 Thorpe House, Sowerby, was purchased to aid expansion. In 2001 The Centre for the Study of Theology and Health was opened. And in December 2005 the Trust received the gift of Hexthorpe Manor in Doncaster.

2 Small notebooks were placed in each bedroom when Holy Rood House was opened by the Bishop of Whitby, the Rt Revd Gordon Bates, in July 1993. The pieces written in the books, including poems, have helped community awareness and development over the years. They are a testimony to the determination and commitment of journeys towards health and well-being between community staff and guests.

3 All prayers and liturgy, unless otherwise stated, are written by Elizabeth Baxter on behalf of the Holy Rood Community.

4 The Anglican Order of The Holy Rood began in Coatham, North Yorkshire in 1854 and closed in Thirsk in 1992.

5 Eucharistic Prayer for Easter, Holy Rood House Publications, 2003.

6 Prayer from the Easter Vigil, Holy Rood House Publications, 2003.

7 The Centre for Health and Pastoral Care is in membership of The Association of Therapeutic Communities and is in Organisational Membership of The British Association for Counselling and Psychotherapy. Therapists and counsellors give voluntary time to guests and visiting clients at Holy Rood House and Hexthorpe Manor.

8 Holy Rood House is registered with Fresh Expressions, a Church of England and Methodist Church initiative encouraging people hoping to establish 'new or different forms of church for our changing culture'.

9 From the Pentecost Eucharist, Holy Rood House Publications, 2003.

10 For example, paedophile rings or self-abuse through addictive, obsessive, ritualistic practices such as hand-washing or cutting.
11 From the Pentecost Eucharistic Prayer, Holy Rood House Publications, 2003.
12 Easter Eucharist, Holy Rood House Publications, 2002.
13 Research and conference weekends have brought together many different people in this dialogue, for example, 'Questioning Security: Strategic and Theological Perspectives' (February 2004), in collaboration with Quaker Peace and Social Witness, Churches Together in Britain and Ireland, International Affairs Office, and Bradford University Department of Peace Studies.
14 From the Liturgy at the Thanksgiving for the Fifth Anniversary of the opening of Thorpe House (Burgess, 2004, p. 87).

References

Boyce-Tillman, J., *The Creative Spirit: Harmonious Living with Hildegard of Bingen*. Canterbury Press, Norwich, 2000.
Burgess, R. (ed.), *Friends and Enemies*. Wild Goose Publications, Glasgow, 2004.
Carston, J. and Hugh-Jones, S., *About the House: Levi Strauss and Beyond*. Cambridge University Press, Cambridge, 1995.
Eiesland, N., *The Disabled God: Toward a Liberatory Theology of Disability*. Abingdon Press, Nashville, 1994.
Grey, M., *Prophecy and Mysticism: The Heart of the Postmodern Church*. T&T Clark, Edinburgh, 1997.
Heyward, C., *The Redemption of God: A Theology of Mutual Relation*. University Press of America, Washington, 1982.
Heyward, C., *Touching our Strength: The Erotic as Power and the Love of God*. HarperSanFrancisco, San Francisco, 1989.
Isherwood, L., *Introducing Feminist Christologies*. Sheffield Academic Press, London, 2001.
Mollenkott, V. R., *Sensuous Spirituality: Out of Fundamentalism*. Crossroad, New York, 1993.
Nouwen, H. J. M., *Reaching Out: The Three Movements of the Spiritual Life*. 8th edition, Zondervan Publishing House, Grand Rapids, Michigan, 1987.
Nouwen, H. J. M., *The Wounded Healer: Ministry in Contemporary Society*. Darton, Longman & Todd, London, 1994.
Palmer, P. J., *The Company of Strangers: Christianity and Renewal of America's Public Life*. Crossroad, New York, 1981.
Pohl, C. D., *Making Room: Recovering Hospitality as a Christian Tradition*. Eerdmans, Grand Rapids, Cambridge, 1999.

Richard, L., *Living Within the Hospitality of God*. Paulist Press, New York, 2000.

Rose, G., *Love's Work*. Vintage/Random House, London, 1997.

Schutz, A., *Collected Papers Vol. II: Studies in Social Theory*. Brodersen, A. (ed.), Martinus Nijhoff, The Hague, 1964.

Sheldrake, P., *Spaces for the Sacred*. SCM Press, London, 2001.

Thomas, R. S., 'The Porch', *Collected Poems 1945–1990*. Phoenix Giant/ Orion Publishing Group, London, 1995.

Ulanov, A. Belford and Barry, *The Witch and The Clown: Two Archetypes of Human Sexuality*. Chiron Publications, Wilmette, Illinois, 1987.

Ward, H. and Wild, J., *Guard the Chaos: Finding Meaning in Change*. Darton, Longman & Todd, London, 1995.

Welch, S., *A Feminist Ethic of Risk*. Augsburg/Fortress Press, Minneapolis, 2000.

3

Ecomysticism: a contemporary path for Christian healing?

MARY GREY

————◆◆————

Beginning with an account of her own experience of breast cancer, Mary Grey describes what she calls the 'lost dimension' of the Christian healing ministry, and names that dimension 'ecomysticism'. Based upon her reading of the Judaeo-Christian narrative, feminism and ecospirituality, Grey places particular emphasis upon the 'ecological self' as a model for ecomysticism, so combining the personal with the political and the mystical with the prophetic. This leads Grey to her 'Challenge to the Churches', as she insists that the concepts of 'relationality' and 'diaconia' (care) must now be 'enlarged to mean care for the whole of creation'.

* * *

A personal introduction

Some years ago, like many other women in Britain and elsewhere, both older and younger, completely out of the blue I discovered that I had breast cancer, from which I have now, hopefully, recovered. I mention this not to chronicle the process of shock, denial, anger and slow recovery that many others have related, but to show that the path to healing revealed surprising insights and that these have inspired the aim of this chapter: to search for and reclaim a lost dimension for Christian Healing, namely, the path of ecomysticism.

One dimension of getting cancer is that one becomes subject to kindly meant interrogations from both friends and family: 'What's wrong with you that you get cancer?' 'We always told you that you were doing too much, sailing close to the wind, and so on

– now look what's happened!' From some male friends came a more surprising reaction: silence, on the part of one dear friend, a priest; *blame* from others: 'How could you give us such a fright?!' Some underlying denial of mortality here?[1]

In other words, one of the most difficult dimensions to deal with was not the medical process of healing I was undergoing that was fairly straightforward – and effective, I am grateful to report – but how to deal with the psychological and spiritual issues raised by these reactions. My spiritual distress was compounded by the fact that I had already made professional decisions about a job in an effort to get the balance right between work and family, and was embarking on a thrilling new job in the Netherlands that had offered me the greatest challenge of my life.[2] Two factors helped me through this crisis.[3] In a context where my family was incredibly supportive, the role played by my sister Barbara and my mother stood out: they were a living witness to the power of relationality and bonding that offered far more than a fragile thread of love. Every day cards arrived with poems, prayers and pictures that they knew would appeal to me. At times when I wanted to give up the struggle, and acquiesce in the overwhelming sense that I had had enough of life and it would be fine to go, these threads of hope would awaken me to the goodness of living and the healing power of relating.

The second factor was what concerns us here: for once I did not turn to books for solace (in fact it seemed that book-learning had let me down!) but to the garden. At this time we lived on a small farm for soft fruit (a 'Pick-your-own-strawberries' enterprise), and, I am ashamed to relate, I had often found this a time-consuming, demanding burden that came between me and my work. Now it was completely otherwise: in working in the garden and on the land I struggled with anger against God: yes, the usual 'Why have you done this to me?' 'Why now, above all times?' But what I discovered was the God of the garden, of the seasons, of diversity, of limits of decay and new blossoming, an invitation to humility and a recognition of the goodness of the different life-spans of the entire web of creation. But it did not happen all at once, and when it did, it set me off on a new path of exploration for Christian spirituality. For the journey I began to follow, ecospirituality and ecomysticism were born.

I: The need for roots

The path to healing in Christianity is criss-crossed with many tracks, not all of them leading in the most helpful direction. Following my very personal introduction, my search here is for witnesses from Christian and Jewish traditions that stress both a *communal* dimension to healing (that does not exclude the personal), and envision healing as including both human beings and the earth. I will argue, first, that this holistic vision of healing is integral to Christianity but frequently lost sight of. And second, I plead for its recovery at a time when the planet's very survival is threatened.

And so to begin, not with the glory of the garden of Eden, but from 'the broken web' (Keller, 1986). This metaphor recalls not only the patience of the spider in constantly remaking the world on the basis of brokenness – 'A passion to make and make again, where such unmaking reigns', as the poet Adrienne Rich has put it (Rich, 1978, p. 64) – but the fact that it does not help us to return in our imaginations to a (supposed) pre-Edenic state of perfection: rather, the task is to tackle the devastation that faces us with all possible resources – spiritual, theological, political and cultural.

Second, justice is an important dimension to be factored in. I never separate the prophetic and mystical dimensions of Christianity and have argued elsewhere that their separation has been a disaster for the Church (Grey, 1997). If we are to recover ecological mysticism for Christian healing it will be within a conviction and commitment to restorative justice to the earth and her creatures. So it will come as no surprise that a first source of inspiration is the Prophet Isaiah of the Hebrew Bible. Isaiah offers a way into the current situation in showing us that we always begin *from the broken web* of ravaged creation. He,[4] like all the prophets, connects devastation of the land with human sin and responsibility, and healing with well-being of both people and earth. He, more than other voices from the Hebrew Bible, is striking in his appeals to the people through the imaginative vision of *shalom* that embraces the flourishing of people, land, and animals. Water springs up in the desert enabling the growth of a diversity of trees (Isaiah 39). But the following, earlier passage emphasizes the human/non-human link I am following:

The wilderness and the dry land will be glad,
The desert shall rejoice and blossom;
Like the crocus it shall blossom abundantly,
and rejoice with joy and singing . . .
Then the eyes of the blind shall be opened,
And the ears of the deaf be unstopped;
then shall the lame leap like a deer,
and the tongue of the speechless sing for joy,
For water shall break forth in the wilderness,
and streams in the desert.

(Isaiah 35.1, 5–6)

Lion, lamb, panther and kid feed together in this messianic vision of redeemed creation (Isaiah 11). Whether this means a vision solely for messianic times – a Jewish conviction – or a compelling prophetic dream of what might be possible, it can nonetheless call us into something radically different from our severely limited human imaginings. For a theology of healing the theme of joy is an important strand.

A second witness as to the beauty yet otherness of divine creation is the wisdom literature of the Book of Job. This may seem a strange move. The point is that the healing of Job's total situation (whatever one thinks about the fact that he is given another set of children!) is enabled only when he acknowledges the revelation of the God of creation. The radical otherness of God's vision for the earth is here revealed. Here, especially in chapters 38–41, we are given magnificent poetry and a cosmology radically different from anything else in the Bible (cf. Grey, 2003, ch. 7). As opposed to apparently being the summit of creation, humanity is toppled from pride of place and placed alongside the animals and humbler forms of life. Radically different views of freedom, justice, the wisdom of creation and the gratuitousness of God's love are presented. This is no Walt Disney view of creation: its wildness, savagery and ambiguity are poured out before our eyes (cf. McKibben, 1994). Where human beings have looked to conquering the land and taming the wilderness, God, who displays intimate knowledge of the ways of birds, gives us the image of the baby vultures being taught to drink the blood of their prey, and a place for the monsters of the deep. Dissonance is revealed not only in the text but also in reality. Otherness, strangeness and the savagery of animals seem to be part of

God's creation. All things may be connected – but not in the comforting way sometimes presumed by romanticists! Not that the savagery and ambiguities of creation are any consolation to those threatened by earthquake, flood and drought: but a severe word of warning is being given to us. In the powers we human beings now have at our disposal to destroy the world with nuclear bombs, to clone human beings and animals, to manipulate the genetic structures of the plant and animal world, we have taken God's role and challenged God's control of creation. Yet God's words to Job are clear:

Have you commanded the morning? (38.12)
Have you entered the storehouses of the snow? (38.22)

The seemingly imperious tones of God recall humanity to a proper sense of humility and a place in the whole web of creation, and to new responsibilities in the current threatened situation of creation. Job's God calls from the whirlwind that we respect the total ecology of place: *ecological* rather than *exclusively economic* objectives must be human priorities.

It is within this grand scheme for healing, embracing people and earth, that Jesus' mission and ministry must be placed. Luke (4.18–30) places Jesus in the prophetic tradition of Isaiah, as well as in the tradition of the Jubilee Laws. Even though the text cited by Luke does not mention the land, the Isaiahan inspiration (61.1–2) recalls the return of the exiled people to Judaea, their need to rebuild ruined cities and devastations, and concludes:

For as the earth brings forth its shoots,
And as a garden causes what is sown in it to spring up,
So the Lord God will cause righteousness and praise
To spring forth before all the nations.

(61.11)

Healing of land, cities and people is caught up with and assumed into the praise of the creator, because God's joy is in the flourishing of creation.

So why is it that Christian healing has frequently been reduced to purely individualistic meanings? Healings and miracles are now mostly understood as affecting the person without reference to either community or the earth. Conversion, especially since the Reformation, is mostly seen as the appeal to the human person to turn away from evil and towards God. The ecological motif has been completely lost.

First, in response we should note that the times of Jesus were not the times of ecological crisis in the way that they are now: yes, they were times of land misuse, of the suffering of the landless and of rapacious landlords, but this was exploitation within an ecological footprint that was far lighter than it is today. Second, Jesus' ministry must be placed within a wider vision. It is usually accepted that this occurred within a proclamation of the coming of the Reign of God, the kingdom (or *kin-dom*, as many of us like to say),[5] a new state of transformed relations where all experience peace and justice. But this does not yet make explicit the fact that the transformed earth is included in the vision. Traditionally, Jesus is seldom portrayed as an ecologist, with the earth at the forefront of his consciousness. Did he not say that humans are of more value than the sparrows, the ravens and the birds of the field (Luke 12.7, 24)? A new lens is needed to glimpse another vision beneath the deep-seated anthropocentrism that blocks deeper perception.

Surely Jesus' focus was actually a holistic one that refused to separate body and spirit? What aroused his compassion was the sight of suffering bodies, bodies of vulnerable categories of people like widows, outcasts, people with disabilities, people both thirsty and hungry. Healing body and spirit in a community setting was the hallmark of his ministry: this is poignantly illustrated by the raising to life of the widow's son (Luke 7). Clearly, it is not just the fact that the boy has died that is the real issue: he will face death again in the future, as would Jesus' dear friend Lazarus. It is the plight of his mother that inspires the Galilean healer to compassionate healing, a mother who has lost her only protector. We do not know whether she would face a Levirate marriage, beggary or even prostitution, which would still be the options in many societies today. Tempted to make the connection between this widow and Jesus' own mother, we can at least say that Jesus made the relational connection in responding to her grief.

Sallie McFague has shown how the image of the messianic feast (again, recall Isaiah's feast on the Holy Mountain – Isaiah 25) is the prospective image of the coming kingdom (McFague, 1993). Not only the healing of bodies but the feeding of bodies is a priority. It is almost impossible for us to move through the barriers of separative dualisms that hinder us today from a holistic view of the human person. We do read that Jesus not only made his table practices the heart of his ministry, but that he longed and desired to eat the Passover with his disciples (Luke 22.15). In liturgy, in sharing a sacred meal, comes the possibility of transformation. And this is true for many faiths.

Another witness to make the links I explore is the late David Toolan SJ, who, like the palaeontologist and mystic Teilhard de Chardin, believed in the sacramental potential of matter and offered a cosmic, earth-based eucharistic vision that is also linked with the idea of transformation. But he earths this vision more concretely than Teilhard de Chardin in the context of Jewish Passover as well as in the context of the looming death of Jesus:

> There are no theatrics here, no magic, simply the highly-charged action of a man who knows he will die on the morrow and must make every word and gesture count. Two great movements converge in what Jesus shows us here: the everlasting desire of cosmic dust to mean something great and God's promise that it shall be done. There is first a centripetal movement. We the followers and the disciples centre in on Jesus, identify, become one with him. Then there is the centrifugal, decentralising movement. Jesus, both conduit of Spirit-Energy and cosmic dust himself, freely identifies himself with us and with the fruits of the earth – the ash of a dying star present in bread and wine – and converts these gifts of earth, the work of human hands, into another story than the nightmarish one we have been telling with them.
>
> (Toolan, 2003, p. 210)

This other story is the fact that Jesus – in a context of unconditioned love and forgiveness – transforms, transmutes and breathes new meaning into all life forms. Jesus, as Toolan says, is 'bidding us take in, to discover in our own soul-space the same Spirit that works in and through him' (Toolan, 2003, p. 211). Toolan also emphasizes that this cosmic dimension of healing is in fact the saving work of the whole Trinitarian Godhead:

> In effect, Jesus is saying that the whole work of transfiguring earth stuff in accord with the Creator's dream is not his solitary work but fundamentally the work of the Father in heaven. . . .

Swallow this, Jesus declares, I am God's promise for the elements, the exemplary inside of nature, its secret wish fulfilled. Swallow my words, let them resonate in the marrow of my bones, and you will tap into the same current of spirit that moves me. Swallow me and you will have taken in what God imagines for matter: that it be spirited, that justice be done to all, according to the vision of the great rainbow covenant.

(Toolan, 2003, p. 212)

It is this rich, multidimensional dimension of cosmic healing that is almost – but not quite – stifled throughout tradition, and now being reclaimed as the ecomystical path.

Another factor that we find almost impossible to recover in our post-Enlightenment Western world is the community mindset as setting for our lives. As healing rituals developed in the early Christian communities, particularly through the sacrament of reconciliation, where sin and not physical sickness was normally the focus, only those sins that wounded community required the expulsion of the individual, the tangible proof of penance, then solemn re-entry into the community (cf. Martos, 1981). As is well known, this communal dimension was gradually lost through the monastic practice of individual penance, originating with eastern monks, then carried to Ireland and thence to the west. This personal focus would become heightened at the Reformation: and after this the link between the Isaiahan holistic vision of the healing of land and people would slowly vanish. To make matters infinitely worse, the expansion into and conquest of the 'new world' at the end of the fifteenth century onwards would mark the beginning of ecocidal policies and rapaciousness of the earth's resources that, far from being condemned as sin, acquired justification in the name of imposing Christianity upon the 'heathen'.

Not only did the concept of sin become interpreted individually, with a loss of the sense of communal responsibility, but the idea of spiritual experience became increasingly seen as a private affair. This meant that mystical experience became increasingly the prerogative of the individual, a state of affairs that the great mediaeval mystics would not have recognized. As Rowan Williams wrote about Teresa of Avila: 'Teresa makes it very clear that the criteria of authenticity do not lie in the character of the experience itself but in how it is related to a pattern of concrete behaviour, the development of dispositions and decisions. There is no one kind of experience that declares itself at once to be an experience of God' (Williams, 1991, p. 147).

The outcome of the long process by which mysticism became understood as being primarily about the exalted experience of an individual would be summed up by the now classic work of William James, who wrote:

> The handiest of marks by which I classify a state of mind as mystical is negative. The subject of it immediately says it defies expression, that no adequate report of its contents can be given in words. . . . In this peculiarity mystical states are more like states of feeling than like states of intellect.
>
> (James, 1960, p. 367, cited Jantzen, 1995, pp. 304–7)

It is not only the reduction of mysticism to the private experience of an individual that is the problem but the issues of power and gender within which it is packaged. As Grace Jantzen has said, reinforcing the way in which mysticism had become privatized:

> The privatised, subjectivised ineffable mysticism of William James and his followers is open to women as well as men; but it plays directly into the hands of modern bourgeois political and gender assumptions. It keeps God (and women) safely out of politics and the public realm; it allows mysticism to flourish as a *secret inner life*, while those who nurture such an inner life can generally be counted on to prop up rather than challenge the status quo of their work places, their gender roles and the public systems by which they are governed, since their anxieties and angers will be allayed in the privacy of their own hearts' search for peace and tranquillity.
>
> (Jantzen, 1995, p. 346)

In summary, what I have attempted to sketch briefly is the way the turn from the earth was accompanied and reinforced by a privatized notion of sin and grace (Grey, 2003, pp. 7–19). This in turn was influenced by a dualistic split between body and spirit that affected both the development of spirituality, and the understanding of healing. Healing of body and healing of soul were not necessarily connected, although the idea that bodily sickness was punishment for sin was never completely lost sight of.

But at the same time there has been an alternative strand that kept the holistic vision from being completely lost. (I am speaking of glimpses rather than a continuous strand; nor do I plead that the writers cited here were free from the dualisms that plagued tradition.) First, where theologians and church leaders had become blind to the connections between the healing of earth and people, poets and musicians kept a vibrant witness, from Caedmon, the seventh-century poet of Hilda's monastery, in his 'Dream of the Rood', to the way that poets and musicians today are recovering Celtic inspiration.[6] The visions of Hildegard of Bingen (1098–1179) offered an integrated picture of the dynamic greenness (*viriditas*) of the Holy Spirit. In this wonderful affirmation of life in its fullness, God's creative presence to the whole of creation as source of its flourishing is affirmed:

> I, the highest and fiery power, have kindled every spark of life, and I emit nothing that is deadly. I decide on all reality.... with wisdom I have rightly put the universe in order. I, the fiery life of divine essence, am aflame beyond the beauty of the mead-ows, I gleam in the waters, and I burn in the sun, moon and stars. With every breeze, as with invisible life, I awaken everything to life. The air lives by turning green and being in bloom. The waters flow as if they were alive ... and thus I remain hidden in everything as fiery power. Every thing burns because of me in such a way as our breath constantly moves us ... I breathe life into everything so that nothing is mortal in respect to its species. *For I am life.*
>
> *I am the Life, whole and entire, (vita integra)* – not struck from stones, not blooming out of twigs, not rooted in a man's power to beget children. Rather, all life has its roots in me.
>
> (Hildegard, in Fox (ed.), 1987, pp. 9–10)

Divine wisdom, beauty, flourishing and the vital presence of God through the entire creation are all formative aspects of this vision, which, I argue, are all ingredients of Christian healing. Hildegard's intuition seems very close to what a more contemporary creation visionary would express, but in his case, the context was the poet's awareness of what humanity has done to the earth:

> And for all this nature is never spent;
> There lives the dearest freshness deep down things;
> And though the last lights of the black West went
> Oh morning, at the brown brink eastward, springs—

Because the Holy Ghost over the bent
world broods with warm breast and with ah! bright wings.
(Hopkins, 1953, p. 27)

In England in the seventeenth century, Thomas Traherne stood
in the same line as the medieval mystics of connecting divine
presence in creation (for him the English countryside) with God's
longing for us: 'For Traherne the countryside is so glorious,
creation itself so wonderful not because it is pretty or even
because humanity is called to care for it, but because it is a direct
outpouring of the wanting of God' (Matthews, 2000, p. 112).

One century later than Traherne, Haydn's Creation Symphony
proclaimed that 'The Heavens are telling the glory of God', and like
Traherne, classical choral music saw nature as part of the grand
divine redemptive scheme in Jesus' suffering and resurrection.

But divine vital presence, beauty and longing are not the only
elements of ecological mysticism. There is another strand not
normally associated with mysticism and that is justice. Whereas
it is difficult to discover this in the mystical or creation traditions
of the mediaeval period and Reformation, it can be discerned
in counter-cultural peace movements – and this will be important
for the contemporary reawakening.

The Emperor Constantine, after 312 CE, when he converted
to Christianity and led his troops to victory under the banner
of the cross, made Christianity the established religion across
the Roman Empire. This appeared to eclipse the nonviolent
ethic of Christianity that had so far prevailed. The *Pax Romana*
turned the notion of peace on its head. 'Peace' was imposed
with the sword and by substituting emperor worship for commitment to the risen Lord, the suffering servant who identified
with the most vulnerable of society. However, I argue that the
culture of radical peace has never quite disappeared: with the
Quakers, the Mennonites and Ana-Baptists, with prophetic teaching on nonviolence, the Poverty movements of the Middle Ages,
including the witness of St Francis, and in the many Communities for Reconciliation since the World Wars, the radicality
of seeking peace with justice in a nonviolent manner has never
been completely lost sight of. By definition this is not an individualistic search but earthed in a specific community and its
cultural symbols. Nonviolent witness is usually accompanied

with love of nature and a simplicity of lifestyle and these are valuable connections for the theme I develop.

II: *The ecofeminist awakening*

Ecofeminism is, as Vandana Shiva and Maria Mies have pointed out, a new word for an old wisdom (Shiva and Mies, 1993). It is a union of two concerns – ecology and justice for women. Whereas ecology explores the interaction and interdependence of all life forms contained in the great web of life, in Christian theology the web of life is creation, sustained by God's love. So ecological theology explores what promotes healing within this sacred web and what makes this impossible – usually through human greed and violence. It does not stop at the level of physical devastation but asks what cultural and religious symbols, what psychological means people have used to distance from the earth and contribute to its domination. The processes of Christian healing will be especially concerned with the links be-tween the damaged psyche and damaged earth, at both personal and communal levels.

My first example is an outstanding contemporary witness to these connections. In 2004 Professor Wangari Maathai, of the Kikuyu tribe in Kenya, was awarded the Nobel Peace Prize for her inspirational Green Belt Movement, founded in 1977. The Committee chairman, Ole Danbolt Mjoes, made the links between peace and the environment clear: 'This is the first time environment sets the agenda for the Nobel Peace Prize, and we have added a new dimension to peace. We have expanded the peace concept to include environmental issues because we believe that a good quality of life on Earth is necessary to promote lasting peace in the world. Peace depends on our ability to secure our living environment' (*The Guardian*, 13.10.04). Professor Maathai herself said simply: 'Many of the wars in Africa are fought over natural resources. Ensuring they are not destroyed is a way of ensuring there is no conflict. In manag-ing our resources . . . we plant the seeds of peace' (*The Guardian*, 01.11.04).

Wangari Maathai illustrates ecofeminist method dramatically. While teaching at the University of Nairobi she would listen to women relating the realities of their lives – their need for water, wood (for fuel), and nutritious food. She came to understand that their problems were symptoms of a poorly managed environment leading to a lack of clean drinking water, insufficient food supply and poor health. Together with these women, she hit on the idea of planting trees to provide food and fuel, slow soil erosion and desertification, offer shade and improve the aesthetic environment. This is a possibility for anyone. And planting a tree means that a person connects with the Earth and has a stake in its survival. So on World Environment Day in 1977, seven trees were planted at a ceremony in Nairobi, and slowly the idea took off. Small tree nurseries that women could manage were planted close to homes, nurseries that evolved into the Green Belt Movement. In the process a growing number of women became 'foresters without diplomas'.

But the influence was wider than just tree-planting: alongside this the Green Belt Movement trained communities in human rights, democratic governance and conflict resolution. For the first time, men and women recognized their responsibilities and their power to combat ecological decline, promote democracy and choose the direction of their lives – a phenomenon I have also experienced with tribal communities in Rajasthan.[7]

Maathai is living proof that twenty-first-century peace work is politically and socially dangerous, and that being an effective environmentalist today is not just about planting trees, but working at the grassroots with the poorest communities and challenging powerful political and commercial forces. She, like many others today in many parts of the world, knows that conflicts are waged over resources such as land, forests, minerals, oil and water (cf. Shiva, 2002; De Villiers, 1999). As the Earth's resources continue to be depleted through poor management and rapacious exploitation, conflicts will flare more often and be more difficult to contain. So protecting local and global environments is therefore essential for achieving lasting peace.

But Wangari Maathai leads the way in another respect: she called for another Bible, or for reading the Bible with different eyes, in order to recover its message of healing in place of the domination of the earth that has now reached a critical stage. Ecofeminist method rethinks vital reference points to create a holistic way of relating between human beings and the earth. I take for granted that the attempt to recover from damaging splits between mind/body/spirit will be at its heart, as it has been with feminist pastoral strategies. Second, the attempt to rethink the human person less individualistically also appeals to feminist anthropological attempts to envision the relational self, or self-in-relation to others. (This process has now become popular in other networks (cf. Kumar, 1992; Grey, 1989/2000).) Here I do not make extravagant claims that women's so-called closeness to nature means that women have superior knowledge and skills. This is both because to associate women with nature and men with culture is now dismissed as essentialist; and also the so-called superior knowledge, claimed by Vandana Shiva and others, has to be carefully contextualized and is now being challenged in different contexts (cf. Jewitt, 2002). Becoming a self-in-relation does not stop with human relations, but links with a person's environment to form the *ecological self*. Becoming an ecological, connected self, I see as event, process and responsibility (cf. Grey, 1993, p. 77; Macy, in Plant (ed.), 1989, pp. 201–11). It is a process that is at the heart of the Bible, especially in the prophetic texts. But in the biblical context it is addressed to the *whole* people, who are continually summoned to turn to the steadfastness and righteousness of God. Jesus of Nazareth's image of prospective kingdom was an inclusive vision of the messianic feast to depict the fullness of the kingdom of God (as was mentioned earlier – Luke 14.7–14), and Sallie McFague has pushed this inclusivity further to ask how animals can be included: are they only present at the great banquet in order to be eaten (McFague, 1993)? This indicates the elasticity of some biblical texts that are capable of further liberating meanings in response to a changed context.

Feminist spirituality has sought to move the non-personhood of women in many societies to an awareness of becoming whole persons, created in the image of God, *imago Dei*. Methods of sharing stories and solidarity struggles, valuing experiences, especially those of diversity, and creating healing rituals that address abuse and wounded sexuality, are common. If the process is then deepened to becoming an *ecological* self, then dimensions of community and justice stand central. Even if ecofeminism focuses on justice for women and earth, the fact that relationality is such a central focus, means that women are considered in relationship, with family, children, partners and the wider community. This is part of the promise of ecofeminist spirituality.

But given that we still live in a dualist and profoundly unjust society, committed to a particularly pernicious form of consumerist individualism, it is also a clarion call to highlight *faith* perspectives of justice specifically. The danger is that middle-class attitudes to nature (sunrise picnics, ethnic clothes, expensive organic food and the enjoyment of nature commodified in the form of aromatherapy and CDs of waterfalls, for example) may distract attention from the justice and poverty issues that form the context for ecological well-being in many parts of the world. Sheer survival rather than flourishing may well be the form that Christian notions of healing must take. How then can following the ecomystical path lead to healing for Christians today?

III: The practice of ecomysticism

I began with a personal story, one that tried to depict a slow movement from an experience of distress into a journey of new discovery. I make no claims that this is original, that there were not pitfalls, backward steps and even times when any sense of journey completely disappeared, or that I have actually achieved any new pinnacles: it is the journey that counts and what the journey makes possible for others.

First, to explain why this should be called a *mystical* or *ecomystical* journey: this harks back to an ecofeminist re-imagining of the concepts of immanence and transcendence and to the earlier cited voices of the presence of God in nature. If God is truly to be encountered *immanently* in the oceans and streams, the animals and birds, what a richness of experience is offered! This is in fact what the Jewish faith offered – with the caveat of the Book of Wisdom that it is *God* who is encountered, and to be worshipped – not the particular stone or flower (Wisdom 13.1–9). What needs stressing – again we need the Book of Job! – is that it is not the cosy God of the ersatz comforters encountered, but God of the terror and the majesty, the *fascinans* and the *tremendum*. This is not a *private* experience but one that draws us into deepening connections and relations: hence a much closer link between immanent and transcendent. Somehow, mystical faith has to be strong enough to take in the sheer power of nature including its destructive elements. Perhaps the newness of the revelation of God for our times is that of the Spirit, not as gentle dove, but as wild bird, leading us to care for the fragile ecosystems before they vanish (cf. Grey, 2003, ch. 6; Wallace, 1996).

Second, the ethical task of an ecospirituality is to discern human responsibility and respond to its urgency: for example, the fact that Haiti suffered so much from hurricanes in 2004 is connected with its having lost all but 2 per cent of forest cover, due to unscrupulous logging. As I write, numerous examples of the effects of climate change are pouring in: the melting ice cap and consequent disappearance of the habitat for penguins and polar bears, for example. For these disasters humans are responsible – as well as suffering the consequence of the narrowing of our own potential experience.

Third, as has been stressed by numerous writers of spirituality, the experience of divine immanence and transcendence – in terms of drawing us onward into the beauty and the terror of God – is dependent on the constant *waiting on God* (Weil, 1949). It is the paying attention to the minute details, rhythms and connections. And this has become an area of great creativity for ecofeminist spirituality, as the poems of Adrienne Rich (1981), Janet Morley (1988), Nicola Slee (2004) and Kathy Galloway (2004) witness. But it is more than simply paying attention: Annie Dillard's novel *Pilgrim at Tinker Creek* (1974) reveals that paying attention nourishes an attitude of caring for where we dwell. In a beautiful example of what is meant by the *ecological self* she declares her identity is rooted in simply being at Tinker Creek. The plot of the novel – if one can call it a plot – consists in simply *dwelling*. The least you can do is be there! Annie Dillard dwells for a year by Tinker Creek, in the Appalachian Mountains, listening and watching. In fact, watching and listening are almost all she does, all the time displaying unflinching courage at the paradoxes she finds there. (It has to be emphasized that contemplation is an *activity*, not an opting out, even if it is not an activity offered for poor communities struggling for survival, deprived of water and food, and frequently suffering violence.) At the same time this dwelling is also a searching for God. Annie Dillard finds the mystery of God is everywhere, even in the perception of flawed beauty and the presence of violence:

'We wake, if we ever wake at all, to mystery, rumours of death, beauty, violence . . . "seem like we're just set down here," a woman said to me recently, "and don't nobody know why" '. And again: 'There is the one simple mystery of creation from nothing, of matter itself, anything at all, the given. Mountains are giant, restful absorbent. . . . The creeks are the world, with all its stimulus and beauty' (Dillard, 1974, p. 2).

Seen through an ecofeminist theological lens, this kind of attention can be called a sacramental perception, the kind of eucharistic perception that David Toolan described in the passage cited earlier. Sallie McFague calls this form of perception *seeing with the loving eye* (McFague, 2001). This is in contrast to *the arrogant eye*, or the eye of detachment, that wants to objectify, possess and control. McFague suggests meditating with the loving eye as a way to develop a different relationship with nature. This is an ecomystical practice – open to all. A similar idea is suggested by Paul Santmire (2000). Is it possible to develop Martin Buber's advocacy of an I–Thou relationship (as opposed to the detachment and control of an I–It attitude), with all living things? Santmire proposes instead of I–Thou, an 'I–ens' relationship ('*ens*' is the Latin word for 'being'). This means developing an attitude of respect, appreciation and reverence for each organism, each eco-system, as appropriate. It is another form of *sacramental perception*, the perception that Annie Dillard practises at Tinker Creek.

But does the quality of what you see depend on the tenderness of a lover, the single-mindedness and purity of heart of the pilgrim? Tenderness, purity of heart, enlarging compassion to take in all life forms are gifts, as well as qualities that develop in the practice of the path I am developing. How does simply being there qualify as part of this path? Annie Dillard's search for the 'tree with lights in it' does manifest something of mystical vision. Seeing is somehow dependent on *being able to receive*. In a powerful passage she tells us:

> I *saw* the backyard cedar where the mourning doves roost charged and transfigured, each cell buzzing with flame. I stood on the grass with lights in it, grass that was wholly fire, utterly focused and utterly dreamed. It was less like seeing than being for the first time seen, knocked breathless by a powerful glance. The flood of fire abated, but I'm still spending the power. . . . The vision

comes and goes, mostly goes, but I live for it, for the moment
when the mountains open and a new light roars in spate through
the crack, and the mountains slam.   (Dillard, 1974, pp. 33–4)

The deepest form of sacramental perception is mystical. What
links with the mystical experience of religious traditions is the
sense of not so much seeing but being seen, held and dreamed:
God's is the initiative, God who holds us in distress, a God
present even when experienced as absent. And God reaching out
to whole communities in their pain. This was the intuition of
Etty Hillesum during the Nazi persecution of World War II,
a young Jewish woman in the camp at Westerbork, before
deportation to Auschwitz, where she would die. The utter
vulnerability of God was what drove her to a prayer life where
she wanted to be the praying heart of the concentration camp,
where every aspect of nature – a twig of jasmine or a piece of
bread – encouraged her appreciation of creation and her desire
to offer everything to God (Hillesum, 1981).

But the mystery of the ecomystical path at its most profound
level is the simple experience that healing is offered through
reverencing the earth, and paying attention to the humblest of
tasks. As I found digging my garden 14 years ago, as Wangari
Maathai discovered when she planted a tree, honouring creation is
earthing our hopes and believing in the earth's future. It is
practising an ecology of care. At the same time the human spirit
is being healed. There are numerous examples of this ancient
truth that is being rediscovered by some contemporary psychotherapeutic practices. But it is actually found in some of the
wisdom of the Eastern Desert Fathers. There is a story of a young
monk brought low with depression and sickness of spirit, not
made any better by being told to stay in his cell:

> For three days the monk did this but then he was overcome
> with *akedia* (spiritual lassitude and apathy). But he found some
> little palm leaves and started trimming them. Next day he started
> plaiting them; when he felt hungry, he said, 'Here are some more
> palm leaves; I'll prepare them. And then have something to eat'.
> He finished them and said, 'Perhaps I'll read for a little bit before
> eating'. When he had done some reading, he said, 'Now let's sing a
> few psalms and then I can eat with a good conscience'. And so
> by God's help he went on little by little.
>
> (cited Williams, 2003, pp. 86–7)

This is the Egyptian desert in the sixth century – but the principle is the same. Do whatever humble job is possible, the simplest task that confronts you, especially where it involves interacting with nature, and in embodied practices that help to heal the split between body and mind. It is also the experience of many women in poor environments where the struggle to maintain life brings both anguish yet moments of contentment and peace.

The ecomystical practice takes diverse routes. What sustains poor women in the droughts of Rajasthan will be different from what sustains communities in the numerous deprivations of a polluted city. But the current hunger for healing experienced by secular society now challenges Christian churches to draw on their resources so as to enrich the entire community in an authentic ecomystical spirituality that will contribute to building up the Christic body.

Conclusion: The ecomystical way – a challenge for the Churches

What gives the ecomystical path its authenticity as healing practice is what it offers to Christian Churches as a whole. Spirituality is not a privatized journey but rooted in God's healing and reconciling actions in Christ. The woundedness of body/spirit discovers hope in the healed, risen life of the resurrection, or redeemed reality. Thus personal body/mind healing is given to us as foretaste, as glimpse of restored new creation. Perhaps it is given so as to fire our imaginations and energies to work for its fulfilment, to inspire our yearning and to reveal the sufferings necessary for its coming. Hence Paul Santmire speaks of the necessity of the recovery of the Martyr Church, where the love of Christ flows into our hearts through the Holy Spirit but also to the creatures of nature:

> How then will this martyr church in this ecological and cosmic era love nature? Passionately, persistently and pervasively. We Christians will be a voice for the voiceless, for the sake of all the creatures who have no voice in human affairs. We will listen to the plaintive cries of the whales and hear the groaning of the rain forests, and we will be their advocates in the village square and in the courts of power by the grace of God. All the more we will

hear the bitter wailing of the little children who live on the trash mountains of this world and who wear clothes washed in streams overflowing with heinous poisons and who sometimes drink those very waters. . . . With comic beauty or with dead seriousness this martyr church will also raise its voice in holy rage against the plundering of this planet's God-given bounty. . . . We will be a martyr church, witnessing in word. But not words only. We will also love nature and all the little ones of this earth in deed.

(Santire, 2000, pp. 119–20)

By becoming again a Martyr Church, the community of those who know themselves beloved along with trees, and plants and earth creatures, our ecomystical yearning for new creation is kept alive. Through the presence of those suffering for justice, the community of witnesses, living and dead, the Spirit will find cracks in the diseased imagination of culture. This is what the Book of Revelation calls the 'subaltern presence': 'When he broke the fifth seal I saw under the altar the souls of those who had been slaughtered for God's word and the testimony they bore. They gave a great cry: "How long, sovereign Lord, holy and true, must it be before Thou wilt vindicate us and avenge our blood on the inhabitants of the earth?"' (Revelations 6.9–10).

Communion with those who have suffered for justice involves our willingness to bear the scars in our own bodies for the sake of this new creation, as those who have chained themselves to trees to avoid their destruction, know too well. But the Church can draw on its ancient tradition of *diaconia*, care, now enlarged to mean care for the whole of creation (cf. Grey, 2001). This is a responsibility crossing all areas of life in community, from practical issues like the ecological justice of our gatherings (light bulbs, heating, recycled paper), to what we read and what we sing in worship, to how we enable awe, wonder and praise to become a shared experience. It means a recovery of the sacred body of creation, not in a sanitized closeted way – sometimes the only way allowed by buildings – but in its rawness, messiness and embodiment. It means facing the horror of natural disaster and not evading the issues.

I am writing this just after the tragic murder of Margaret Hassan in Iraq.[8] In so doing I would like to honour her efforts to sustain life in the deteriorating situation in Baghdad through bringing water and food to the poorest people. Remembering and celebrating the presence and the witness of the community of saints, from *all* faiths all over the world, suffering and being murdered because they stand for truth and justice awakens a new awareness of the transgressive Spirit kindling the fires of resistance and creating a new source of mutuality across and beyond boundaries. This is a mystical spirituality in the pursuit of justice. It is ecological because the faithful animals are included in the cloud of witnesses/martyrs (as they have appeared in Celtic spirituality and in the stories of the early monks in the desert) as well as the sacred trees of all religions, the mountains of revelation and the deserts of solitude.

And finally, in this pilgrimage of reconversion to the earth, ecomysticism is the shared path of recovery of hope and recovery of joy. There was joy at creation's birth, joy offered by the great vision of the Feast of Life (Isaiah 25) and again by the vision of the redeemed city where the leaves of the tree of life are for the healing of nations (Revelation 22): these images nurture a great hope that the restraint and transformation of lifestyles, necessary if creation is to be redeemed, are in the service of a joy that all may share, enabling the participation in the joy and desire of God.

Notes

1 I was not alone in experiencing this: in a discussion group of women friends who had also experienced cancer – more than once in some cases – we shared this common reaction emerging *especially* among priests.

2 I had been appointed two years earlier to the Chair of Feminism and Christendom at the Catholic University of Nijmegen.

3 The fact that I do not mention my husband Nicholas's role here is because he shared so much of the distress with me: he too needed support and strength.

4 I realize Isaiah is a composite figure, covering the pre-exilic period, exile and return from Babylon.

5 The word was first used by Ada Maria Isasi-Daiz and points to the transformation of relations that the kingdom heralds, the fact that we are sisters and brothers in this new creation.

6 I am aware that this is controversial: much that passes for Celtic revival is inauthentic and appeals to the popular taste in an unhistorical way.

7 This is as part of my involvement with Wells for India, a small NGO working with partners in the desert state of Rajasthan (see <www.wellsforindia.org>).
8 Margaret Hassan was the Director of *Care International* in Iraq. She had converted from Christianity to Islam after marriage to an Iraqi and had displayed remarkable courage before and during the war.

References

De Villiers, M., *Water Wars: Is The World's Water Running out?* Weidenfeld and Nicholson, London, 1999.

Dillard, A., *Pilgrim at Tinker Creek*. Harper Perennial, New York, 1974.

Galloway, K., *The Dream of Learning our True Name*. Wild Goose Publications, Glasgow, 2004.

Grey, M., *Redeeming the Dream*. SPCK, London, 1989; Sahitya Prakash, Gujarat, 2000.

Grey, M., *The Wisdom of Fools? Seeking Revelation for Today*. SPCK, London, 1993.

Grey, M., *Prophecy and Mysticism – the Heart of the Post-modern Church*. T&T Clark, Edinburgh, 1997.

Grey, M., *Earth-Keeping: Pastoral Theology in a climate of Globalisation*. Inaugural Lecture for the University of Wales, Lampeter, 2001.

Grey, M., *Sacred Longings: the Ecological Spirit and Globalisation*. Fortress/ Augsburg, Philadelphia, 2003.

Hildegard of Bingen, *Book of Divine Works*. Fox, M. (ed. and intro.), Bear and Co, Santa Fe, 1987.

Hillesum, E., *Etty: an Interrupted Life: the Diaries of Etty Hillesum, 1941–43*. Washington Square Press, New York, 1981.

Hopkins, G. M., 'God's Grandeur' in *Poems*. Penguin, Harmondsworth, 1953.

James, W., *The Varieties of Religious Experience: the Gifford Lectures of 1901–2*. Collins, Glasgow, 1960.

Jantzen, G., *Power, Gender and Mysticism*. Cambridge University Press, Cambridge, 1995.

Jewitt, S., *Environment, Knowledge and Gender: Local Development in India's Jharkhand*. Ashgate, Aldershot, 2002.

Keller, C., *From a Broken Web*. Beacon, Boston, 1986.

Kumar, S., *You Are, Therefore I Am: a Declaration of Independence*. Green Book, Dartington, Totnes, 1992.

Macy, J., 'Awakening to the Ecological Self', in Plant, J. L. (ed.), *Healing the Wounds: The Promise of Ecofeminism*. New Society, Philadelphia, 1989.

Martos, J., *Doors to the Sacred: a Historical Introduction to Sacraments in the Christian Church*. SCM Press, London, 1981.

Matthews, M., *Both Alike to Thee: the Retrieval of the Mystical Way.* SPCK, London, 2000.

McFague, S., *The Body of God.* SCM Press, London, 1993.

McFague, S., *Life Abundant.* Fortress/Augsburg, Minneapolis, 2001.

McKibben, B., *The Comforting Whirlwind.* Eerdmans, Grand Rapids, Michigan, 1994.

Morley, J., *All Desires Known.* Women in Theology, London, 1988.

Rich, A., 'Natural Resources', in *The Dream of a Common Language.* W. & W. Norton, New York, 1978.

Rich, A., *A Wild Patience has taken me thus far.* W. & W. Norton, New York, 1981.

Santmire, P., *Nature Reborn.* Fortress/Augsburg, Philadelphia, 2000.

Shiva, V. and Mies, M., *Ecofeminism.* Zed Books, London, 1993.

Shiva, V., *Water Wars: Privatisation, Pollution and Profit.* Pluto, London, 2002.

Slee, N., *Praying Like a Woman.* SPCK, London, 2004.

Toolan, D., *At Home in the Cosmos.* Orbis, Maryknoll, 2003.

Wallace, M., *Fragments of the Spirit.* Continuum, New York, 1996.

Weil, S., *Waiting on God.* Crauford, E. (tr.), Fontana, London 1949.

Williams, R., *Teresa of Avila.* Geoffrey Chapman, London, 1991.

Williams, R., *Silence and Honey Cakes: the Wisdom of the Desert.* Lion Publishing, Oxford, 2003.

4

Healing and peace

CLIVE BARRETT

———◆———

Clive Barrett demonstrates how a Judaeo-Christian understanding of peace is integral to the Christian healing ministry. Taking his definition of peace from the Hebrew word *shalom*, Barrett emphasizes the relational component of peace as 'right relationship with everyone and everything'. In this way Barrett extends the commonly accepted understanding of peace as 'right relationship with God', to include right relationship 'with oneself', 'with one another', 'in community', 'in the world' and 'with our planet'. This leads Barrett to explore how the Church as an institution, and its members personally, are called to bring healing and peace to the world.

* * *

It was Europe's darkest hour, 1941, and the continent was in the grip of a terrible war. Not everyone believed that the war had been inevitable. Not everyone had acquiesced in the vindictiveness of Versailles 1919, or the refusal of petty-minded national leaders to embrace opportunities for universal disarmament. A group of Anglican pacifists had worked tirelessly between the wars to find alternatives to militarism, to promote a climate of peace and to find a route to continental justice more equitable than the right's policy of appeasement of Fascism. One of that group was Gilbert Shuldam Shaw, a rebellious priest in Poplar, East London, and later Warden of the Community of the Sisters of the Love of God, at Fairacres, Oxford.[1] Shaw was a contributor to a Christian pacifist symposium, published in 1941 by those committed to the ways of peace, even in a time of war. His chapter, entitled 'Prayer for peace', includes a paragraph worthy of further reflection:

God is peace. He is not only the God of peace but He Himself is peace itself in the same manner that He is not merely the God of love but He Himself is love. Peace is a positive attribute of being, of the same order as love and truth, for peace is *the state of harmonious relationship* between the several parts of a living organism, each perfectly fulfilling its contribution to the whole and to each other. Peace, as it belongs to absolute being, is therefore in our relative existence only expressible as *a state of becoming*, that is being manifested rather than being an accomplished fact at any given moment of expression. Peace, the flow and reflow of harmony in unbroken relationship, is *the goal of prayer* . . . Our Blessed Lord promises to those who are in *the way of reconciliation* with Him, His own peace: 'My peace I give unto you' . . .   (Hartill (ed.), 1941, p. 96, my italics)

God is peace

'In the beginning, God . . .' (Genesis 1.1)

That it is in the nature of God to be loving was known to the Hebrew prophets from the time of Hosea (3.1). In Jesus' parable of the prodigal and his brother (Luke 15.11–31) the most significant figure is the boys' loving father, an image of God that would have seemed strange to many of his audience. Beyond this, the Johannine insight into the nature of God was that God actually is Love (1 John 4.8, 16). There is an identity, an equivalence, a sine qua non. That equivalence relation means that the Hymn of Love in 1 Corinthians 13.4ff. can be read, at least devotionally, as 'God is patient, God is kind . . .' Yet such glimpses into the nature of God have more than devotional consequences: the Johannine revelation was immediately used to admonish those who did not love their brothers and sisters and to encourage those who did. Doctrinal insights have implications for moral behaviour.

Shaw's insight takes us further. Peace, too, is part of the Godhead, the peace that passes all understanding. Perhaps 1 Corinthians 13.4–8 could be read as 'peace is patient, peace is kind . . .' To consider peace as an aspect of God is to revisit the doctrinal formulations of the Catholic Church. Among the consistent teachings of the early Church were the assertions that the followers of Christ were not able to take part in battle, and that God was Trinity *in Unity.*

Tertullian (c.160–220), who said that Jesus' disarming of Peter was the disarming of every soldier, was the first theologian to explore *tres Personae, una Substantia* in the debate on the nature of God.[2] Similarly Irenaeus (c.177–202), Bishop of Lyons, stressed the absolute oneness of God in the same document wherein he rejoiced that Christians had indeed turned their swords into ploughshares.[3] Doctrinal insights do indeed have implications for moral behaviour. That was understood of old by Levitical scribes: 'You shall not take vengeance or bear a grudge against any of your people, but you shall love your neighbour as yourself: I am the LORD' (Leviticus 19.18). The peaceful and united nature of God as peace requires a peaceful, reconciling, nonviolent ethic in Christian life. With God as peace permeating all aspects of our being, the call to walk the way of God's healing peacemakers is to be lived in our daily lives, our community affairs, our international relations.

On a number of occasions in the twentieth century, the Lambeth Conferences of Anglican bishops worldwide addressed issues of faith and peace. From 1930 onwards, most conferences endorsed a statement that, 'War, as a means of settling international disputes, is incompatible with the teaching and example of our Lord Jesus Christ.' That teaching and example are consistent and clear.

The teaching of Matthew 5 is well known, including the present-tense blessing being received by those who are actively being makers of peace, as well as their future appellation as children of God. The Mosaic prohibition of murder is strengthened to address not only murderous intent, but the anger that fuels so many smaller acts of violence. The acceptability of altar offerings is dependent on prior reconciliation. *Lex talionis* is superseded by love for enemies. An essential dimension of Jesus' sermon is that it addresses the here and now. The in-bursting of the kingdom of peace is associated with the coincident living of the values of the kingdom of peace. Eschatology is for today. This is not an avoidable counsel of perfection, to be postponed until such time as God determines to bring about the fulfilment of the kingdom. Rather, this is the way of God for today, God's kingdom of peace being lived and anticipated in the values and actions of God's people.

Jesus' example was even more radical than his teaching. Jesus the physical healer is the Jesus whose humble birth was proclaimed to be that of the prince of peace, whose healing extended to the household of a member of the hated occupying forces, whose embrace knew no bounds, extending to terrorist Zealots and collaborating tax-collectors alike, who broke down barriers between Samaritan and Jew, male and female, who refused (John 6.15) to become a military Messiah, who rode on a humble donkey rather than a warrior-king's steed, who resisted the opportunity to take up arms in Gethsemane ('Put your sword back into its place; for all who take the sword will perish by the sword' – Matthew 26.53; Luke's account, 22.51, even includes Jesus healing the wounded), whose Passion was met with non-violence and a prayer for forgiveness. The Passion narratives contain repeated prophetic allusions, including Isaiah 53.9, where the suffering servant endured the final insult of being buried in a grave of the despised rich, even though, it stressed, unlike them, 'he had done no violence'.

Seen in this light, one of the primary lessons of the resurrection is God's vindication of the way of nonviolent love. No wonder that the greeting of the risen Christ was 'Peace be with you' (John 20.19–20, 26). Jesus' way of nonviolent love is the pathway to reconciliation with God, to peace in God's world. It is the pathway that the followers of Jesus are called to walk, the way of the cross that is to be taken up. Paul spoke of having peace with God through our Lord Jesus Christ (Romans 5.1). Such is the way to God, the way to God's kingdom. The earliest Christians were known as followers of 'The Way'.

In the age of Pentecost, there was constant allusion to God the Spirit of peace. 'To settle the mind on the Spirit is life and peace,' wrote Paul, adding, 'The kingdom of God . . . is righteousness and peace and joy in the Holy Spirit' (Romans 8.8; 14.17). The fruits of the Spirit listed in Galatians 5.22–23 begin, 'Love, joy, peace patience . . .' The coupling of ειρηνη and μακροθυμια is significant, as in many instances 'patience' or 'longsuffering' could just as easily be translated as 'nonviolence'.

There was considerable early emphasis on peace in community, about maintaining 'the unity of the Spirit in the bond of peace' (Ephesians 4.2–3). The primitive communism of Acts 2.42–47 and 4.32 indicated a peaceful, nonviolent community ideal, marked by an awareness of justice and each other's need (James 2.15–16). This was a peace that needed building, hence the encouragement of 1 Peter 3.11 to 'seek peace and pursue it', and of Hebrews 12.14 to 'pursue peace with everyone'.

Paul's relationships with the imperial powers were tactically astute, as mission opportunities were greater for those who stayed out of trouble. Hence Romans 13, which can hardly be seen to justify a meek acceptance of a state's call to arms when read alongside the explicitly pacifist 12.9–21, with its conclusion that evil should be overcome with good. One of the most striking New Testament rejections of militarism is seen in the imagery of Ephesians 6.12–17. Out go breastplates, shields, helmets and swords and in come righteousness, faith, salvation and the Spirit, and 'as shoes for your feet put on whatever will make you ready to proclaim the gospel of peace'. Christians are to walk in the light, as those who have beaten their swords into ploughshares, who learn war no more (Isaiah 2.4–5).

If the healing miracles are seen as signs of the in-bursting of the kingdom of the God who is peace then the example of Jesus' life is a sign of the living out of the way of that kingdom: nonviolent, reconciling, recognizing the human worth of all people. The teaching and example of Christ, as reflected upon by the early Church, indicates that God's desire for healing, wholeness, unity and peace includes and moves beyond the individual. Indeed, a healing that is limited to the individual in isolation is a partial healing. Few, if any, have a vocation to live as a hermit. Each person is an individual in community, in the global village of a small planet. Concerns for healing move out beyond oneself, to embrace the violence, fractures and divisions in personal relationships, in the condition of society, and in the principalities and powers at work in the international order.

The state of harmonious relationship

The Greeks, as we have seen above, thought of peace in terms of the often spiritualized *eirene*; the Romans maintained a sometimes brutal *pax*; more all-encompassing was the Hebrew concept of peace, *Shalom*. Shalom implied a sense of well-being, of the security that arises through being in a right relationship with everyone and everything. Peace was not a solitary concern, but fundamentally an issue of relationships. If any relationship was unhealthy there was the risk of joining the false prophets who cried peace when there was no peace (Jeremiah 6.14). Consider the breadth of peace as a right relationship:

• with God

See Peace as the goal of prayer (pp. 73–5)

• with oneself

At different times in life, all people suffer from what the Book of Common Prayer describes as 'trouble, sorrow, need, sickness or any other adversity'. For internal or external reasons, one's peace is shattered, one's physical, mental or emotional well-being is fragmented, and one stands in need of healing. Scientific research and the advances of modern medicine have increased the quantity and quality of life for everyone in the western world. The Centre for Health and Pastoral Care, commonly known as Holy Rood House, is one of a number of mainstream independent centres, which may or may not have a faith basis, working in close co-operation with health authorities to provide the caring, listening space within which personal healing can take root. This is the building or rebuilding of wholeness, in body, mind and spirit. For some this means the addressing of personal memories, for others it means coming to terms with issues of addiction, forgiveness, self-esteem, self-confidence, empowerment. It is an enabling process, freeing each person from their walls and letting them become more fully the person that God wants them to be, letting them find peace in and with themselves.

• with one another

Human beings are social creatures, designed to interact with other people. Yet in each person's experience is a catalogue of failure to conduct relationships, casual or more meaningful, with appropriate care and respect. Daily anger and frustrations contribute to the diminution of peace. Inappropriate dealings with others, from shop customer to road user, add to the stress and violence in the world. This is most likely of all in the places where people spend most time, possibly in the workplace, more often than not in the home. Relationships with those in one's own household are the ones most likely to be tense, imbalanced, unpeaceful. As every counsellor knows, in all too many cases these relationships disintegrate into the most horrendous domestic violence, with abused partners and children undergoing appalling suffering behind a closed front door.

- in community

It is hard to believe that a myopic leading politician could once claim that there was no such thing as society. Consideration of the needs of one's neighbours reveals requirements that can be addressed, patterns of behaviour that can be changed, to lessen the violence and enhance the peace in local communities. Is there an elderly person dying alone? A teenager feeling alienated from society? A member of a minority group feeling threatened because of their race or religion? A pedestrian fearful of a random attack? A drug-user desperate for the next fix? A homeless person who has fallen through the safety-net of our society? An ex-prisoner wondering how he might ever fit in again? A woman anticipating the next beating from her violent partner? A single parent struggling with the demands of young children and a part-time job? A refugee in anguish at the prospect of being sent back to the perils of the past? An ambitious employee ground down by long hours and overwork? A family struggling to survive on the minimum wage, mindful of the affluence of others? Where there is violence there is no peace, including all the countless ways local communities cry out against structural violence, injustice and inequality.

- in the world

Development campaigns have highlighted the injustices that shatter the peace: fair trade, drop the debt, make poverty history. Such campaigns contribute to peacemaking in the world. While banks and corporate conglomerates share fatter profits among their shareholders than the poorest nations have to share out in GDP, then there is injustice, then there is no peace. Yet it is simplistic, even dangerous, to say that there is no peace without justice. That slogan has too often been used by those in power to impose a 'justice' favourable to them, by military means. We have seen it, to our shame, in the military action undertaken by the USA and the UK in Iraq. The slogan needs to be balanced by the realization that neither is there justice without peace. One example will suffice. In a world of traded armaments, the arms industries that drain the budgets of developing nations, often as a condition of receiving supposedly generous aid contributions made by the industrialized nations, take bread from the mouths of the starving. The very existence of armaments producers is an abomination. Until their abolition is taken as seriously as an earlier generation approached the scandal of slave trading, there can be no peace and there certainly can be no justice. A few years ago I was visited by a Sri Lankan theologian, at a time when the civil war in that island was at its height. I asked him what we in the UK could do to help. He said that there were no armaments factories in Sri Lanka, that all weapons on both sides were imported. At that time there was a tank factory in my city. The theologian told me that, although there were no tanks in Sri Lanka, the best thing we could do would be to try to close that tank factory. While ever the rich make money from any form of arms, the poor will suffer the world over.

- with our planet

The created order is wounded and in need of healing. War is a major polluter and abuser of the earth, but even apart from war, human greed, ambition, ignorance and overpopulation are damaging this fragile planet. From deforestation and desertification, from nuclear waste to the ozone layer, from climate change to coral reefs, human beings are drawing on resources that have taken longer than human history to produce, with consequences that will take even longer to repair.

These categories are not rigidly separate parts of human life and behaviour. The stressed worker is the person more likely to express his or her frustration through violence in the home. An imbalanced head of state is not the best person to entrust with weapons of mass destruction. After a number of international conflicts from Vietnam onwards, more western soldiers have subsequently committed suicide than were killed in action during the war. As violence crosses the boundaries of human activity, so must our search for healing and peace. It includes making the kind of protest enunciated by Canon Samuel Barnett at the Annual Meeting of the Peace Society back in 1899, when talk of imperial war in South Africa was rife. Barnett was warden of the Toynbee Hall university settlement in the poverty-stricken East End of London. In those paternalistic days he was regarded as the 'voice' of the people of East London. Barnett contrasted military spending with the deprivation, squalor and brutal attitudes he found. There was an economic component to the violence:

> East Londoners have not the equal means for a healthy and happy life; they have not the same clean and well-lighted streets as their neighbours in the City have. They have not houses through which the air can freely blow, and in which the children can grow up healthy and strong; they have not . . . ; they have not . . .
>
> Why? . . . The expenditure, we are told, is too great. . . . The taxes could not endure it; but the taxes are used in keeping up the war instruments. Well, sires, the money that is being spent yearly in the instruments of death might be spent in keeping thousands and thousands of children alive, and in making more healthy and strong the men and women who are alive. . . . It is, therefore, sir, on the part of these people who starve and die that I protest against this great expenditure on war material, and claim that a far wiser expenditure would be in making the conditions such that the children should grow up to be men and women, and that when they do grow up they shall be healthy in body, happy in mind, home lovers, real patriots . . .
>
> (Barnett, 1899, p. 234)

Barnett was able to make the connection between violence at an international level and the community and domestic violence he saw daily. He observed how war abroad affected human behaviour at home. (In modern terms, attempts to stop playground bullying will never be totally successful while Britain possesses nuclear weapons or goes to war in Iraq.) The rich were affected by a spirit of war in developing a sense of 'masterfulness', which led landlords and employers to become more contemptible of the poor. (So our age of war coincides with an era of contempt for refugees.) Barnett spoke too of his poorer neighbours in East London who were 'brutalised', who enjoyed tales of horror, whose 'conduct is often coarse and their manners are rough'. These people were on the edge of being extremely cruel and likely to regard violence as a remedy for wrong.

These people then are 'brutalised', and war, as I understand it, has always thrown a sort of halo over a character, and war has enabled people to be brutal by making them believe that they are heroes. The consequence is that whenever there is a talk about war, and when men are worshipping the heroes of war, and when they are thinking about what war is going to do, they themselves are more easily inclined to brutal pleasures, and are themselves more proud of being brutal. . . . In the name, therefore, of the people, of my neighbours, who are capable of being tender, who are capable of being considerate for the weak, who are capable of the highest pleasures of thought and feeling, who are capable, at any rate, of following the Prince of Peace, and of admiring Him, I protest against this light talk about war, which allows them to live a more degraded life than they ever meant to live.   (Barnett, 1899, p. 234)

Any consideration of peace and healing, therefore, needs to recognize and address the wholeness of peace, the need for Shalom, for right relationships in every aspect of our lives, from the interpersonal to the international. To say there is a wholeness to healing may sound tautological. Addressing only the personal, say, or the interpersonal *in vacuo* can only produce a partial healing. The 'original sin' of the fractured world in which we are born and brought up has wounded us all, and it is not possible in any real context to produce completely whole and healthy persons. The wholeness of peace requires us to consider the wholeness of opportunities for healing. Similarly, campaigning groups need to realize that the creation of a just and peaceful international order cannot be separated from the need to address issues of healing and peace in each person's spiritual and emotional life, and the interpersonal relationships of each household and group. Peace is a whole and God is peace and God is one.

A state of becoming

1 Accepting vulnerability

Defining 'peace' is non-trivial. I once heard a suggestion that the only sensible way to represent peace would be as a hologram, something that could be glimpsed but never completely grasped. It is far more than an absence of war, an absence of violent conflict. It may not even include an absence of conflict in general, as conflict, nonviolently handled, can bring understanding and growth. Similarly, it could be noisy, adventurous. Part of the more familiar biblical imagery, however, is the vision of each person beneath their vine or fig tree, with sufficient prosperity to guarantee food, shelter, contentment and security.

The relationship between peace and security is one that has recently been considered by the Norwegian churches. Instead of military state security they explored human security, environmental security and economic security. What is the relationship, they asked, between the right to protection from calamity or malice and the essential vulnerability of every human being? Vulnerability, trust, compassion and a desire for cooperation go hand in hand, yet alongside them is a need for protection, against the elements, against disease, against persecution. The prophets stressed God's favour for the persecuted and outcast, the crucifixion can be interpreted as a sign of God's solidarity with the nonviolent victims of society, but neither means that it is good to face persecution, that it is desirable to be a victim.

The search for security is part of the search for peace, but what if that search becomes obsessive, what if it denies one's humanity by attempting to take away the essential vulnerability that is part of what it is to be human? Excessively striving to reduce the risk in life can become counter-productive. A child brought up in an over-protective environment can become susceptible to disease in later life through not having acquired an ability to withstand infection; a risk-obsessed society penalizes genuine mishaps and accidents in a greed-induced litigious culture; a democracy can destroy ancient freedoms in an attempt to defend a society whose worth is measured in those freedoms. These all show that security is a false god. Of course it is right and good to reduce the avoidable risks of life, but it is a dangerous fallacy to act as if individually or nationally we are or could ever be inviolable, added to which it is observably true that those who believe themselves to be invulnerable are the most likely to be tempted into violent conflict. The tightrope walked by a democratic society post 9/11 is to protect people against the violation of vulnerability, while defending their essential right to live vulnerably. 'The vulnerable human being is entitled to protection *for the sake of his/her vulnerability* so that he/she can *continue to be vulnerable* and therefore human.'[4]

The Norwegian report notes that one of the aims of those engaged in terrorism is to promote discord. An essential component, therefore, in overcoming terrorism is the promotion of cooperation between religious and ethnic groups, with a valuing of diversity, of what Jonathan Sacks called the 'dignity of difference' (Sacks, 2002). Trust is built through coming face to face with the other and coming to recognize one's mutual interdependence.

2 Listening

A key ingredient in any process of bridge-building is the ability to listen. That is more than being in a forum where different opinions are being expressed in order to express one's own opinions. Rather, it is the recognition that there are other ways of looking at the world, other experiences and insights, other understandings with which one has yet to engage. True listening implies an openness, a preparedness to be challenged, to grow, to change. It means acknowledging that one may not have all the answers, may know only in part and may prophesy only in part. Peacemaking requires daring to listen, and listening means being open to the possibility of hearing the voices of those whose presence could not be seen, whose stories could not have been imagined.

Listening is a well-established practice in the therapeutic care of individuals. The Centre for Health and Pastoral Care is a classic example of a safe environment where active listening is encouraged in the process of healing the emotional wounds and painful memories of individuals. Victims of violence, and especially survivors of sexual abuse, appreciate the healing that is opened up by being listened to and taken seriously. In a noisy world, such voices may not otherwise be heard, may not otherwise dare to whisper.

There is also a political dimension to listening. Alongside the UN International Decade for a Culture of Peace and Nonviolence for the Children of the World, the World Council of Churches is promoting 2001–10 as a Decade to Overcome Violence (DOV). The Central Committee of the World Council of Churches, under the heading 'Seek peace and pursue it'

(Psalm 34.14), noted that 'Part of the contribution to building a culture of peace involves listening to the stories of those who are the primary victims of violence, including people who are poor, women, youth and children, people with disabilities, and Indigenous Peoples.'

3 Being Church in a new way

The DOV has impacted across international ecclesial structures. The Conference on World Mission and Evangelism has acknowledged not only that a church can be a healing community for the most vulnerable, but also that there are many aspects of church provision of ministries of healing and reconciliation in situations of violent conflict. The churches are specially equipped with the theological language, pastoral experience and sacramental resources to be able to work alongside both victims and perpetrators in addressing such issues as repentance, forgiveness, the healing of memories, and reconciliation. Churches Together in Britain and Ireland has begun to explore similar themes but has been hampered by the shameful lack of financial commitment to ecumenical peacemaking by its constituent churches. It is hardly surprising, therefore, that British Christians have been largely unaffected by the challenges of the DOV.

A more positive response has come for the international Lutheran community. The Lutheran World Federation (LWF) has addressed the wounded world's need of healing, realizing that amid the suffering and brokenness, God is using human beings to effect healing in marvellous and unexpected ways. Such healing was not limited to the individual or intimate sphere, but included the social, political and ecological: 'Where healing takes place, justice is restored.' In particular, the LWF has called upon member churches to listen, not only to Christians from minority groups, but also to members of other faiths, being open to recognizing God's presence among them and, through '*diapraxis*' (dialogue in praxis) striving with them 'for the healing of the world through reconciliation, peace and justice for all God's children'.[5] Children and families need to be free from the fear of violence, whether internal violence within the family, or the violence of war, poverty, drugs and disease that devastate families the world over. Sometimes nonviolent resistance can break these cycles of violence and be used to confront militarism and the manufacture of armaments. The LWF affirmed the use and power of nonviolence to transform situations of violence and injustice; it is a lead that British churches should follow.

Accepting vulnerability, actively listening, being Church in a new way – these are all parts of making peace, in oneself, in relation to others, as Christ's community in the world. The beatitude to the peacemakers is in the present tense: both the peacemaking and the blessings are for now, with only the appellation of 'children of God' left to the future. There is not peace now, only wars and rumours of wars, so the task for this now and every now is to be a peacemaker, for the end is yet to come. Peace is for now on. Individually and collectively the challenge is to live lives that are nonviolent and peaceable, to become more truly God's people, the people of peace, of the God who is peace.

As mentioned above, the first followers of Christ were known as 'The Way'. The realization that peace is not so much a goal, a destination, as a way to travel is a Gandhian insight into nonviolence. A. J. Muste, from the US Fellowship of Reconciliation, is credited with the dictum, 'There is no way to peace – peace is the way.' Mother Teresa is reputed to have said something similar, that 'Peace is not something you wish for, it is something you make, something you do, something you are, something you give away' (Mavunduse and Oxley, 2002, p. 4).[6] Peace is not only in the vision, its essence is in the action; it is as much a verb as a noun. That means that it is impossible to make war in order to achieve peace, to undertake violence in order to bring about Shalom, for the means chosen become the end achieved (cf. Iraq). One reaps what one sows. The only way to peace is peace; the only winner in choosing war is war.

If peace is indeed a noun, it is not a future fantasy, it is a state of becoming, it is about the way lives are lived today. It is about living peaceably with oneself, with each other, with the planet. It is about standing alongside the most vulnerable, striving to reduce their vulnerability, while affirming that our vulnerability is an essential part of our humanity. It is about trusting and listening, even when that trust is abused or one recoils from what one hears. It is about finding new ways to be Church, in which the resolve to overcome and heal all aspects of violence in the world lasts not only for a decade but for ever.

Peace . . . the goal of prayer

From the Hebrew Shekinah to the threefold call of Isaiah, the nature of God is mysterious, other, holy. The etymological root of holiness implies separation, a paradoxical concept in the study of wholeness. Yet it is a separation that leads to an appreciation of the need for healing and forgiveness, hence Isaiah's response that he was lost, a man of unclean lips dwelling amid a people of unclean lips (Isaiah 6.5). Cleansed and restored to health he was able to proclaim a moral and spiritual holiness, a reflection of a holy God that implied a wholeness of being. In his seminal volume on *The Christian Healing Ministry*, Maddocks noted that 'To be made whole is to be "at-oned" with all those who are enjoying salvation and healing', and with the holy God (Maddocks, 1981, p. 15). The Gospel begins with Zechariah being struck dumb by his engagement with the holy God. Nine months later when he reclaimed his tongue he proclaimed the need to respond to God by service in 'holiness and righteousness' (Luke 1.75). These two terms are inseparable; spirituality and morality go hand in hand. There can be no wholeness, no healing of self or society, without both holiness and righteousness, prayer and prophecy, inner peace and outer.

The Faith and Order Team of the World Council of Churches, in a 2003 reflection entitled 'Nurturing peace', suggested that upholding Shalom calls for a new way to be Christian, a new spirituality committed to the inter-relatedness of life, a spirituality that is creative and inclusive, confronting and transforming cultures of violence. Such an inclusive spirituality has implications for both our personal and corporate relationship with God.

Holiness is a new way for each person to see the world, with eyes open to the God-perspective in the created order, in human structures, in oneself and one's relationships. Holiness is also a way of hearing or, more precisely, of attentive listening. It is an invitation to be still, freely to choose to be silent, to listen to God in the prayer of the heart, the Quakerly silence of attentiveness to the Spirit. Here again is the call to patience, to nonviolent waiting, to foregoing the immediate, to immersion in God's time, acknowledging the eschatological fullness of the kingdom (cf. Hauerwas and Fodor, in Hauerwas, 2004, pp. 99ff.). This prayer is a channel for God to change the one who prays, for in listening to God one hears also the silence and the cries of the world's victims. Such prayer is a personal openness to the God who is peace, an openness to personal change, for changing one's way of relating to others. Prayer is a means of being one with God who is alongside victims of violence; it is a means to become in solidarity with those victims. In intercession, those who pray are one with God with the world on their heart. In that peace with God is found a commitment to God's peace.

There is a tendency for postmodern spirituality to become narcissistic, a pastime for introspective individuals. Nothing could be further from the Judaeo-Christian model of community. To become a spiritual being requires life in community, sharing one's journey with others variously journeying within a Christian community. Even the desert fathers and mothers of the fourth and fifth centuries developed a spirituality of community (cf. Williams, 2003). The praying community, despite its inevitable tensions, should lead in to the essential wholeness of the Church catholic. The corporate worship of the Church should reflect on the nature of God as peace, should enable greater insight into the God of peace. What anniversaries and commemorations, ancient or modern, are marked liturgically? Do liturgical anniversaries speak of war or peace? Do they engage with holocaust memorials or the US acknowledgement of Martin Luther King in January? How many churches keep the Week of Prayer for World Peace, with its opportunities for interfaith bridge-building? Or note St Hugh's rejection of war taxes on 17 November? What canticles, hymns, anthems are chosen? (A recent Anglican office book recommends the Song of Moses and Miriam, Exodus 15, for daily use in Eastertide; the regular rejoicing in the slaughter of Pharaoh's army by a God of battles is hardly an appropriate way to celebrate the Easter vindication of a nonviolent Christ.) In particular, in what way is 11 November marked? Is Remembrance Day a time for yet more militarism and nationalism, fuelling the very sentiments that led millions to perish in the twentieth century? Or is it a proclamation of peace, of 'Never again' in the face of governments that repeat the sins of their ancestors in Kosovo, Afghanistan, Iraq . . . ? What place is given to the saint commemorated on that day, Martin of Tours, a policing soldier who rejected 'the king's shilling' and left the imperial army rather than engage in fighting? Corporate worship, and especially the music of the Church, forms the nature and character of Christian people in society. Christian festivals, music and healing liturgies in particular must embrace the healing needs of the world. Only then will the Church's worship start to become worthy of the God who is peace.

The way of reconciliation

The interconnectedness between forgiveness, healing and peace is substantial. There are issues concerning one's own need for forgiveness, for individual sins of commission and omission that build barriers between oneself and God, barriers that disturb one's spiritual peace and equilibrium. These lead into the realm of spiritual direction and sacramental confession. There are issues concerning one's own need for forgiveness for being part of a group (e.g. the Church, the nation) that has been responsible for adding to the violence of the world. On the occasion of the founding of the DOV in 2001, the World Council of Churches stated, 'We launch this decade in a spirit of repentance that as Christians we have been among those who have inflicted or justified violence.'[7] Such awareness of sin (for example, historically, in creating the philosophical basis for the Holocaust) should not paralyse us and prevent us from working for peace today (in Israel–Palestine, say), doing justice and loving kindness, but it should certainly make us walk more humbly with our God (Micah 6.8). There are wrongs to be righted, in humility, with patience (that is, nonviolence).

Related issues concern the ability of a person or a group to offer forgiveness to those who have committed wrong – 'as we forgive those who have sinned against us'. There can be a perverse comfort, even a cause for identity, in wallowing in a victim culture. How many times in human history have persecuted minorities revelled in the strength induced by their persecution? It certainly worked for the early Church. Even knowing that a refusal to forgive is a refusal to embrace one's own healing does not make that act of forgiveness any easier. Memories can be long and extremely painful. One of the initial DOV themes was 'Healing the memories of violence'. Archbishop Tutu and the 'Truth and Reconciliation Commission' in South Africa were a classic paradigm of their age. Their approach led to a surge of interest in processes of memory and reconciliation.

A powerful vehicle for exploring such themes and processes is the 'peace museum', and one of the signs of hope in the world is the plethora of museums for peace springing up in all continents. The search is not only, in the words of the founder of the Transcend organization, Johan Galtung, for *'une histoire subjective'*, a 'what if' approach to historical alternatives, showing that violent conflicts are not inevitable.[8] More than that, in many contexts, there is an attempt to reclaim real memory, the fullness of truth, not to have the future determined by hegemonic memory of the official historians of past victors. Memory is the space for political struggle. In societies that have faced crimes against humanity, even telling stories can take courage when the consequences for one's political well-being, let alone one's psychological health, are unknown. To enable such stories to be told in a way that neither reinforces a victim mentality nor promotes a desire for vengeance, but rather enables the possibility of reconciliation, requires considerable skill and patience. *Memoria Abierta* and other peace groups in Argentina strive to stimulate critical memory of the recent age of military government and missing persons. Grassroots plans for a peace museum in Cambodia, a space for healing memories in a land where genocide and consequent starvation claimed two million lives in the late 1970s, could be more practical than vast expenditure on a formal international tribunal. In the UK, The Peace Museum, Bradford, is a repository of artefacts and stories of all levels of peacemaking, and it is now possible to obtain a postgraduate degree in Peace and Reconciliation at Coventry University.[9]

The way of reconciliation, of bridge-building, of peace making does not have to wait until violent conflicts arise. The more that communities can be brought together before animosities boil over, the more governments can be persuaded to tackle seriously the differences between obscene wealth and desperate poverty, the more that the causes of conflicts are addressed, the less chance there is of violence growing. It is normal to look to inoculations to prevent future disease in one's body, to provide a pre-emptive healing; it must become the norm to look to peacemaking and the search for justice to prevent future violence, both in society and in the wider world.

Healing and peace

Gilbert Shaw was right. God is peace. Peace is within the divine identity. In consequence, all human doing and being should be consistent, compatible and conformed to the way of peace. Health and healing, wholeness and holiness, cannot be separated from the way of peace. It infuses one's prayer, informs one's decision making, inspires one's actions. At all levels one strives to find harmony within relationship, even living in a world where manifestly 'there is no peace'. The fulfilment, then, of one's peacemaking, one's coming to healing in a healthy universe, is clearly in the future. Peace is the goal of one's being, yet, in the present living out of the eschatological values of the kingdom, peace is seen as the means to achieving the goal that is peace. Peace, therefore, is a state of becoming, a way of becoming, indeed the only way that leads to the goal of peace.

The promise of Jesus was that 'my peace I give to you'. It was not a privatized peace of escapism; it was not a peace of a militarized world; it was not a peace where there is no peace. Rather, it is the Shalom of God, bringing wholeness and healing to all aspects of our being, our community, our world. It is for us to pray, to live, and to make that peace of God.

Notes

1 The Russian Archbishop Metropolitan Anthony referred to Shaw as 'the greatest priest I have ever known in any tradition, Orthodox, Catholic or Anglican' (Hacking, 1988, p. 4).
2 Tertullian: 'The patience of the Lord was wounded in (the wound of) Malchus. And so, too, He cursed for ever the works of the sword' (Tertullian, *De Patentia*, 3; *Adversus Praxean*).
3 Irenaeus, *Adversus Haereses* IV.XXXIV.4.
4 'Vulnerability and Security', 3.5. The Commission on International Affairs in the Church of Norway Council on Ecumenical and International Relations, 2001.
5 Message of the Tenth Assembly of the Lutheran World Federation, Winnipeg, 2003.
6 Elsewhere this comment has been attributed to Robert Fulghum in a related article, 'I Believe in Mother Teresa', *Saturday Evening Post*, 1989.

7 Message on the Occasion of the Launch of the Decade to Overcome Violence: Churches Seeking Reconciliation and Peace.
8 Proceedings of the Fifth International Conference of Peace Museums, Gernika, 2005; see <www.transcend.org>.
9 For further information concerning this paragraph see: <www. museumsforpeace.org>; <www.sitesofconscience.org>; <www.act-cambodia. org>; <www.peacemuseum.org.uk>; <www.coventry.ac.uk>.

References

Barnett, S., Annual Meeting of the Peace Society, 'Herald of Peace', *The Peace Society*. London, June 1899.

Hacking, R. D., *Such a Long Journey: A Biography of Gilbert Shaw, Priest*. Mowbray, London, 1988.

Hartill, P. (ed.), *Into the Way of Peace*. James Clarke & Co., London, 1941.

Hauerwas, S., and Fodor, J., 'Performing Faith: The Peaceable Rhetoric of God's Church', in Hauerwas, S., *Performing the Faith*. SPCK, London, 2004.

Irenaeus, 'Adversus Haereses' in *Ante-Nicene Christian Library, Vol. V*. T&T Clark, Edinburgh, 1868. Also available at <http://www.ccel.org/fathers2/ANF-01/TOC.htm>.

Maddocks, M., *The Christian Healing Ministry*. SPCK, London, 1981.

Mavunduse, D., and Oxley, S., *Why Violence? Why Not Peace?* A study guide produced by the World Council of Churches for the Decade to Overcome Violence, 2002.

Sacks, J., *The Dignity of Difference*. Continuum, London, 2002.

Tertullian, 'De Patienta' in *Ante-Nicene Christian Library, Vol. XI*. T&T Clark, Edinburgh, 1869. Also available at <http://tertullian.org/works/de_patientia.htm>.

Tertullian, 'Adversus Praxean' in *Ante-Nicene Christian Library, Vol. XV*. T&T Clark, Edinburgh, 1870. Also available at <http://www.tertullian.org/works/adversus_praxean.htm>.

Williams, R., *Silence and Honey Cakes*. Lion, Oxford, 2003.

Additional website information:

The Norwegian Churches report, 'Vulnerability and Security', <www.gechs.org/activities/opening/stalsett.pdf>.
The World Council of Churches, 'Decade to Overcome Violence', <www.overcomingviolence.org>.
The World Council of Churches, Faith and Order Team reflection, 'Nurturing Peace', <www.wcc-coe.org/wcc/what/faith/nurturingpeace.html>.

5

Forgiveness as permission to live

HADDON WILLMER

———•◆•———

Forgiveness is central to the Judaeo-Christian narrative and pivotal to the Christian healing ministry. But here Haddon Willmer teases out the difference between forgiveness and healing in order to explore forgiveness 'in itself'. This he does, first, by describing what forgiveness is not: for forgiveness 'is not to be ripped out of its space, but is observed in its active contribution and dependencies with all that goes on there'. To get closer to this contextual reality Willmer then proceeds to explore forgiveness as represented biblically and within two novels, arguing, as he does so, for a picture of forgiveness that can be seen as 'a hard, honest and yet hopeful path'.

* * *

Introduction

> Bless the Lord, O my soul,
> and do not forget all his benefits –
> who forgives all your iniquity,
> who heals all your diseases . . .
> (Psalm 103.2)

Forgiveness and healing are like two hands working together to redeem 'your life from the Pit' (Psalm 103.4). The link between them is ancient and still vibrant. But how are they related? In contemporary Christian concern with health and healing, forgiving is often slotted into a niche as a specialist form of healing. That, in my view, diminishes and distorts forgiveness. I want to contribute to the partnership of healing and forgiving by affirming the independence of forgiveness from healing, refusing to assimilate the two. So this paper aims to explore forgiving in itself.

But what is 'forgiving in itself'? I will explain why I do not trust dictionaries to give us the answer, and how my present search is structured by a set of points of orientation. Within this search field I then pursue one aspect of forgiveness in the Bible and in a couple of novels, where it can be seen taking basic, modest and patient form as *permission to live.*

The framework

Words in the forgiveness family are used in many different ways. That needs sorting out. One reason why it does not get sorted out is that many assume they know instinctively what forgiveness is. So our talk goes on at cross-purposes. The confusion cannot be sorted out by laying down definitions of what is held to be 'real' rather than ersatz forgiveness; definition may be good for policing discourse but does little to set free reality-friendly imagination. Forgiving needs to be understood by discerning it in practice even where it is not named. The dictionary is not a reliable guide to forgiving that matches the messiness of life where forgiving turns out to be as needed as it is difficult. In pointing out the limits of definition, I am not supporting a lazy tolerance of an unclarified multiplicity of meanings. Forgiveness is too important for that.

An alternative to proceeding from a definition is to explore a field that is marked out by various interacting considerations. Forgiving may then be discovered living in an environment. Forgiving is not to be ripped out of its space, but is observed in its active contribution and dependencies with all that goes on there.

To explore forgiving we need some initial idea of what we are looking for. This idea is open to correction and development as a result of the search. What we started looking for may not be there: our searching may discover something unexpected but worth finding. Columbus looked for a way to the Indies and found what we call America. I have been thinking seriously about forgiveness for forty years. What I look for is not the same as what I thought I was looking for when I began, though it is not another creature altogether, and I am sure it is there in the field. I am still looking, with an initial idea that is the outcome of years of looking. My idea of forgiveness and of the field in which I am looking for it is a search engine, not the capture of a definitive answer.

Some sides of my idea collide head-on with opinions so widely held that they seem to be self-evident truths. For example, forgiving is not, in my approach, optional. We are *commanded* to love God and our neighbour as ourselves. Love includes forgiving because love of the actual neighbour breaks down quickly unless love works itself out in forgiving. But what if we do not believe in God, or make the mistake of thinking God's command only applies to believers? There are other ways to decide that forgiving is not a matter of choice. Humanity requires us to be simultaneously and appropriately hopeful and truthful about human being. In that simultaneity is forgiveness. Of course, we can choose to abandon the project of being human; there is often much to make it implausible. In the same way, we *can* choose death, for ourselves or for others, but we *may* not. To give up the project of being human may seem to free us from the obligation to forgive, but unless despair becomes absolute, in spiritual death, forgiving is merely postponed, so that when we get round to it, forgiving will have more on its agenda. It will have to bear the burden of our despair about humanity, and its practical consequences, and bring us back to start again not just in truth but also in hope.

Second, forgiveness is not essentially an intransitive or reflexive action, therapy for the victim, but transitive, releasing the *wrong-doer* from the moral and social consequences of wrongdoing. The hurt victim who decides to look after himself, and not to be consumed by bitterness, is on a path of healing wisdom, but it should not be called forgiveness. The victim's liberation from bitterness is only forgiving if somehow it contributes to the release of the wrongdoer. Forgiving is not to be assimilated to any therapy of selfhood (Jones, 1995, pp. 35ff.).

Third, forgiving is not an exclusive possession or right of the victim, though the contribution of victims has a special potential. The right and duty of judging is not restricted to direct victims, let alone to indirect victims. Forgiving is a form of judgement. Judgement is not to be left to victims.

Fourth, forgiving is not to be seen as a dangerous alternative to justice. It is not exceptional marginal practice, while justice is the norm, but it is an indispensable criterion and mode of justice. Justice without forgiving is unjust (Volf, 1996, p. 224).

Fifth, forgiveness is not merely personal or interpersonal, but is to be thought and practised politically.

Sixth, forgiveness and healing are not synonyms, and are not as close as is often imagined. Healing is not a more accessible, contemporary word for forgiveness, and their assimilation can be seriously misleading. In particular, there are vast areas of human living where the word healing gives false expectations: people suffer irreparable losses. There are some hurts for which there is no healing. Where healing is not given, forgiving is possible. The point of this argument is to distinguish healing from forgiving, not to restrict forgiving to the unhealable. There is much of life when both are feasible and they work together, but they are not the same (cf. Parker, 1993).

Seventh, forgiveness is not adequately understood via models that present a simple innocent victim over against a simple guilty aggressor. Such models reflect what occasionally shows up in real life, but mostly people on all sides of a conflictual history are, in varying proportions, victim–victimizers. To read complex situations by squeezing them into the simple model is not merely to render ourselves unable to deal with the reality, but may be an unforgiving device for discrediting the idea of forgiveness, making it seem unintelligible and impracticable. We need to face the sad truth that, sometimes, our thinking about forgiveness is shaped by a will not to forgive. To use a simple model of forgiveness to help with the tangles of human relations is a convincing way to discredit forgiving. It loads too heavy a burden on to the isolated victims.

Eighth, in accord with the gospel of Jesus and with our humanity, forgiving is to be practised on earth as in heaven, by human beings. It is not reserved to God. The Son of Man is given authority *on earth* to forgive sin (Mark 2.1–12).

Last, forgiving is not to be understood, as it overwhelmingly is, in a primarily backward-looking way. Its essential move is not to write off the past, nor is it a healing of memories. Forgiving opens the door to new and liveable possibilities. The door opens out from a closed room that has been built by the mess we have made of things. There is no help in messing about with the mess in itself. If there is no door open forwards from the mess, we will never be able to see it in a different way, and will not find the freedom that goes with forgiveness. Desmond Tutu argued that there is no future without forgiveness; it is equally true that there is no forgiveness without the future. This point is one of the main preoccupations of this chapter.

Forgiving is action in which there is achieved, simultaneously, *truthfulness about and hope for human beings*. Forgiving frees the wrongdoer for a different liveable future. But all the futures open to us in this world are imperfect. Forgiving does not alter this fact but is a way of living hopefully and truthfully with it. Here we encounter what might be called the constant regress of forgiving so that we have to pray, 'Forgive us our forgivings'. No forgiving action is perfect, indeed it can only be sustained *as forgiving* if it is interpreted and followed up forgivingly. If we imagine that an action of 'forgiving' puts an issue to rest, safely insulates us from the past, and is a sure basis for a different, simply happy, good kind of life, we are working with an illusion. Forgiving is real change, opening the door to a different and better future, but because that future is connected to the past, imperfect, unfinished, finite, any act of forgiving is vulnerable; it can be judged to be wrong or empty. People sometimes have reason for so judging: because it does not solve the whole problem for ever, we despise it and say it is not real forgiving at all. And when we judge any act of forgiving out of an expectation of perfection, it comes to nothing. We despise the day of small things (Zechariah 4.10); we quench the smoking flax and break the bruised reed (Isaiah 42.3). We end up in fruitless sterile righteousness because we do not have patience with the weak and imperfect. So to forgive forgivings is indispensable.

Any initial act of forgiveness is dependent on the way it is interpreted and built on by others. It invites a response from those who need forgiveness: repentance is best understood, not as a preparatory condition for forgiveness, but as accepting the opportunity provided by forgiveness. Repentance therefore follows and is shaped by forgiveness. But it is not the wrongdoer alone whose response is crucial to the achievement of forgiveness. Much depends on people and agencies who constitute the environment of the infant forgiveness. If the surrounding culture, media and politics is hostile to forgiving or fails to understand the value and the necessary means of forgiving, forgiving people will struggle to get beyond the stage of wishful dreams. The act of forgiving is thus a practice of interdependence. Jesus' command to forgive seventy times seven points us towards a community whose practice and spirit is forgiving. Spirit calls for embodiment, in standing process, in routine and institution.

The rest of this chapter discusses forgiveness as the permission to live. This is a basic image of forgiveness, which encapsulates both its promise, as opening the future, and its vulnerability to being stifled on the grounds that it achieves so little.

'For the wages of sin is death but the free gift of God is eternal life in Christ Jesus our Lord' (Romans 6.23). This is a central Evangelical text; at least it was in my upbringing, though I am not sure that it is now, when Evangelicals are well into abundant living understood in a hedonist culture of self-realization. In this text, sin, judgement (wages), and death have weight; but grace abounds much more. Conservatives belittle the text, liberals shun it, both for the same reason: we have largely lost the capacity to live with the metaphorical complexity and flexibility of this language and experience. Death is simply the termination of this temporal life. When we have so dim a sense of living before God, talk of the second death, or the death of the soul, becomes thin and unimportant. We are left with physical death which we aim to postpone for as long as possible – except when we are dealing with the wicked we hate, fear and judge unworthy of life, and the many unnamed, uncounted victims of our allegedly necessary wars.

We have good reason to abhor the punitive correlation of sin and death, which is not merely endorsed, but relished, by so much religion. Undoubtedly we go wrong, religiously, if we give unbalanced emphasis to the first half of the text. But it is foolish to refuse to meditate on the reality of sin and death. Their metaphorical depth gives them personal and social relevance: they illuminate dark places for us. It is dangerous work. How can we walk in the valley of the shadow of death, theologically, without being overcome by fear (Psalm 23; Hebrews 2)? The only ways to find a tolerable meaning are either to give up on God or to read the text whole: 'the wages of sin is death *but the free gift of God is eternal life*'.

We should not read the text with a frightening or punitive intent. Rather we take the first part in the light of the second. God in the Bible, God in Christ, sets this relation of sin–death in a forgiving perspective and intention. It is not a detached principle, complete in itself, which can then be wielded by cruel punitive people, as a justification for their negativity or sadism – their refusal to love or hope for those they perceive as sinners. The correlation of sin and death calls us to consider the weight of sin, but it only enables true perception when it is itself seen and interpreted within the perspective of forgiveness.

The Bible

The biblical narrative, as read in Christian faith, sets sin with death in the perspective of forgiveness. God said: 'You shall not eat of the fruit of the tree . . . lest you die.' The Serpent countered: 'You will not die' (Genesis 3.3–4). God's response confirmed the connection of sin and death, but death is transmuted into continuous human living on earth. Personal bodily death does not follow directly upon the sin. While life will be limited, painful, sweaty – signed by the death towards which it travels – it also goes on within the inaugurated promise of victory and redemption. The serpent bites the heel of the woman's offspring, but his heel crushes the serpent's head. The truth and hope of humanity are together present in this promise. Expelled from the garden, Adam and Eve get on living the reality of what life has become *within the promise*. Their existence is not finally determined by sin, nor shut up to death, but has meaning and value and joy within the forgiving order God makes.

We are invited by the Bible not to think of Adam and Eve as two individuals, with their daily ups and downs, as though they were celebrities arousing curiosity. Rather, they are the parents of humanity, not in any creationist scenario, but in an *anthropological theological symbolism* – especially is this so when they are read in the light of the second Adam, Jesus Christ (Romans 5.12–21; 1 Corinthians 15.45–50). The life that is enabled by God's foundational forgiving in response to the first sin is the *life of the whole human community*. Adam and Eve do not die; instead outside the garden they become parents of the race. They enable life and it is found to be permitted, but complicated by what has already happened to it.

We are thus invited by this story to *see the life of the whole of humanity as permitted and enabled*. It is not a life that is doomed to death without meaning and without delay. It is not a perfectly unblemished, satisfactory and competent existence. It is rather a forgiven existence. It is not therefore to be despised or belittled. Its sin is not to be counted against it. *Forgiveness* permits and enables us to live after the sin whose wages is death. The idea of being permitted to live irks us. Life is our right: it does not depend on permission, from anyone or any organization. Yet death does not respect our right. Is it only death that takes the liberty to transcend our rights? Is God there too? If so, then the ground of life is gift and comes to us more like a permission than a right.

Since they did not die, we may ask why the serpent was wrong to say, 'You will not die'? Why was he a destructive seducer rather than a life-enhancing truth-teller? His fault was not that he invited them to believe they would not die, but that he turned the forgiving faithfulness of God into a cheap grace to be exploited, rather than respected. If they had known to ask, the serpent might have told why they could expect to get away with it: he might have anticipated the cynical assurance of 'God will forgive: that's his *métier*'. But if they had known how to argue that much with the serpent, they would have known cheap grace is not worth the price.

'You will not die' was said by the serpent with destructive intent. It is also heard in the story of David, in the mouth of the prophet Nathan forgivingly: 'The Lord ... has put away your sin; you shall not die' (2 Samuel 12.13).

Unlike Adam and Eve, David does not symbolize universal foundational forgiveness in human history. David is not the Father of the race, nor the Father of Israel. For Christians, Jesus is 'great David's greater Son', but even so, David's individuality impresses itself, from our first hearing of his meeting Goliath onwards. We are told enough of his life to get some sense of his character, his intentions and skills, his strong and weak points, how he dealt with other people and what God was for him. By comparison, nothing biographical is given us about Adam and Eve. David was of course an unusually gifted and lucky person, a hero even as a boy and a great King, at least in that little corner of the world. So the story of his sin and his being forgiven may tell us something about politicians and other really or supposedly great people. But the story of David's sin and its forgiving has democratic potential. It is not only great men who have the leisure to see other men's wives while their husbands are away working. Not only great men want the beautiful woman when they see her, and go to any lengths to have her. It is not only great men who go from one terrible invention to another to cover up their wrongdoing, to gain the freedom to live without paying for the damage they cause, protecting their ill-gotten gains. David's action, and the spirit it reveals, is everyday moral squalor – there is not much that is great about it.

What David did, displeased the Lord (2 Samuel 11.27). But the Lord did not strike him down immediately. He sent Nathan to him. Nathan did not come to pronounce absolution from all his sins – he was not an authoritative priest. Nor was Nathan a simple accuser, seeking to expose and destroy his victim. Nathan's was a service of forgiving. Forgiving has to be done in the right way, respecting the link of sin and death. Forgiving does not spare the exposure of sin, nor euphemize the looming of death.

Nathan did not accuse David or attack him directly. He told a story that seemed to have nothing to do with David's case. It was not about an adulterous king, but about a rich man – of whom there were many in David's kingdom, under his rule. Nathan may have been helped by the fact that David had got to the point of being sure he was getting away with his sin – Uriah safely dead, no outcry for an inquiry, Bathsheba in his house and with their new baby thriving. David was not looking around him suspiciously. He was not oversensitive. He did not think, as soon as Nathan appeared, 'The prophet has come to get me.' His conscience was quiescent, not accusing him. But his ruler's sense of justice was still there, looking over his kingdom. So he listened to Nathan's story not thinking about his own action, but as a king who was to give judgement for the poor.

Nathan put the case well. A guest comes to a rich man's home. The rich man will not take an animal from his own huge flock to entertain him, but takes the precious lamb of a poor neighbour and kills it for his dinner party. David did not have to be a clever judge to see where right or wrong lay in this story. He was righteously angry. He pronounced death upon the man who did such a wicked thing. He had forfeited his basic right to life. David wished the world to be free of his presence. He would permit him no future. And the wrongdoer must make restoration fourfold.

Nathan was thus on common ground with David: they shared an understanding of right and justice in their reading of the story. He gave David the story to enable David to articulate his principles and commit himself to act on them.

So Nathan had only to say: 'You are the man' (2 Samuel 12.7). He could tell David's story to David with the leverage of David's sense of justice. And just as David had said: 'the man who has done this deserves to die' (2 Samuel 12.5), Nathan went on: 'the sword will never depart from your house, evil will always beset it, and you will see and suffer it' (2 Samuel 12.10 – paraphrase).

David acknowledged: 'I have sinned against the Lord' (2 Samuel 12.13). In the context, does that not imply David accepted his doom: he deserved to die?

Nathan said: 'The Lord also has put away your sin . . . you shall not die' (2 Samuel 12.13). David is forgiven, in the sense that he has permission to live even after such grievous sin. But this is *not a permission to live any kind of life*. Options for the future have been narrowed. Forgiveness cannot take David out of the narrative of his life up to that point. Forgiveness is permission to go on living truthfully and hopefully from where we are. We are in sin: the truth of it forbids hope. And we are in the Lord's hands: there is hope in the full truth.

David could not avoid living through the history he had made for himself. He was permitted to live – indeed, required to live through the dying of the child, which he took hard. Once the child was dead, he got on with life. The death had come and had to be accepted. And in the child's death, David foresaw his own destination: 'I shall go to him' (2 Samuel 12.14–26). This openness to and acceptance of the judgement of God was characteristic of David. He did not look for forgiveness outside the judgement and the freedom of God. Sooner or later, David would come to death and he did not presume otherwise. So implicitly David had a profound sense of life as a gift direct from God.

There is something terrible about this forgiving. It is morally shocking. We might think we could do without it, if it is like this. The death is not prevented but suffered immediately by this baby, who did no wrong. And perhaps it was suffered by David, through the baby, not as David's immediate death but as his loss of what he loved, the baby, and as a powerful reminder of where he was headed: to death. But before then there is permitted life: David is able to live with Bathsheba, comfort her, and father the boy he called Solomon, who was loved by the Lord, so that Nathan the prophet called him Jedidiah. One baby dies and is death for him; another is God's loving permission to live. This forgiving is not merely an incomplete unstable fragment, it is morally questionable in its ramifications.

David's being forgiven is thus worked out in a narrative involving other people. It is not a pious individualistic story of David sinning against the Lord, and achieving some kind of inward change of heart. The account of sin and forgiveness offered in Psalm 51, traditionally taken as David's penitential prayer after this great sin, is very different from the narrative in 2 Samuel 12. The Psalmist says: 'Against thee, thee only, have I sinned', whereas Nathan makes it quite plain that David sinned against the Lord and against Uriah. The Psalmist confesses to being conceived in sin – but never confesses to adultery and murder. The Psalmist sees that God wants truth in the inward being, but never confesses truthfully anything like David did in his public life. The Psalmist looks for cleansing of the heart, and for a willing spirit. This may invite us to see that forgiveness opens up, permits and enables a new life, but that is not spelt out here with any concrete detail. The penitent in the Psalm is not committed to live by working through the mess and sadness which is left behind by what he has done. Instead, his spirit is renewed in freedom so that he can teach sinners the ways of the Lord. And the Psalm at the end sounds as though the fruit of forgiveness will be the restoration of Jerusalem and God's delight in animal sacrifices accompanying the acceptable sacrifice of a broken heart. Psalm 51 has done much to shape conventional religious views of sin and forgiveness, perhaps with a resulting loss in social and narrative realism.

If we read 'You shall not die' as permission to live, it translates as a requirement that we live on, affirming life as a blessing full of hope, even though we are living after sin and within its reshaping of human being. After mortal illness, after accident, simply being alive comes to light as a wonderful gift – wonderful in its reality, but also in its precariousness and contingency. As never before, we see living as gift. So also, is it possible that the life which is still to be lived, after wrong done, may be found again as a good and precious gift? Forgiveness is the invitation to accept life, *as it has become*, in the present. Where it seems that life has become death, and is not liveable, forgiving works to find and invent renewed possibilities. Forgiving gives courage to live. Forgiving is closely linked with resurrection (Williams, 1982, p. 52).

Forgiveness is life in the knowledge of sin, of wrong done, of consequent losses. But it is life given again, given in spite of what has been done which is against it. The future flows out of forgiveness, and is shaped by it. Sin tends to bind and constrict the future. People who have done or suffered wrong are strongly and reasonably tempted to feel their options are determined by the wrong done: revenge is valid. Victims succumb or resist as avengers, but either way their resources seem to be deployed along the path imposed by the evil that has been done. Perpetrators often feel themselves committed to persist in the path they have opened for themselves, justifying it glumly beside their burned boats: evil be thou my good. Sin thus pretends to sovereign overwhelming control of life. But it is life not death that is sovereign; where sin abounds, grace much more abounds. Sin is given its true weight in shaping life only when it is known as forgiven sin. Forgiven sin is not sin denied or condoned. Forgiveness includes necessarily the exposure and judgement of sin as sin. 'To forgive is to blame, not to punish' (Volf, 2005, pp. 138, 170). Forgiving takes the sin into itself. As it permits and enables future living, the sin is disempowered to the extent that it no longer shapes, controls and commands the future. It becomes a problem to be dealt with, a burden to be carried, but has no veto on living and no right to say how or for what the future should be lived.

This modest, sober view of forgiveness lives in the tangles of real life. It does not picture forgiveness in such a way that it can only be realized in special cases or conditions, in church, in heaven, or by moral heroes. Forgiveness meets and helps people whose living is always broken and falling short. If David is one example, Cain is another. Cain killed his brother Abel, out of jealousy which grew because Cain did not heed the advice of God. He refused to be his brother's keeper, but Abel's blood cried from the ground and was heard by God. Cain was punished: cursed from the ground where Abel's blood was spilt, so that it is no longer his friend, Cain could only be a fugitive and a wanderer. This was more than Cain could bear: it means, he thought, that 'whoever finds me will slay me' (Genesis 4.14). His permission to live had been withdrawn. Being driven from the ground not only made him vulnerable to other people, but hid Cain from God's face, excluding him from God's care and respect. The prayer for blessing, 'The Lord lift up the light of his countenance upon you and give you his peace' (Numbers 6.26) was not to be said for him.

The outright though just negative did not quite suit the God who forgives. Cain had to live on in the world he had made – and away from the presence of the Lord. But the Lord set his mark on Cain, not to make him a target for punishing avengers, but to protect him, so that he might live, even though he could never rest on the earth. Cain was punished, and yet there was a forgiving in it as well.

Novels

I have come to this view of forgiving partly as Luther said he found his theology: 'Living, nay, rather dying and being damned make a theologian, not understanding, reading or speculation' (cited Rupp, 1953, p. 102), partly by trying to think forgiveness politically rather than individualistically and piously; and partly by being a child of my times, reading novels. A novel may show us persons and predicaments in some detail. Slick polarizing approval or disapproval makes a novel dull and bad: in good ones, we see human beings in their moral and spiritual questionableness. Some lead us into the shadow of death: having accompanied people through hundreds of pages, we can see that for them there is no easy hope left. But (at least in a few novels I can make something of) our empathy is won for some questionable, compromised characters so that we want them at the end of the story to have permission to live, with at least Cain's measure of viability. In such a story, we have been shown too much of the limits and maybe sin of the person to be deceived by a simply happy ending. The tale told has revealed the constricted options left to people. They have finite, even undermined capacity for living. But we still look for signs of a road opening and we are heartened by any hint that after the end of the book, they will walk it. So Milton ended *Paradise Lost*:

They looking back all th' eastern side beheld
Of Paradise, so late their happy seat,
Waved over by that flaming brand, the gate
With dreadful faces throng'd and fiery arms:
Some natural tears they dropp'd, but wiped them soon;
The world was all before them, where to choose
Their place of rest, and Providence their guide.
They, hand in hand, with wand'ring steps and slow,
Through Eden took their solitary way.

So, in a thoroughly post-Christian idiom, Ian McEwan's *Saturday* (2006) tells, on its last page, how Henry decides what to do in response to the day's devastating encounters with Baxter. He will try to keep the dying man from being brought to trial, as he deserves, and then ending his days in prison, suffering the inevitable 'descent into nightmare hallucination' because of his incurable illness. Baxter has a 'diminishing slice of life worth living' before him: Henry will do what he can to secure it for him. A faint echo of permission to live is audible. 'Is this forgiveness? Probably not, he doesn't know and he's not the one to be granting it anyway.' Thus, Henry (and McEwan?), like many contemporaries, shies away from the word forgiveness, yet, at the same time, shows an alert sensibility to its possible relevance in a pressing and complex situation. I think this degree of shyness is unnecessary – we are inhibited by too narrow and rigidly defined conceptions of forgiveness (what it is, who may grant it). It is wiser, and more in tune with its intrinsic boundary-transgressing generosity and creativity, to notice and celebrate forgiveness even when it comes in fragments, shadows and improper disguises.

Saturday is a very recent book. *Johanna at Daybreak* (1969/1983), by the profoundly Christian writer R. C. Hutchinson, has nourished my thinking about forgiveness for many years, since I first discovered it by accident on a railway bookstore.

Johanna was married to Josef, who was a Jew, a wealthy industrialist. They had two children. She was tricked by Nazis and by her own weakness and fear into persuading Josef to return to Germany from Switzerland. So she was responsible for his death. She lost the children who suffered immensely. At the beginning of the story we meet her as a displaced person, after war's end, taking refuge in amnesia, in denial of a past so terrible she cannot get herself to face it. Johanna wishes no permission to live and sees none. She tries suicide. She tries detachment, just going away from life, from others, from herself. Repeatedly, in various ways, she is prevented from achieving this evasion. There is resistance deep within herself as well as from her inescapable social existence. She is repeatedly required to live, not given permission to die. But can this living become to her anything more than a death she cannot achieve? Even though it can never be a life without the memory and the record of the wrong she has done and its consequences, can it be life rather than a living death?

Albrecht, a relative of Josef, finds her and leads her, cleverly, forcefully, without her free or informed consent, to remember and face her past. As her amnesia is stripped away, layer by layer, she gets involved with members of Josef's family, who are living in a hostel; she meets again her children, Felix now a hardened young man, and Ruth, a severely mentally damaged timid sweet child. Her 'sedative pretence that I could go on living as if in a different universe' was demolished (Hutchinson, 1983, p. 238).

Towards the end of the novel various strands of the story are woven together. She has a conversation with Felix, now the head of the family and its main provider. He makes it clear that she can stay with them and be provided for; she is useful as a carer for the old invalid members of the family; but she can expect no emotional relation, no reconciliation, with him or with others (p. 303). She knew that 'even if he proposed to annul the past, to forget that the crippling of his life resulted simply from my dereliction, I could not imagine myself accepting such forgiveness' (p. 238).

At this point the word forgiveness is used in a way that indicates it means full personal reconciliation and coming to a freedom in relation with others, including those harmed by her. Forgiveness of that sort is ruled out by Felix: he says no one in her family can offer that – and she accepts it.

She reacts immediately by deciding to flee again into detachment, this time with radical totality (pp. 305–6). She cannot go back to amnesia; but an irrevocable conscious break with her past and her roots is required. As she runs from all she is and all her connections, she is prevented first by a sense of terror at finding herself in the empty space of the city. She escaped from 'one state of misery only to an infinite loneliness': 'there came a time that night when I found myself mouthing incoherent prayers as a terrified child would; but without the hopefulness of children; for when you cease to talk to fellow-creatures you put between yourself and any imaginable God a boundless and impenetrable silence' (p. 309). So she wanders back towards the hostel, and as she gets near, she is given the news that Tilka died in the night *triumphantly*.

That word 'triumphantly', spoken of *this* death, moves Johanna. To understand, we must go back to Tilka's part in the story of Johanna. Tilka injects into the narrative of the whole novel, the gospel of Jesus Christ, in a properly veiled form. She was a profoundly Christian, life-loving, Polish woman, who in the postwar time of the novel is bedridden and dying. Johanna shared a room with her and came to see her life as having been 'nothing but goodness and courage' (p. 251). That is a view of herself Tilka will not accept and will not allow Johanna to work with.

To get Johanna to think more truly about her, Tilka gets her friend Lore to tell Johanna the story of the prisoners. In the war Tilka was nursing in an army hospital when she got the news that her husband had been killed. She was responsible for four German prisoners whose bomber had crashed. Tilka told them their friends had killed her husband so they would get no more nursing from her. She locked the door and left them to die. That was her revenge on the Germans and also – the novel is explicit – on God. 'He had taken Wladyslaw – I meant to take four lives in return, to defy and insult Him.' As she was going away from the locked ward, 'He met me in the passage and told me to give him the key. He said if I wouldn't look after the airmen he must do it himself, in spite of his condition – and you could see the trail of blood where he'd come across the snow. So I had to give in and nurse them' (p. 252). ('He', here, is the crucified Lord – who appears significantly, cryptically in other novels by Hutchinson.)

Tilka was a forgiven person – she was not 'nothing but (self-possessed) goodness and courage' (p. 251). She knew in herself she could kill the Germans and defy God. She did not forget her sin. Her being forgiven did not come about through confession and absolution, so that her sin was washed away and she was clean. It came to her through the requirement that she enact forgiving. She responded to the permission to live, the command to live, for the Lord in the Lord's way. The form and content of her being forgiven was to be a practical forgiver, embodying forgiveness in caring appropriately for others and so representing the Lord, to spare him having to do it himself. Since he was her Lord, since she was devoted to him, she was open to this command. Her discovery that she was not all goodness came when she decided to defy God by not forgiving and was met by the forgiveness of God, not in the form of the cheap grace of a let-off, but in the requirement to forgive even at cost to her own feelings and identity. Forgiveness in this form was of a piece with the whole of her being, as an invalid, with her carer Lore. The triumph Johanna saw in her did not consist in her courage only; 'it was . . . a special gift for being at once involved in the drudgeries of living and detached from their smallness, for watching even their own distress with eyes which contained a larger scenery' (p. 313).

Being reminded of Tilka, and understanding why she died triumphantly, gave Johanna a clue to the way forward for herself. So she returned to the hostel, found by Ruth, her daughter, who simply takes her hand – unlike Felix, Ruth can make no speeches or moral judgements. And this act completes the change for her: her path is clear. *She has permission to live a certain kind of life, with a promise and a discipline.*

And that might be a better way of understanding forgiveness than the more common idea of being freed from the past sin or hurt. Johanna could not find escape in amnesia, nor could she find forgiveness as the restoration to relationships as they once were or might have turned out had nothing gone wrong. Nothing could alter the past, or give her the future that would have flowed from a different past. She had to accept all that and recognize what her life was in the present, with all its pain and difficulty. She had to accept it as her responsibility and then to get on with it. She comes to see she cannot expect forgiveness if it is understood as restoration which makes the past as though it never had been – invisible repairs. Instead, we read at the end:

> I echoed 'Ruth', and again, 'Ruth'. But my body was slow to share in this meeting: it was she who, with a grave simplicity, stretched out to touch my hand.

Side by side – our hands still touching – we went into the
house, to be greeted by the fumes from a pan of milk which
someone had let boil over and by the pervasive bickering of
children. Enveloped in that orchestra of inveterate sounds
and smells, I realised I was back on the painful course I could
never finally escape from – itself my one escape from the
despotism of the past; the only course which could lead towards
an ultimate tranquillity; the harsh, acceptable, exalting road.

(p. 314)

The permission, the requirement, to live without amnesia, without dehumanizing detachment (in which the original sin of
betraying her husband and family would simply be continued
down to death), but also free from the 'despotism of the past' is
the form forgiveness often takes in this present life, in this
world where God comes to bring forgiveness of sins. (God does
not take away the sin of the world by abolishing the world,
does he?) It took Johanna a long time, a hard struggle, to come
to this point. She accepted forgiveness as a belonging to a community which would always be, on one side, a silent accuser,
because it is the community of those damaged by her wrongdoing. She accepts forgiveness through living truly who she is
and has become: there is no more running from it into some
dishonesty. She accepts forgiveness as a harsh road. But it is
acceptable – it is a possible road for her; it does not ask an
impossible repentance and transformation from her. But maybe
'acceptable' here does not mean merely that it is feasible for
Johanna, but rather that it is acceptable to God – it is God's
will (Romans 12.2). And it is exalting, it is the road to 'ultimate
tranquillity' – but not immediate ease. It is only by accepting
and living in this painful course, indicated partly by the irksome-
ness of life in a family hostel, that she finds the reality of what
I suggest amounts to forgiveness.

It is significant that the novel is careful not to call it forgiveness at the end. Hutchinson reckoned with the fact that the
word forgiveness is commonly understood as a taking away of
all grievance and dissension, so as to make possible a full and
unrestrained reconciliation. Forgiveness in that form was not
plausible in his story. The deep realistic sympathy which informs
its telling of all the people here was not to be voided at the end.

We might judge that the way Johanna finds is not to be called 'forgiveness'. But what other word shall we use? Hutchinson did not look for or find a *single word* to label the outcome for Johanna. He described it only by the *proleptic narrative of the final paragraph*, indicating the way Johanna could and would take, a hard, honest and yet hopeful path. The story would fail if the conclusion were advertised directly as 'forgiveness'. Not being a crass incompetent novelist, Hutchinson did nothing like that. But as an enquirer, seeking to understand forgiveness, I find his conclusion illuminating, not only as a relief from the obscure superficiality of conventional uses of the word, but more as a clue to its active embodiment. There is much talk about forgiveness, which reflects genuine need and serious desire, but it is hampered because the word has been worn down by usage, like a stone staircase whose steps no longer offer a flat, safe foothold. This is a family of words which cannot be used without exploring and explaining and renewing the meaning. And the explanation, let alone the renewal, cannot be achieved by explicit definition. It needs to go via exploratory and experimental narrative, fictional and historical, so that the word comes alive again and grows afresh.

The permission to live is not a definition of forgiveness, but rather an angle of view and approach, by which we may search for it. Forgiveness cannot be found in the evasion or denial of life. It is clear from the story and spirituality Hutchinson gives us that permission to live puts forgiveness in austere garb. Where is the joy and freedom, the goal and the heart of forgiveness? Is forgiveness then no more than a hard path of discipline? There is more, in Hutchinson's telling. It is still hidden for Johanna, still before her on the way. But nevertheless, in another segment of her story, the witness of Tilka dares the word 'triumphant'. Johanna could not grasp such a word for herself, in herself. If she did, it would merely substitute the amnesia of triumphalism for her amnesia of grief; it would dissolve all that she has discovered and begun to enter into on her own way to forgiveness. But for all that, it brings the light and lift of grace to her when she hears it. The austerity of her way is not a Sisyphean futility, hard labour without hope. The same Christ who met Tilka is there for her with costly grace.

References

Hutchinson, R. C., *Johanna at Daybreak*. Zenith, Feltham, Middlesex, 1983 (original edn 1969).

Jones, L. G., *Embodying Forgiveness*. Eerdmans, Grand Rapids, Michigan, 1995.

McEwan, I., *Saturday*. Vintage, London, 2006.

Milton, J., *The Poetical Works*, Frederick Warne, London, n.d.

Parker, R., *Forgiveness is Healing*. Darton Longman & Todd, London, 1993.

Rupp, E. G., *The Righteousness of God*. Hodder & Stoughton, London, 1953.

Tutu, D., *No Future without Forgiveness*. Rider, London, 1999.

Volf, M., *Exclusion and Embrace*. Abingdon, Nashville, 1996.

Volf, M., *Free of Charge*. Zondervan, Grand Rapids, Michigan, 2005.

Williams, R., *Resurrection*. Darton, Longman & Todd, London, 1982.

Willmer, H., *Forgiveness and Politics*. Centre for Contemporary Christianity in Ireland, Belfast, 2003.

6

A necessary angel

JONATHAN BAXTER

Jonathan Baxter focuses on the biblical understanding of God's covenant promising peace when read in light of healing and embodiment. Exploring the relationship between reality and imagination as a 'precise equilibrium', Baxter develops a realist symbolic interpretation of peace as health – when peace is understood as a 'difficult peace'. Further to this, Baxter argues that love, not health, should be the lens through which we interpret illness, so that health is relativized as a dominant narrative and illness is assumed into God's covenant promising peace.

* * *

Overview

In the following chapter I explore one (possible) theological interpretation of illness by assuming illness into God's covenant promising peace. In doing so I adopt Gregory Nazianzen's injunction that 'what is not assumed is not healed' (cited Avis, 1989, p. 40).

Illness, as I understand the term, implies a multidimensional definition that includes biomedical, psychological, sociological and subjective interpretations (cf. Hardey, 1999). Here I give particular attention to the sociological and subjective interpretations as formed (or deformed) within the socio-symbolic of Western patriarchy.[1]

As dialogue partners within this chapter I look briefly at the work of the American modernist poet Wallace Stevens and the process-oriented psychology of Arnold Mindell. I relate my reading of Stevens' understanding of reality and imagination to St Paul's understanding of 'hope [that] is no fantasy' (Romans 5.5), and I develop their insights into an embodied epistemology based upon the work of Mindell.

The overall aim of this chapter is to wrestle a blessing for embodiment and by association for illness, just as Jacob wrestled a blessing from, and perhaps on behalf of, an unnamed stranger God (Genesis 32.22–33).

A more difficult peace

Illness is an experience that happens to all of us. It is a natural consequence of physiological and mental life. And it is thus, fundamentally, an experience of embodiment, when embodiment is understood as a mind–body continuum.

> Change is the essence of life, and the body is subject to change in so many dimensions that . . . the complexity is unimaginable. Periods of breakdown of equilibrium are periods of relative illness between peaks of relative health. Perfect health is an impossibility in the relative world, and any person or system promising it is not to be believed. (Weil, 1998, p. 55)

But illness is not reducible to biomedical description alone, for it is also a subjective and, more broadly, a collective narrative experience that assumes personal interpretations. Thus while illness is experienced as a material and/or bodily reality, we interpret and respond to illness in ways that *transcend* materiality. And it is this transcendent, or more specifically, *imaginative* response, that I want to develop within this chapter.

According to the writers of *Mud and Stars: The Impact of Hospice Experience on the Church's Ministry of Healing*, 'Christian faith is not [about] problem-solving but mystery encountering, so that any sickness is part of a much wider and deeper picture' (Report of a Working Party, 1991, p. 85). This definition is useful if we bear in mind the distinction between 'mystery encountering' and mystification. So while drawing attention to the 'wider and deeper picture', I do not want to downplay the often painful and constricting experiences of illness as they impact upon our lives. Nevertheless, I do want to emphasize the (potentially) transformative experience of illness, as a form of *metanoia* – a change of heart or rite of passage? – to which the Judaeo-Christian tradition bears witness.

100

This it does in three ways. First, it draws on the Old Testament understanding of God's covenant promising peace.

> Though the mountains may move and the hills shake
> My love will be immovable and never fail,
> And my covenant promising peace will not be shaken,
> Says the Lord in his compassion for you.
>   (Isaiah 54.10)

This covenant assumes the Doctrine of Creation and makes explicit the emphasis upon God's unfailing love as a prophetic hope within Creation.[2]

Added to this a Christian must also take seriously *the way* in which Jesus incarnates God's love, so that the life of Jesus (including his death and resurrection) becomes a model for witnessing God's covenant promising peace. Here Paul is instructive:

> ... through faith, we are at peace with God through our Lord Jesus Christ, who has given us access to that grace in which we now live; and we exult in the hope of the divine glory that is to be ours. More than this: we even exult in our present sufferings, because we know that suffering is a source of endurance, endurance of approval, and approval of hope. Such hope is no fantasy; through the Holy Spirit he has given us, God's love has flooded our hearts.   (Romans 5.1–5)

Now without getting distracted by a possible misreading of Paul that emphasizes suffering as somehow valuable in itself, what is significant here, among other things, is Paul's binding together of suffering and hope – which I will later explore in terms of reality and imagination. In short, Paul suggests that in addition to 'the divine glory that is to be ours' sometime in the future, there also exists, 'in our present sufferings', a (potential) experience of the 'Holy Spirit' as 'God's love [that] has flooded our hearts'. And it is this experience of an embodied spirituality – what Rowan Williams, in this volume, calls 'a spirit-inhabited body' – that provides the foundation for Paul's claim that 'hope' is irreducible to 'fantasy'.

Bearing the above in mind I want to weave these three strands together and argue in favour of a more *difficult peace* than traditional interpretations of the Christian healing ministry have prescribed. And I want to do this by following the New Testament tradition in translating the Hebrew word for wholeness (*shalom*) through the Greek word for peace (*eirene*). In this way I hope to draw attention to the *act* of healing as a participative and relational process – with God, oneself, one another and the world – rather than, for example, a harmonious *state* per se. Thus I want to step beyond John Wilkinson's definition of *shalom* as 'the presence of wholeness, completeness and well-being in all spheres of life whether physical, mental and spiritual, or individual, social and national' (Wilkinson, 1998, p. 12), and argue, instead, for a more *disturbing peace* in line with Isabel Carter Heyward's interpretation of power (*dunamis*) as a power 'unmediated by official social legitimation' (Heyward, 1982, p. 41).[3]

I emphasize *dunamis*, rather than the Greek word *exousia* – the two key words used to signify 'power' and 'authority' in the New Testament narratives – because *exousia* implies a 'power that is socially-licensed or allowed', while *dunamis*, as stated above, implies a power 'unmediated by official social legitimation' and one that is often 'experienced by others as raw . . . , spontaneous, uncontrollable and often fearful' (Heyward, 1982, p. 41). And I want to suggest that this quality of *dunamis*, described by Heyward as the relational power that Jesus incarnates,[4] bears a striking resemblance to our experience of illness.

This it does in at least two ways. First, illness, as a quality of *dunamis*, can be experienced by ourselves and others as 'raw . . . , spontaneous, uncontrollable and often fearful'. Second, illness spills out of the *authoritative* dualisms – good/ bad, healthy/unhealthy – that binary discourse sets for it. Hence Foucault:

> [O]nce power [in this case 'authority' (*exousia*)] produces [its] effect [for example, the diagnosis of an illness upon the body], there inevitably emerge the responding claims and affirmations, those of one's own body against power, of health against the economic system, of pleasure against the moral norms of sexuality, marriage, decency. Suddenly, what had made power strong becomes used to attack it. Power, after investing itself in the body, finds itself exposed to a counter attack in that same body.   (Foucault, 1980, p. 56)[5]

In line with the above I want to suggest that illness defined as a quality of *dunamis* – what in following Foucault we might call its 'counter attack' quality – can be said to contain its own power: a power commensurate with God's covenant promising peace. And I want to argue, in accordance with the threefold interpretation of Christian faith outlined above, that God's covenant promising peace is an incarnate possibility, embodied by Jesus and expressed by us through the 'love [that] has flooded our hearts'. To explore this possibility I now want to *hear into speech* (Morton, 1986) the experiences of those who struggle with illness.[6]

A difficult life

Nancy Mairs, an essayist and poet reflecting upon her experience of multiple sclerosis writes:

> [I]f a cure was found, would I take it? In a minute. I may be a cripple, but I'm only occasionally a loony and never a saint. Anyway, in my brand of theology God doesn't give bonus points for a limp. I'd take a cure; I just don't need one. A friend who also has MS startled me once by asking, 'Do you ever say to yourself, "Why me, Lord?"' 'No, Michael, I don't,' I told him, 'because whenever I try, the only response I can think of is "Why not?"' If I could make a cosmic deal, who would I put in my place? What in my life would I give up in exchange for sound limbs and a thrilling rush of energy? No one. Nothing. I might as well do the job myself. Now that I am getting the hang of it. (cited Eiesland, 1994, p. 46)

Here Mairs testifies to what I have been calling a difficult peace by moving beyond the 'why me?' phase of illness and into a more expansive understanding of human identity.[7] Thus Mairs accepts that being 'a cripple' is who she is. She is a person who suffers from multiple sclerosis. And the desire to be a person with 'sound limbs and a thrilling rush of energy' would be, for Mairs, a denial of reality. Thus for Mairs emphasis is placed upon 'a true generosity of spirit' (cited Eiesland, 1994, p. 46) in response to the life that she actually lives and not upon an abstract, oppositional definition of health as a harmonious state of 'wholeness, completeness and wellbeing'.

Commenting upon Mairs' experience, Nancy L. Eiesland writes:

> These horrible things need not diminish us; they can make us more fully aware of the full range of things human. Performing an authentic alchemy using disability and honesty, Mairs has fashioned a difficult life, in contrast to our constant search for ease and painlessness. Her difficult life need not be denied or descried. It need only be lived. (Eiesland, 1994, p. 46)

To live this 'difficult life' – what in my terminology I call a difficult peace – there needs to be a re-evaluation of what we consider normative, including the values we recognize as constituting peace and health. And it is the aim of this chapter to show that peace as health, when understood from a Judaeo-Christian perspective, is not what we as a society normally understand by 'ease and painlessness' (Eiesland). Rather, Christian notions of peace as health will be a scandal to normative discourse because there is always something more than, less timely and fitting than authoritative/normative discourse allows. And this is because the Judaeo-Christian story is a story in excess of *self*-definition, for it includes what is *other than* and orientates itself accordingly.[8]

> The self is formed in creative responsiveness to the influences received from the whole world. . . . But while the self emerges in response to these influences, it is impossible ever to bring them all to awareness. There is always that which eludes us: we are not 'self-contained.' We are essentially each an open self, embedded within a world touched by infinity. Neither the totality of our selfhood nor, even less so, the totality of the other can ever be apprehended by the necessarily selective function of consciousness that is always intuited, but never grasped. We *sense* the infinity in which we participate.
> (Suchocki, 1999, p. 39, my italics)

Taking this to heart I want to define but not constrict, if that is possible, a (potential) interpretation of God's covenant promising peace as a *love without limit*. A love that assumes the failure of peace and well-being as a vital, and therefore life-giving, power (*dunamis*) within creation.[9]

Accordingly love, not health – as 'a constant search for ease and painlessness' (Eiesland) – should be the lens through which we interpret illness. And in order to glimpse why this interpretation is 'no fantasy', I now want to turn to the writings of Wallace Stevens, in particular his reflections on reality and imagination, as developed in *The Necessary Angel: Essays on Reality and the Imagination* (Stevens, 1984).

Reality and imagination

Stevens was not a Christian poet. Nor, indeed, was he a Christian believer – or not until his death-bed conversion, at least.[10] But he does offer a resource for Judaeo-Christian theology by negotiating a middle way between the either/or tendency to privilege reality or imagination in what is commonly referred to as the realist/anti-realist debate (cf. Crowder (ed.), 1997).

In short, Stevens contends that reality is shot through with imagination just as imagination is infused with reality, so that 'the relation between the imagination and reality is a question, more or less, of precise equilibrium' (Stevens, 1984, p. 9). Therefore Stevens holds in tension the somewhat arid dispute between what can or cannot be said about reality. That is, the tension between the usual modernist (realist) and therefore normative, scientific, medical contention in support of empirical fact (discovered by observation and confirmed by verification) and the textual relativism (anti-realism) of *some* postmodern and/or new age philosophies in their assertion that there is nothing beyond or below the excess of signification or imagination.

Indeed, Stevens demonstrates in his poetry and argues in his prose that there is more to reality than 'bare fact' alone (Stevens, 1984, p. 60) – what passes naïvely for 'objective' fact[11] – and more to the imagination than signification alone because it is the task of the imagination to face the 'pressure of reality', a pressure that Stevens defined within the socio-political context of his life as physical and spiritual violence (Stevens, 1984, pp. 26–7).

So while Stevens may not be concerned with the question of what constitutes illness or health per se, his reflections upon reality are, I suggest, applicable to anyone experiencing first hand, or reflecting upon, illness and its (potential) interpretations. In short, the question becomes: how do we transform the 'pressure of reality' – including our experiences of illness – into what Eiesland calls 'an authentic alchemy' or what Stevens' calls '[a]n elixir, an excitation, a pure power' (Stevens, 1970, p. 101)?

Thus I am suggesting that illness, and therefore pain and suffering, are not *merely* reducible to the 'pressure of reality' – what in psychoanalytic terms we might call an experience of impingement – for they are also shot through with our imaginative responses – what in relation to Paul we might call our imaginative hopes. And although these hopes should never *deny* reality – they should not, in Paul's sense, become *mere* fantasy – they can, nevertheless, *illuminate* reality, so that they 'become part of our vital experience of life' (Stevens, 1984, p. 65).

Therefore illness, as a 'vital experience of life', can be said to pierce us 'with strange relation' (Stevens, 1970, p. 102). And it is in response to this 'strange relation' that we, as Christians, are called to a 'total response' (Jeanrond, 1995, p. 118).

The body: sacred or profane?

It might be thought that what I have said so far was an accepted insight within Judaeo-Christian theology, especially bearing in mind the centrality of the cross (reality) and the recurrent theological emphasis upon the parabolic imagination (cf. McFague, 2002; McIntyre, 1987). But unfortunately such insights have been sidelined within Christian theology (as distinct from *Judaeo*-Christian theology) due, in part, to a profound ambivalence towards the material/finite body.[12] This can be seen in the early Gnostic debates concerning the divine or human status of Jesus, Augustine's early post-conversion antipathy towards the body, and the Church's current 'crisis' concerning the ordination, or not, of sexually 'deviant' followers of Jesus. All of which, I suggest, has led to the corruption of our theological imaginations and the consequent distortion of much theological reflection upon illness and health.

To remedy this distortion I want to develop the suggestion that we re-imagine or re-inscribe our understanding of the body – including its socio-symbolic structure – in terms of its Godly/divine signification (cf. Jantzen, 1998; Raphael, 1996). Therefore I advocate in this chapter a 'feminist movement' (hooks, 2000-a)[13] that has the power (*dunamis*) to transform Christian understandings of illness to become compatible with God's covenant promising peace.

One contribution to this re-inscription would be to argue that the health/illness dichotomy is a residue of the sacred/profane dichotomy that has historically alienated men from their bodies and tied women too closely to the 'crushing embrace' that equates women with the body and profanity (Isherwood and Stuart, 1998, p. 80). Thus in order to liberate the body from the socio-symbolics of this ambivalent profanity, Christianity needs to assume the body's (potential) sacrality and ask how the body bears witness to God's covenant promising peace.

The body speaks

As a way of assuming the (potential) sacrality of the body I want to explore the work of Arnold Mindell and his theory of process-oriented psychology. As with any theory there are questions to be asked when assessing process-oriented psychology's contribution to theology and the creation of a *biophilic* world. But given the constraints of this chapter I want to state my conviction that process-oriented psychology offers an imaginative tool for *hearing the body into speech*.[14]

Process work (shorthand for process-oriented psychology), has its roots in two overlapping disciplines: Jungian depth psychology and contemporary physics. But it also draws on yesterday's wisdom traditions, in particular Taoism and Buddhism, and on a pluralistic interpretation of the monotheistic traditions. In response to this genealogy Mindell presents his work as a unifying paradigm, one strand in a web of 'rainbow medicine', 'another name for multidimensional approaches in medicine' (Mindell, 2004, p. 15).[15] And he argues that the main task of process work is to train one's awareness and not necessarily cure illness.[16]

To do this, process work interprets body symptoms *creatively* as 'gateways to a new kind of wisdom', as 'apparently unanswerable questions meant to increase our consciousness' (Mindell, 2004, p. 42; p. 5). And it puts this interpretation into practice by 'amplifying' body symptoms within six complementary 'channels': body feelings (or proprioception), visualization, hearing, movement (or kinaesthesis), relationships (as we experience ourselves through and with others) and the world channel (including myths and collective narratives) (Mindell, 1990, p. 23). In this way process work encourages individuals to find meaning within their symptoms, thus letting their symptoms *speak for themselves*. Furthermore, by amplifying body symptoms in this way – by bringing them to awareness and exploring them in more detail – Mindell suggests that our habitual ways of experiencing the world will find themselves challenged and enlivened.[17]

This reinterpretation or re-employment of symptoms is made possible, according to Mindell, due to a threefold layering of reality – a schema described by most contemporary medical paradigms as 'reality', 'mind' and 'universe' (cf. Salmon, 1985, p. 272). Here are Mindell's own descriptions:

- *Consensus reality*: observations of time, space, weight, and repeatable measurements.
- *Dreamland*: experiences of fantasies, subjective feelings, dreams, and dreamlike figures.
- *Essence*: perceptions of subtle tendencies and a lucid sense of the force of silence from which dreams arise.

(Mindell, 2004, p. 17)

The key layers here, for the purpose of this chapter, are what Mindell calls 'dreamland' and 'essence' and which I translate as imagination and God-Spirit.[18] And I want to suggest that by applying the above three layers to our interpretation of reality, Judaeo-Christian theology can develop a more adequate understanding of the body's (potential) sacrality as symptomatic of God's covenant promising peace.

Observant readers will have noticed, however, that by arguing for this triadic integration I am stepping beyond Stevens' 'more or less . . . precise equilibrium' by including the possibility of a third layer, translated here as God-Spirit. And here it has to be acknowledged that I am interpreting process work in line with the Judaeo-Christian tradition and not within a purely secular, and arguably Stevensian, account. This being the case I now need to ask how an understanding of God-Spirit relates to consensus reality and the Judaeo-Christian imaginary.

Faith as practice

To answer this question I want to quote Hans Urs von Balthasar at some length, and I would ask the reader to pay particular attention to the material and bodily metaphors von Balthasar employs.[19]

> No limb of the body of Christian faith remains motionless when it meets its neighbour. All these members of the body are asleep, lifeless and theoretical, between the covers of a catechism; but they all stretch and strain to move effectively when they meet one another, when, in this encounter, theory becomes practice. A practical Christian is a man [or woman] who undergoes this resurrection of truth in the reality of his [or her] life. When this happens the practical Christian becomes a practising Christian. And a practising Christian is one who loves Jesus and 'keeps his commandments'. Practising means putting these commandments into practice, and we know that all the commandments of Christ are embodied in the one commandment of love. We shall be justified by this commandment alone: according to the practice in our lives of practical, active love – or our lack of practice. This unique commandment is also the standard for finding out whether we know God: 'He [or she] who does not love does not know God; for God is love' (1 John 4.8). There is no such thing as theoretical faith, or being a Christian 'in theory'. Christianity is a form that can't exist without the matter just as the form of a piece of sculpture can't be actual apart from the stone, wood or metal that takes that form. The matter is where love manifests itself, where it shines; the matter is the object of love's self-sacrifice: the neighbour who can only be so close to us because God in Christ is present in him [or her]. My neighbour can be loved so much only because in him [or her] there appears the everlasting love of God for me and for him [or her]; the love which is the First and Last of all things, and of our encounter as well.　　　　　　　　(von Balthasar, 1970, pp. 95–6)

In line with the above, and with a particular emphasis upon the resurrection imagery von Balthasar uses – which to paraphrase Melanie May we might call our *practice of resurrection* (May, 1995, p. 19) – I suggest that a Judaeo-Christian understanding of peace as health finds its definition, its physical 'form', within the 'stretch[ing] and strain[ing]' of our relational lives as '*embodied in the one commandment of love*' (my italics). Therefore illness, as with any 'vital experience of life', provides the material context for this 'practical, active love', and this it does in three familiar ways:

- *Consensus reality*: experiencing the contingency of embodiment.
- *Dreamland (imagination)*: being open to empathic care[20] and the stories that sustain us.
- *Essence (God-Spirit)*: attending to the silence within our bodily symptoms.

Now the first two practices are common enough (although the significance of the imagination is often downplayed), providing as they do the foundational resources for coping with, caring for and reflecting upon illness. But the third practice, that of attending to the silence of God-Spirit within our bodily symptoms, remains curiously neglected within both normative-secular and traditional Christian discourses.

This is because – to put it simply[21] – in the Western world our twofold emphasis upon Spirit (pre-enlightenment) and Matter (post-enlightenment) has distorted (in complementary ways) our experience of embodiment. Consequently, we have suffered an *authoritative* dissociation from the body. This is not merely because we fear 'experiencing something bad', or because we fear 're-experiencing all the old hurts that were never allowed to unfold in the first place' (Campbell and McMahon, 1985, p. 16). More specifically it is because we, through the socio-symbolic structures within which we live, have 'denied' and 'descried' (Eiesland) our body's 'felt sense'.

> Eugene Gendlin [the founder of a therapeutic process called Focusing] has referred to the broader substratum beneath this visible tip [of our rational mind] as a *felt sense*. This term embraces a wider, initially nebulous meaning that is felt rather than conceptualized in our awareness. It is called *felt* because it is felt in the body. It is called *sense*, not like the five senses but more like *the sense of something* or *he [or she] makes good sense*. *Sense*, here, is a meaning word. It is a meaning that is felt – as yet unclear and vague. A meaning prior to symbolization.
> (Campbell and McMahon, 1985, p. 25)

Now putting to one side any contentious discussion about the pros and cons of defining *meaning* as 'prior to symbolization', it is certainly the case that all of our experiences are filtered through the socio-symbolic structures that give meaning (or its lack) to our lives. And here I suggest that the authoritative/dominant socio-symbolic structures upon which both Western Christianity and secular discourses are predominantly based have privileged, respectively, a profane (traditional Christian) and a reductive (modernist, secular) interpretation of the body *over and against* the body's (potential) sacrality.

Embodied sense: where else would it be?

To remedy this distortion I want to suggest that Gendlin's definition of 'felt sense' might be usefully expanded to include what Huston Smith defines as our 'religious sense' (Smith, 2001, p. 274), and that Smith's 'religious sense' might appropriately be interpreted as an experience of embodiment.[22] In this way I want to bring these two senses, felt and religious, together as a way of reflecting upon the body and its (potential) sacrality.

Smith's 'religious sense' includes four distinct features:

- The religious sense recognizes instinctively that the ultimate questions human beings ask – What is the meaning of existence? Why are there pain and death? Why, in the end, is life worth living? What does reality consist of and what is its object? – are the defining essence of our humanity.
- [T]he religious sense is visited by a desperate, at times frightening, realization of the distance between these questions and their answers. As the urgency of the questions increases, we see with alarming finality that our finitude precludes all possibility of our answering them.
- The conviction that the questions have answers never wavers, however, and this keeps us from giving up on them.
- [W]e [religious believers] conduct our search together – collectively, in congregations as you [scientists and keepers of the high culture] do in your laboratories and professional societies.   (Smith, 2001, p. 274)

From the above we can see that the 'religious sense' is vitally concerned with questions of meaning while acknowledging that the ultimate answers remain beyond our grasp. Furthermore, this quest, when understood as a religious quest, is irreducible to the individual, for it is a journey that we 'conduct . . . together', and one that we narrate and celebrate within the socio-symbolic structures within which we live. Therefore by bringing what Gendlin calls our 'felt sense' and what Mindell calls 'perceptions of subtle tendencies and a lucid sense of the force of silence' into play with Smith's 'religious sense', we have, or so I suggest, a useful model for imagining and engaging with God's covenant promising peace as a personal and political practice.

This is because, as Jonathan Miller puts it, it is only through the body as 'the medium of experience and the instrument of action' that we, as humans, are able to 'shape and organise our experiences and distinguish our perceptions of the outside world from the sensations that arise within the body itself' (Miller, 2000, p. 2). Therefore any disembodied description of God's covenant promising peace will fail, by dint of our own embodiment, to do justice to our 'felt sense', our 'religious sense', and even to the material world as it is currently expounded within the sciences.[23]

God's silence

That said, the question of what the body can or cannot communicate is subtle, and the tension between the 'felt sense' and felt absence of God-Spirit needs to be examined in relation to illness and God's silence. This is because God-Spirit is not always, or overtly, experienced as a 'felt sense' (or *presence*) within the body. And it is often through such *absence* that we make our way.

Here, then, I want to return to Mindell's understanding of 'the force of silence', his translation for '[t]he Tao that cannot be said' (Mindell, 2004, p. 49) when interpreted in light of contemporary physics.[24] And I want to give an example of both the 'felt sense' and felt absence of God-Spirit in order to articulate the inevitable tension within my understanding of God's covenant promising peace.

The first example is drawn from Julian of Norwich. Here Julian demonstrates the connection between our bodily experiences and our religious interpretations – when religion is understood as a binding together, a sense of connection.

A man [sic] walks upright, and the food in his body is shut in as if in a well-made purse. When the time of his necessity comes, the purse is opened and then shut again, in most seemly fashion. And it is God who does this, as it is shown when he says that he comes down to us in our humblest needs. For he does not despise what he has made, nor does he disdain to serve us in the simplest natural functions of our body, for love of the soul which he created in his own likeness.

(Julian of Norwich, 1978, p. 186)

Here, then, we have a clear, symbiotic relationship between God and embodiment; one that demonstrates something about the body's sacrality and how the crudest of bodily functions can evoke and/or remind us of the 'felt sense' of God-Spirit. Yet the above passage can only take us so far. For in this example we have an account of a healthy 'well-made' body, not a body suffering from illness.[25] So what happens when the connection between our body and the 'felt sense' of God-Spirit breaks down?

To answer this question I want to turn to Mark's Gospel and his account of Jesus in the garden of Gethsemane. This is a time when Jesus knows he is about to face arrest, trial and likely execution (although the divine inevitability of this process should not be overstated). And while this account fails to deal with the question of illness per se, it does, by analogy, tell us something (disturbing and perhaps surprising?) about a Christlike attitude to illness, especially if in the face of illness we experience the silence of God (that primary threat to Judaeo-Christian theodicy).

Aware, then, of the risk to his life, Jesus goes to Gethsemane to pray: 'Abba, Father, all things are possible to you; take this cup from me. Yet not my will but yours' (Mark 14.36). And what is salient about this prayer when reflecting upon the (potentially) transformative power of illness is the recognition that while Jesus has no desire to meet his death neither does he expect to be *rescued* from his life.[26]

Jesus speaks and, when he has spoken, there is silence. There is no suggestion, in the structure of the narrative, that he expected a reply. . . . In Gethsemane [in contrast to the Book of Job] there is no divine fulmination, no thunderous theophany. Jewish and Christian understanding of God has now reached the point where we do not expect, nor do we have any reason to suppose that Jesus

113

expected, a reply. His duty, his obedience, goes all the way into the dark; his whole identity is given over into silence.

(Lash, 2004, pp. 75–6)

This emphasis upon God's silence refusing any easy answers is, I suggest, a key to understanding what it might mean to imagine the felt absence or silence of God-Spirit as encountered in times of illness and other times of crisis. Because it indicates, at least as I read it, that our lives are contingent and that contingency is where we belong. Thus for us, as for Jesus, there is no escape from the fact of embodiment (or incarnation). Rather, in Lash's terms, we must go 'all the way' into the silence, as into God's covenant promising peace. And the fact that this bears little resemblance to what we have *authoritatively* come to imagine as 'ease and painlessness' (Eiesland) – as an abstract definition of peace or health – is simply a reminder of how far we have strayed from the suffering and hope that Paul binds together in his understanding of the 'grace in which we now live'.[27]

This is a point made well by Werner G. Jeanrond's *Call and Response: The Challenge of the Christian Life* (Jeanrond, 1995). Here Jeanrond takes issue with a tendency within the Christian tradition to deny 'the biologically oriented concept of death' by mistaking the limitations of mortality for the limitations of God (Jeanrond, 1995, p. 54). And I suggest that a similar tendency needs to be taken into account when reflecting upon a Christian understanding of illness, so that illness is not interpreted to signify the *absence* of God-Spirit but is rather interpreted as a necessary, although difficult, fact of embodiment, and as a vital component of God's covenant promising peace – what we might want to call the *real presence* of God-Spirit. Hence Shuman and Meador:

> It is not wrong to beseech God to remove our suffering or extend our lives or magnify our vigor. But we err if we act as if that is mainly what God is *for*. And we are, perhaps importantly, simply mistaken if we abandon hope when suffering continues or health is illusory, or if we despair of God when sickness persists or death seems imminent. For Christians, these are not conclusions but starting places. The hard work of Christian discipleship begins here, in the face of the difficult task of negotiating life as mortal and broken bodies in a finite and broken world, and of doing so without losing hope.   (Shuman and Meador, 2003, p. 116)

A necessary angel

I want to conclude this chapter with a brief meditation on Jacob's wrestling. And I want to interpret Jacob's story as a primary resource for a Judaeo-Christian understanding of God's covenant promising peace: one that challenges us 'to imagine more, to feel more, to think more – in short, to love more. And so to be inwardly changed' (Shanks, 2001, p. 5).

In brief, Jacob in the course of his difficult life – a life, we should note, that flies in the face of *authoritative* definitions of morality and justice (cf. Burdon, in Walton and Hass (eds.), 2000, pp. 160–74) – finds himself at a crossroads. He is about to meet his brother whom he hasn't seen for a number of years and who has good reason to treat him harshly.

> During the night Jacob rose, and taking his two wives, his two slave girls, and his eleven sons, he crossed the ford of Jabbok. After he had sent them across the wadi with all he had, Jacob was left alone, and a man wrestled with him there until daybreak. When the man saw that he could not get the better of Jacob, he struck him in the hollow of his thigh, so that Jacob's hip was dislocated as they wrestled. The man said, 'Let me go, for day is breaking,' but Jacob replied, 'I will not let you go unless you bless me.' The man asked 'What is your name?' 'Jacob,' he answered. The man said, 'Your name shall no longer be Jacob but Israel, because you have striven with God and with mortals, and have prevailed.' Jacob said, 'Tell me your name, I pray.' He replied, 'Why do you ask my name?' but he gave him his blessing there. Jacob called the place Peniel, 'because', he said, 'I have seen God face to face yet my life is spared'. The sun rose as Jacob passed through Penuel, limping because of his hip. That is why to this day the Israelites do not eat the sinew that is on the hollow of the thigh, because the man had struck Jacob on that sinew.
>
> (Genesis 32.22–33)

Now without saying all that might be said about this story[28] there are three points I want to highlight. The first is that Jacob faces his antagonist alone in a direct bodily confrontation. The second is that Jacob is not daunted by this encounter, for he wrestles and is prepared to wrestle until daybreak. And the third is that Jacob, despite being wounded, is determined to receive a blessing for his troubles. Additionally we should note that the blessing Jacob receives is not *contained* in or by this encounter, rather it *spills out* into Jacob's future (and thus the life of Israel). Also the name he receives, 'Israel' (God strives), might also tell us something about a (possible) Judaeo-Christian attitude to illness.

Reading the story analogously for our own experiences of illness, we can interpret the first point to mean that we meet God face to face: that we encounter God's presence in the 'felt-sense' of our embodiment and that this encounter will always have a quality of aloneness.

> Man's [or woman's] consciously lived fragility, individuality, and relatedness make the experience of pain, of sickness, and of death an integral part of his [or her] life. The ability to cope with this trio autonomously is fundamental to his [or her] health.
> (Illich, 2002, p. 275)

This emphasizes the point that we are personally, and therefore deeply and imaginatively, involved in our experiences of illness. That illness is not merely a passive occurrence, but a reality within which we find ourselves 'more truly and more strange' (Stevens, 1970, p. 29). This leads to the second point, that illness is a challenge that demands our 'total response' (Jeanrond), and that how we confront this challenge will substantially determine the experiences we are likely to have. Hence Jacob challenges his protagonist, 'I will not let you go unless you bless me.'[29] A challenge for which we are also accountable, I suggest.

Finally, the third and perhaps key point tells us that the content of this encounter remains *objectively* empty; that there is no meaning to the encounter other than that which we wrestle from it.[30] Hence Jacob asks his protagonist, 'Tell me your name, I pray.' And in response to this petition no name is given.[31] Yet it is precisely for this reason that the story of Jacob is a healing story.

> The story of Jacob's confrontation with the angel is a narrative of healing precisely because it shows he is innocent. There is nothing he has done to anger the angel. The adversarial conflict is not of his making. He is not accountable. And he is not to blame for his wound. However, healing happens when he is able to embrace the wound as a blessing and assume responsibility for his actions. (hooks, 2000-b, p. 233)

However, while I agree with bell hooks that Jacob is not to be blamed for his wound – that there is no value judgement or name appended to woundedness as such – nevertheless, hooks distorts the story by conflating Jacob's blessing with his wound. For it is not the wound that Jacob receives that is a blessing. That, put simply, is part and parcel of life. Rather, his blessing is a promise, the renewal of God's covenant, signified, but not contained, in the name he is given.[32]

Specifically, then, it is not the heroism of Jacob that is at stake in this story, but the way this encounter becomes a *collective* 'chain of memory' (Hervieu-Léger, 2000). For it is in the imaginative appropriation of this story – that the Israelites to this day 'do not eat the sinew that is on the hollow of the thigh, because the man had struck Jacob on that sinew' – that a clue is given for binding suffering (reality) and hope (imagination) together in a way that embodies God's covenant promising peace. This is because both Jacob (individually) and Israel (as a community) have been schooled, through their evolving understanding of God, to believe that a blessing is possible. Therefore it is neither through a singular and obdurate heroism nor through the avoidance or denial of our difficult lives, but rather as a way of giving *shape* to our lives, that we are able, however 'disabled', to wrestle a blessing for our embodiment and give a name to that blessing which is 'no fantasy'. This is a point expressed eloquently by Mary Grey:

> From out of the chaos of fragmentation, the isolation of illness and disability, the lack of a future, a spirituality of hope moulds and shapes whatever will keep the flickering candle burning. It may be that the grand dream does not materialise yet; as Isaiah and his followers grew to understand, the constant reshaping of hope in new situations was the prophetic task. It may be that there is not an end to darkness, only a way of seeing in the dark, only lighting a candle within it. But that is why we keep the feast, in ceremonial time, Sabbath time, mythic time, the time of telling the stories that give substance to our hope.
>
> (Grey, 2000, p. 17)

And it is significant that this 'reshaping of hope', as re-enacted, in part, through the threefold mission of the Church to proclaim the Word, administer the sacraments and provide pastoral care (Avis, 2003, p. 50), is not reducible to the present tense. For the hope that is Israel and the hope that Christians strive for is not the fantasy of a quick-fix solution – what Stanley Hauerwas calls a 'cruel peace' (Hauerwas, 1998, pp. 245–8) – but the difficult wrestling of an unfolding covenant at odds with 'ease and painlessness' (Eiesland).

Therefore when the darkness comes as it did for Jesus, and if illness is such a darkness, which symbolically it (still) is, then we must go 'all the way' into it, not resigned but wrestling, as a witness, no doubt difficult, to God's covenant promising peace. A peace, as Harold Brodkey reminds us, that 'was never in the world', but is, paradoxically, 'all around me' (Brodkey, 1996, p. 177). And to which, a Christian might add, we are given access through the life, death and resurrection of Jesus (Romans 5.1).

Notes

1 By 'socio-symbolic' I mean the language structure and dominant ordering of society (cf. Chopp, 1992, p. 14).

2 Although an interpretation of God as creator is implicit within this chapter, I cannot do justice here to some of the more problematic and 'disabling' interpretations of the Doctrine of Creation as critiqued by Dawn DeVries (1994) and Catherine Keller (2003) among others. For that reason I have put to one side any explicit discussion of the Doctrine of Creation.

3 By arguing thus I am not downplaying the insights of the Old Testament understanding of *shalom*, a truly radical interpretation of peace as wholeness, justice, and interconnection. Neither am I favouring a spiritualized interpretation of peace. But I do want to disrupt the hegemonic definition of *shalom*, which implicitly favoured Israel as a chosen people over and against other nations and so privileged 'wholeness, completeness and well-being' as to practically and ideologically exclude brokenness, incompleteness and uncertainty from full integration and compatibility with God's covenant promising peace (cf. Shuman and Meador, 2003, pp. 126–7).

4 Here I emphasize the disturbing quality of *dunamis*. This emphasis needs to be read alongside its mutual and co-operative qualities. See, for example, Elizabeth Baxter's and Mary Grey's emphasis upon relationality in this volume.

5 It is also possible to argue that we 'choose' illness as a way of attacking various forms of authority. However, in the current chapter I want to focus on the authoritative imposition of illness and the subversive power of a liberating God.

6 In what follows I interpret illness to include 'disability' and do not, in this chapter, distinguish between them.

7 The question 'why me?' requires 'an explanation which transcends the individual body and the medical diagnoses. The response to these questions goes beyond a search for causes and becomes a quest for meaning. We are trying to relate illness to the order of the world and to the social order' (Herzlich and Pierret, in Currer and Stacey (ed.), 1991, p. 75).

8 Here I have in mind Anselm's statement in the *Proslogion*, that God is that than which nothing greater can be conceived.

9 '[O]ur failures in helping so often provide the richest material for our growth and development as pastoral counsellors. After all, those who seek our help come not because of their successes but because of their failures and their difficulties' (Foskett, 1984, p. 7).

10 For a reductive reading of Stevens' conversion to Catholicism see Critchley, 2005, p. 21. Here Critchley dismisses Stevens' conversion as 'the act of a dying, lonely man who confessed to "a certain emptiness in his life" and who hadn't been on speaking terms with his wife for years'. Thus he is able to say of Stevens that '[p]oetry takes the place of religion as that medium which offers the possibility, or at least pursues the question, of life's redemption. [Therefore . . .] there is no sense in claiming, for Stevens, that there is anything that transcends the world.' In what follows I try to maintain a critical difference (whether or not that is necessary) between what Stevens says of poetry and what I *use* Stevens to say about God's covenant promising peace.

11 For a critique of objectivity see Polanyi, 1969: '. . . as human beings, we must inevitably see the universe from a centre lying within ourselves and speak about it in terms of a human language shaped by the exigencies of human intercourse. Any attempt rigorously to eliminate our human perspective from our picture of the world must lead to absurdity' (p. 3).

12 'These traditions ['philosophical suppositions that privilege the mind and [a] theology crafted coherently in constructionist concepts'] did not and do not tolerate the ambiguity attendant to the mysterious and often tragic cycle of birth and death at the heart of life itself. Trying to transcend the body, and accordingly women, these traditions have tried to transcend finitude and, most of all, mortality' (May, 1995, pp. 16, 19).

13 It is perhaps worth noting that bell hooks' vision of 'feminist movement' has developed from a purely secular presentation to acknowledge what she calls the 'spiritual life', that 'commitment

to a way of thinking and behaving that honors principles of inter-being and interconnectedness' (hooks, 2000-b, p. 77). In what follows I connect hooks' earlier analysis of 'power' with her renewed understanding of the 'divine spirit'.

14 Unlike much depth psychology, Mindell's emphasis upon the body anchors his theory in a biophilic world-view. For a critique of Jungian and other depth psychologies, including their disassociation from the body and re-inscription of sexist archetypes, see Goldenberg, 1990.

15 Mindell uses the term 'medicine' perhaps a little too loosely. He is not referring to 'scientific medicine' as we currently understand it, but to a range of healing practices that includes modern medicine alongside other religious/wisdom traditions.

16 The Christian healing ministry also distinguishes between cure and healing, placing greater emphasis upon the latter (right-relationship with God and community) than upon the former (perfect heath) (cf. Shuman and Meador, 2003 p. 116; Young, in Montefiore (ed.), 1992, p. 155).

17 For an in-depth discussion of the political application of process work, see Mindell, 1989.

18 This translation is in keeping with Mindell's overall schema, but it also serves to challenge his superficial reading of the body and its significance within the Judaeo-Christian tradition (cf. Mindell, 1984, p. 9).

19 By reading the following passage as a metaphor for bodily practice I may well be reading von Balthasar against the grain, but I am not misinterpreting his emphasis upon 'practical, active love'.

20 Under the heading 'empathic care' I include the *positive* contribution of biomedical and technological developments in modern medicine. However, by emphasizing the role of empathy I mean to imply, but do not have space to develop the idea here, an ethical-empathetic application for the use of such developments.

21 There are, of course, exceptions to the rule, but the dominant trend is, I believe, sufficiently established (cf. Keller, 1988).

22 Although I appreciate Smith's thesis and make use of his definition, in the context of this chapter I want to distance myself from his 'metaphysical' emphasis.

23 See, for example, Frijof Capra's presentation of systems theory and its application to models of wholeness and health (Capra, 1982).

24 Mindell draws on the work of David Bohm, who 're-conceived quantum waves in terms of what he called "pilot waves," which he imagined somehow informed or guided material objects [. . .

much] as a radar wave guides ships at sea' (Mindell, 2004, p. 26).

25 For a more detailed discussion of Julian's attitude to embodiment and illness, including the above quotation, see Grace Jantzen's chapter in this volume.

26 An emphasis, we should note, that might affect the way we interpret definitions of salvation as 'rescue' or 'release'.

27 From a process work perspective the above story can be read as an example of Jesus' ability to follow his process – or, we might say, the process of God-Spirit. In short, Jesus moves fluidly between various channels, e.g. the proprioceptive and auditory channels (prayer), the relationship channel (with God, Jesus' disciples and the guards who come to capture him) and the world channel (into which he moves as the only way to manifest God's covenant promising peace). Jesus' primary process (or identity) is that of an ordinary man (he is alone, vulnerable and in need of company) but his secondary process (or identity), and the one he is challenged to integrate and so become, is that of the love which *is* God.

28 Although I cannot develop the point here, it is worth bearing in mind Arnold Van Gennep's description of a rite of passage that passes through three successive phases: separation, transition and aggregation (cf. Miller, 2000, p. 30).

29 There are, of course, circumstances in which we cannot participate, some of which are the result of severe physical and/or mental impairment. In these circumstances it is a faith claim to say that God is present in our absence. Hence, to adapt a quote of Jeanrond's, '[w]here we become totally powerless in death [or illness], God becomes power-full. Where we cannot do anything any longer, God [in the form of God's community] is there for us' (Jeanrond, 1995, p. 54).

30 It is worth bearing in mind James Alison's warning that we risk propagating a lie when we 'create social order and meaning out of a sacred space of victimisation' (Alison, 2003, p. 6). And while Alison is writing specifically about September 11th 2001, and by analogy Jesus' crucifixion, a similar warning applies when attempting to attach prescriptive meanings to either the Jacob story or experiences of illness and crisis per se.

31 It should be noted, however, that this silence can be read to denote the unnameable Elohim.

32 It is also appropriate to note that while Jacob is innocent as regards being wounded in this encounter, he is not, by any reckoning, innocent of the incredibly complicated and compromised life he has previously lived and continues to live after this encounter.

References

Alison, J., *On Being Liked*. Darton, Longman & Todd, London, 2003.

Avis, P., *Eros and the Sacred*. SPCK, London, 1989.

Avis, P., *A Church Drawing Near: Spirituality and Mission in a Post-Christian Culture*. T&T Clark International, Continuum Imprint, London and New York, 2003.

Brodkey, H., *This Wild Darkness: The Story of My Death*. Fourth Estate, London, 1996.

Burdon, C., 'Jacob, Esau and the Strife of Meanings', in Walton, H. and Hass, A. W. (eds), *Self / Same / Other: Re-visioning the Subject in Literature and Theology*. Sheffield Academic Press, Sheffield, 2000, pp. 160–74.

Campbell, P. A. and McMahon, E. M., *Bio-spirituality: Focussing as a Way to Grow*. Loyola University Press, Chicago, 1985.

Capra, F., *The Turning Point: Science, Society and the Rising Culture*. Wildwood House, London, 1982.

Chopp, R. S., *The Power to Speak: Feminism, Language, God*. Crossroad, New York, 1992.

Critchley, S., *Things Merely Are: Philosophy in the Poetry of Wallace Stevens*. Routledge, London and New York, 2005.

Crowder, C. (ed.), *God and Reality: Essays on Christian Non-Realism*. Mowbray, London, 1997.

DeVries, D., 'Creation, Handicappism, and the Community of Differing Abilities', in Chopp, R. S. and Taylor, M. L. (eds), *Reconstructing Christian Theology*. Fortress Press, Minneapolis, 1994.

Eiesland, N. L., *The Disabled God: Towards a Liberatory Theology of Disability*. Abingdon Press, Nashville, 1994.

Foskett, J., *Meaning in Madness: The Pastor and the Mentally Ill*. SPCK, London, 1984.

Foucault, M., *Power/Knowledge: Selected Interviews and Other Writings 1972–1977*. Gordon, C. (ed.), Harvester Wheatsheaf, Hemel Hempstead, 1980.

Grey, M. C., *The Outrageous Pursuit of Hope: Prophetic Dreams for the Twenty-first Century*. Darton, Longman & Todd, London, 2000.

Goldenberg, N. R., *Returning Words to Flesh: Feminism, Psychoanalysis, and the Resurrection of the Body*. Beacon Press, Boston, 1990.

Hardey, M., *The Social Context of Health*. Open University Press, Buckingham, 1999.

Hauerwas, S., *Sanctify Them in the Truth: Holiness Exemplified*. T&T Clark, Edinburgh, 1998.

Hervieu-Léger, D., *Religion as a Chain of Memory*. Polity Press, Cambridge, 2000.

Herzlich, C. and Pierret, J., 'Illness: From Causes to Meaning', in Currer, C. and Stacey, M. (eds), *Concepts of Health, Illness and Disease: A Comparative Perspective*. Berg, Oxford, 1991.

Heyward, I. C., *The Redemption of God: A Theology of Mutual Relation*. University Press of America, Lanham, 1982.

hooks, b., *Feminist Theory: From Margin to Centre*. (2nd edn), Pluto Books, London, 2000-a.

hooks, b., *All About Love: New Visions*. HarperCollins Publishing, New York, 2000-b.

Illich, I., *Limits to Medicine* (the definitive version of) *Medical Nemesis: The Exploration of Health*. Marion Boyars, London, 2002.

Isherwood, L. and Stuart, E., *Introducing Body Theology*. Sheffield Academic Press, Sheffield, 1998.

Jantzen, G. M., *Becoming Divine: Towards a Feminist Philosophy of Religion*. Manchester University Press, Manchester, 1998.

Jeanrond, W. G., *Call and Response: The Challenge of Christian Life*. Continuum, New York, 1995.

Julian of Norwich, *Showings*. Colledge, E. and Walsh, J. (tr.), Classics of Western Spirituality. Paulist Press, New York, and SPCK, London, 1978.

Keller, C., *From a Broken Web: Separation, Sexism, and Self*. Beacon Press, Boston, 1988.

Keller, C., *Face of the Deep: A Theology of Becoming*. Routledge, London and New York, 2003.

Lash, N., *Holiness, Speech and Silence: Reflections on the Question of God*. Ashgate, Aldershot, 2004.

May, M. A., *A Body Knows: A Theopoetics of Death and Resurrection*. Continuum, New York, 1995.

McFague, S., *Speaking in Parables: A Study in Metaphor and Theology*. SCM Press, London, 2002.

McIntyre, J., *Faith, Theology and Imagination*. The Handsel Press, Edinburgh, 1987.

Miller, J., *The Body in Question*. Pimlico, London, 2000.

Mindell, A., *Dreambody: The Body's Role in Revealing the Self*. Routledge & Kegan Paul, London, Melbourne and Henley, 1984.

Mindell, A., *The Year I: Global Process Work*. Arkana/Penguin, Harmondsworth, 1989.

Mindell, A., *Working on Yourself Alone: Inner Dreambody Work*. Arkana/Penguin, Harmondsworth, 1990.

Mindell, A., *The Quantum Mind and Healing: How to Listen and Respond to Your Body's Symptoms*. Hampton Roads, Charlottesville, 2004.

Morton, N., *The Journey is Home*. Beacon, Boston, 1986.

Polanyi, M., *Personal Knowledge: Towards a Post-Critical Philosophy*. Routledge & Kegan Paul, London, 1969.

Raphael, M., *Thealogy and Embodiment: The Post-Patriarchal Reconstruction of Female Sacrality*. Sheffield Academic Press, Sheffield, 1996.

Report of a Working Party, *Mud and Stars: The Impact of Hospice Experience on the Church's Ministry of Healing*. Sorbell, Oxford, 1991.

Salmon, J. Warren, 'Defining Health and Reorganising Medicine', in Salmon, J. Warren (ed.), *Alternative Medicines: Popular and Policy Perspectives*. Tavistock Publications, London and New York, 1985.

Shanks, A., *'What is Truth?': Towards a Theological Poetics*. Routledge, London, 2001.

Shuman, J. J. and Meador, K. G., *Heal Thyself: Spirituality, Medicine, and the Distortion of Christianity*. Oxford University Press, New York, 2003.

Smith, H., *Why Religion Matters: The Fate of the Human Spirit in an Age of Disbelief*. HarperCollins, New York, 2001.

Stevens, W., *Selected Poems*. Faber and Faber, London, 1970.

Stevens, W., *The Necessary Angel: Essays on Reality and the Imagination*. Faber and Faber, London, 1984.

Suchocki, M. H., *The Fall to Violence: Original Sin in Relational Theology*. Continuum, New York, 1999.

von Balthasar, H. U., *Who is a Christian?* Burns and Oates, London, 1970.

Weil, A., *Health and Healing*. Houghton Mifflin Company, New York, 1998.

Wilkinson, J., *The Bible and Healing: A Medical and Theological Commentary*. The Handsell Press, Edinburgh, 1998.

Young, J., 'Health, Healing and Modern Medicine', in Montefiore, H. (ed.), *The Gospel and Contemporary Culture*. Mowbray, London, 1992, pp. 149–58.

7

Embodying technology, becoming our tools: discussing the post/human

ELAINE GRAHAM

———◆◆◆———

Who we are as human beings, the whole process of our biological and cultural evolution, is inextricably bound up with the tools we use. However, as Elaine Graham makes clear in her 2005 Hildegard Lecture, we are now at a crossroads. This is because the tools we use, both digital and biotechnological, are beginning to render 'problematic taken-for-granted boundaries between humans, machines and what we call "nature"'. This leads Graham to explore, through both text and film, the question of what it means to be 'post/human', and what resources a Judaeo-Christian theology has to inform the outcome of that question.

* * *

The issues that technological culture throws into sharp relief are those of values, and the value judgements on which decisions about ends and the restrictions (if any) on the means to achieve those ends, have to be taken. More particularly, at the heart of the problem of value judgements is the issue of the nature of the person. What does it mean to be human? is a question that has taken on a new urgency in a culture where behaviour can be manipulated by increasingly sophisticated technology.

(Brown and Wesson, 1991, p. 22)

... the question can never be first of all 'what are we *doing* with our technology?' but it must be 'what are we *becoming* with our technology?' (Hefner, 2003, p. 9)

125

Introduction

At eleven o'clock on the morning of 21 June 1948, in a workshop in a tiny side street on the campus of the University of Manchester, a team of mathematicians and engineers conducted the world's first successful electronic stored-program computing sequence on a machine they named 'Baby'. Since then, the size of computing machines has reduced from a main-frame structure the size of a lecture theatre into desk-top, hand-held personal machines. Their speed and power has increased a millionfold. Computer-mediated communications have transformed the abilities of their users to store and process information, but more widely, have also changed leisure habits, the jobs many people do, the types of machines that fill offices, shops and homes. Together with the identification, half a decade later, of the structure of DNA, the birth of 'Baby' has triggered a technological and cultural revolution.

And it is the impact of these technologies, the digital and genetic respectively, not just upon our material and economic existence, but – as I shall argue – upon our very experiences and understandings of what it means to be human, that I want to focus on in this paper. I want to concentrate on ways in which the digital and biotechnological age is rendering problematic taken-for-granted boundaries between humans, machines and what we call 'nature'; and in turn, how it raises questions about how we – as humans, as builders and users of tools, artefacts and technologies – think about ourselves.

The 'posthuman condition': being and becoming

Reference to the so-called 'posthuman condition' (Pepperell, 1995) is becoming commonplace to denote a world in which humans are mixtures of machine and organism, where nature has been modified by technology, and technology has become assimilated to form a functioning component of organic bodies. But the impact of digital and genetic technologies is not simply a scientific or ethical issue; it carries a number of deeper, existential implications.

First, the digital and biotechnological age[1] challenges our assumptions about what it means to be human because new technologies are transforming our experiences of things like embodiment, communication, intelligence and disease, even blurring the very distinctions between the 'organic' and the 'technological', or between humans, machines and nature. For some, this is not simply a matter of coming to terms with the economic and cultural impact of new technologies, but as the opening quotations suggest, it also challenges the very nature of human ontology – our being and becoming.

Second, it raises questions of the kinds of images, discourses, authorities and narratives that will be decisive in helping us to debate the very question of what it will mean to be human in the twenty-first century. I am particularly concerned with the relative influence wielded by scientific institutions and discourses, by the media, by popular culture and by religion in advancing and adjudicating this question. It is intriguing to note how much debate about the impact of new technologies on Western culture involves a further blurring of supposedly impermeable boundaries: between scientific objectivity (the world of fact) and that of cultural representation (the world of fiction). A number of recent works (Graham, 2002; Hayles, 1999; Bukatman, 1993; Herzfeld, 2002) draw on popular culture as an important measure of the values informing reception of new technologies.

As Katharine Hayles argues, '. . . culture circulates through science no less than science circulates through culture' (Hayles, 1999, p. 21) – in itself, perhaps, a postmodern acknowledgement of the constructedness of scientific theories, a contention that science does not report on or portray an a priori reality, but is dependent on wider cultural metaphors to weave a narrative about the world. This will often draw on images, analogies, other narratives, to achieve rhetorical effect. Thus, the Human Genome Project is depicted not only as a scientific exercise but as a heroic quest for the 'holy grail' or the 'code of codes'; Francis Bacon's discourse of science rests on an image of the male appropriator seizing nature and forcing her to relinquish her secrets; and witness the continuing potency of the Frankenstein myth in informing public reception of genetic technologies. All of these suggest a creative interplay between science and culture. But similarly, popular culture (Science Fiction especially) becomes both enthusiastic advocate and critical opponent of science and technology.

So different representations of the 'posthuman' (in scientific literature and popular culture) may serve as *refractions* of normative and exemplary models of what it means to be human. They will not simply be neutral depictions, but will rather be expressions of deep value judgements as to what is distinctive about humanity, and what should be the relationship between humans and their tools and technologies.

And so the theme of this chapter, essentially, is this. If the future is one of augmented, modified, virtual, post-biological humanity – the era of posthumanity – then what are the implications? What choices and opportunities are implicit in the hopes and anxieties engendered by the technologies that surround us? What understandings of exemplary and normative humanity will be privileged in the process; but also, who will be included or excluded from that vision?

These are questions about identity, about the future, about community, about technologies themselves; but as we shall see they are also about theology: how we practise religion, speak of God, envisage the sacred, in a digital and biotechnological age. For these questions have added relevance due to the way in which religious and theological metaphors are invoked in the midst of many of these visions of the future, but prompting us, perhaps, to realize that these issues are not only about viewing technology as 'saviour' or 'servant', but about our own very existence: about the nature of life and death, the potential (and limits) of human creativity, about humanity's very place in the created order.

An age of technology

What makes a discussion about the impact of such technologies in 2006 any different from one in 1906, 1956, even 1996? Is it really the case that our understandings and experiences of ourselves are radically affected by the Human Genome Project and the internet any more than by the aeroplane, the telephone, or even the hammer or the hydroelectric dam?

While there may be grounds for regarding the technological (and accompanying cultural) developments over the past 50–60 years as new departures, in other respects the intensification of digital, cybernetic and biomedical technologies merely returns us to long-standing questions about the metaphysics and philosophy of human relationships with their tools, artefacts and technologies. Whether it be the celebration of a kind of technological sublime, or anxiety in the face of the loss of the spiritual integrity of humanity and nature, the possibility of the posthuman is part of a continuing exploration into what it means to be human, and how that vision is expressed in the context of our relationships with other humans, with non-human nature, and how it affects our understandings of, and language about, the divine.

The 'posthuman condition'

Let me begin by identifying some of the ways in which digital and biomedical technologies are said to redefine taken-for-granted understandings of what it means to be human, such that commentators have argued that we are witnessing a transition from the 'human' to the 'posthuman'.

The mechanization of the human and technologization of the natural

The miniaturization of components such as microchips means that it is possible for technologies now to be placed into or grafted on to the human body. In July 2002 the AbioCor artificial heart, constructed out of plastic and titanium and powered by external batteries, was implanted into a patient called Robert Tools. Mr Tools was not expected to survive more than a month, but he died the following November, five months after surgery. More rudimentary implants, such as heart pacemakers and cochlear implants, are more commonplace, at least in the West; but in all cases, 'natural' processes are mimicked by technological or cybernetic means, rectifying abnormalities, replacing lost faculties or assisting depleted physical functions.

Once the province of military experiment and science fiction, 'cyborgs' (mixtures of organic and cybernetic) are now moving from fantasy into reality (Gray, 1995). The term 'cyborg' was first used in a paper published in 1960 by two aeronautics experts, Manfred Clynes and Nathan Kline. Their paper speculated how technological adaptations of physical functioning might enhance human performance in hostile environments such as outer space (Clynes and Kline, 1995). Subsequently, cyborg technologies have been developed to restore impaired functions (such as prosthesis or implants), or modify existing capabilities, enhancing bodies into stronger, better, faster systems.

Cyborgs thus inhabit a world simultaneously 'biological' and 'technological'. A living fusion of the human and non-human animal, the human and the mechanical, and the organic and the fabricated, the cyborg exposes the collapse of taken-for-granted boundaries between species and categories (Haraway, 1991, pp. 152–3). However, for many the cyborg occupies a larger, metaphorical place in social theory, symbolizing the increasing interconnections between humans and technologies, a kind of 'thought experiment' in our understanding of being human in an age of advanced technologies.

For cultural theorist Donna Haraway, the cyborg represents the potential for a *renewed* relationship between humanity and what have been characterized as nature and technology, a greater intimacy and complicity with environment and artefact, a true interdependence in which human nature is no longer characterized through mastery and exclusion of its designated others. Others are more mindful, however, of the classic Sci-Fi cyborg, such as *Terminator* or *Robocop*:[2] the hypermasculine fighting machine, who is rendered invulnerable (and *inhuman*) by technological enhancements and modifications.

Blurring of species boundaries

A side effect of these medical technologies is the emergence of transgenic transplants, where genetic material is transferred from one species to another. Donna Haraway writes about OncoMouse™, a laboratory rodent at MIT who has been bred with a carcinogenic gene in order to facilitate research into breast cancer. She argues that this creature is a kind of cyborg, too, a hybrid of organism and machine, straddling the boundaries of nature, economics and technology, simultaneously mammal, laboratory animal, transgenic species and biotechnological commodity (Haraway, 1992, p. 38ff.).

When we ask, What is OncoMouse™? Where does she belong in the taxonomy of species? we discover her/it occupying a variety of categorical and discursive spaces. As a creature of technologized and commercialized biology, OncoMouse™ defies categorizations that depend on ontological purity and discreteness (Haraway, 1997, p. 119).

So OncoMouse™ is a living being, but also a lucrative commodity, a piece of patented information harnessed by corporate biotechnology in its fight to achieve a therapeutic 'good', namely a cure for cancer. An example, then, of the hybrid and uncertain status of many of the products of biotechnological intervention; but also a signal that we are dealing with a world not only of material technologies, of the manipulation of the physical world, but a world compromised by ethical and political decisions and replete with meanings and myths. And we can begin to get hints of the values underlying cultural representations of new technologies, from the manner in which, for Haraway, OncoMouse™ is portrayed as the bearer of deeper narratives about human suffering and salvation. In the rhetoric of ameliorative medicine, she argues, this little rodent is elevated to a salvific status:

> Although her promise is decidedly secular, s/he is a figure in the sense developed within Christian realism: s/he is our scapegoat; s/he bears our suffering; s/he signifies and enacts our mortality in a powerful, historically specific way that promises a culturally privileged kind of salvation – a 'cure for cancer'. Whether I agree to her existence and use or not, s/he suffers, physically, repeatedly, and profoundly, that I and my sisters may live.
>
> (Haraway, 1997, p. 79)

Thus, OncoMouse™ is not only an empirical or material phenomenon, a product of scientific experimentation, but a cultural icon too, embodying moral, emotional, even theological aspirations.

Blurring of bodily boundaries

But another blurring takes place at the boundaries of the human body. Whereas it was appropriate to think of tools such as the knife, the hammer and the water pot as simple instruments of extension and containment, in the highly technologized societies of the twenty-first century we are increasingly engaging with technologies that actually reshape the very boundaries and contours of the human body itself.

We might think of two dimensions to this: first, the ways in which prostheses, implants and synthetic drugs are internalized by the organic body, so that technology is not as an extension or appendage to the human body, but is *incorporated*, assimilated into its very structures. In the words of Stelarc, the Australian performance artist who specializes in installations which depict human fusions with technologies, 'The skin has been a boundary for the soul, for the self, and simultaneously a beginning to the world. Once technology stretches and pierces the skin, the skin as a barrier is erased' (Atzori and Woolford, 1995).

A second characteristic of the digital and biotechnological age – alongside that of incorporation – is its *immersive* nature, as new habitats for the containment and circulation of communication are created. The epitome of this, of course, would be the creation of digitally generated virtual realities. The philosophical question here is how 'real' such 'imaginary' environments are: whether they represent a flight from embodiment, or a continuation of corporeal and physical extension and augmentation already available via technologies such as the telephone.

Creation of new personal and social worlds

To continue this theme, it is arguable that in their capacity to engender new immersive worlds that authentically mimic organic reality, digital technologies have become not so much *tools* – extensions of the body – as total *environments* (Poster, 1996, pp. 188–9). Digital technology will soon be of such sophistication as to be capable of synthesizing an entire virtual environment, creating cyberspace into which a person can be sensorially if not physically assimilated.

Virtual reality allows the user to project a digitally generated self into cyberspace, synthesizing new spatial and temporal contexts within which alternative subjectivities are constructed. Digitally generated virtual worlds thereby offer new forms of 'post-bodied' activity, and the unitary face-to-face self is superseded by the multiple self – the simulated, fictive identity of the electronic chat room or the multi-user domain. So just as the boundaries between humans, animals and machines erode, so do the distinctions between the virtual and the real.

Some of these confusions of boundaries (bodily, real/virtual) are well illustrated in David Cronenberg's film, *eXistenZ* (1999). This particular movie was one of a number of cinematic explorations of humanity's encounter with cutting-edge technologies to be released at the end of the 1990s. I might also mention *Total*

Recall, *Johnny Mnemonic, Strange Days* and *The Matrix*. *eXistenZ* focuses on the implications of digitally generated multi-sensory 'virtual reality' (VR), its title referring to the name of a software program that runs a complex interactive role-play game. The female and male lead characters in the film are, respectively, Allegra Geller, the confident and adept designer of the software game, and her hapless bodyguard, Ted Pikel, who by contrast is very inexperienced and awkward around new technologies. In one sequence, in which Ted takes his first journey into virtual reality, we see his anxiety at being 'plugged in' via a special bioport embedded at the base of his spine: a fear of bodily penetration (the orifice resembles an anal sphincter or navel), as well as his mixture of incredulity and relief at his 'safe' transport into the digital world. Allegra, by contrast, takes a sensual pleasure in the game and relishes the experience of entering an imaginary world in which multiple identities and outcomes can be explored.

The film thus offers us vivid examples of the blurring of boundaries, of the transgression of clear demarcations between inside/outside of bodies, mechanical and organic, artificial and natural; and these themes are played out throughout *eXistenZ* to the final denouement itself. Indeed, the confusion between layers of 'reality' and 'illusion' gets increasingly complicated as the film progresses. But one of the most original things about *eXistenZ* is the way that the very technology itself subverts these dichotomies, by transgressing assumptions that machines should be plastic or metal. The 'pod' containing the software for *eXistenZ* is actually made of genetically modified organic material. It is thus not conventionally machinic and cold, but fleshy, visceral, organic, sensual. This imagined world thus causes us to rethink all our assumptions about the distinctions between 'hardware' (machines or robots), 'software' (computer programmes) and 'wetware' (organic beings or biological materials).

eXistenZ also draws intriguing distinctions between the characters of Allegra and Ted: they represent two opposing but typical reactions to new technologies. Ted exemplifies an almost hysterical fear at the prospect of the encroachment of technology upon his body. The erosion of corporeal boundaries, along with the confusion of fact and fantasy, is symptomatic of widespread anxiety, or 'technophobia', about the diminishment of human uniqueness in the face of new technologies, portraying them as a sinister and enigmatic alien force, likely to engulf the distinctively human.

Alternatively, the character of Allegra Geller regards her transport into virtual reality as empowering, mind-expanding, exhilarating. She is a keen advocate for the potential of virtual gaming as a means of intellectual and physical enhancement. This represents an alternative, more 'technophilic' tradition that celebrates their potential for good: medical treatments, greater communication, comfort, convenience.

To present this as a crude dichotomy between technophobia and technophilia, however, is not quite accurate. Rather, I think that the various responses to the potential effects of digital and genetic technologies on our assumptions about what it means to be human may be most helpfully grouped in some kind of continuum. I would like to map some of the positions between the extremes of reactions to technology as 'liberation or enslavement' (Cooper, 1995).

Technology: liberation or enslavement?

1 Creation out of control

In the mid-1990s, public concern over the effects of genetically modified crops was accompanied – and fuelled – by media references to 'Frankenstein Foods' (Newton et al., 1999; Wood, 1999). Even Monsanto, the multinational biotechnology corporation, saw fit to counter what it regarded as the negative publicity this occasioned (Monsanto™ Corporation, 1999). Associations with mad scientists and monstrosity evokes (deliberately?) a reaction of horror and suspicion – of creation turning on its creator who dares to 'play God'. The alliterative quality of the term adds to its impact; but in comparison to more neutral terms such as 'genetically modified crops', we are presented already with a powerful set of allusions and associations. Note again, as with OncoMouse™, how science and popular culture/myth are interwoven in the way these issues are represented.

Note also how theological themes are evoked, however incoherently: the notion of 'playing God' plays on fears that humanity has in some way usurped the creator, which is of course a long-standing theme in cultural engagement with technologies. The subtitle to *Frankenstein* was, after all, *The New Prometheus*; Mary Shelley evoking the Greek myth of the mortal who stole fire from the gods and who was punished as a consequence.

2 Dehumanization

Fritz Lang's *Metropolis*, made in 1926, articulates both the wonders of mechanization, but corresponding fears too. Set in the year 2000, the city from which the film takes its name is fatally divided. While the sons and heirs of the factory magnates disport themselves in a roof-top garden of delights, the working populace is enclosed in a subterranean world of unremitting drudgery.

The opening scenes of the film depict 'The Day Shift' as a human collective robbed of individual will or personality. The lethargy of the workers, their movement as one, suggests a fear of the loss of individuality in the era of mass production and central planning. Interspersed with shots of the pumping of pistons and the spinning of cogs and wheels are pictures of a futuristic, decimal clock-face, a juxtaposition that communicates how the relentlessness of time, the rhythms of machinery and the imperatives of productivity take precedence over human need.

So the wealth and technological sophistication of the city has its downside: and the workers in their underground labyrinth have become dehumanized by their routine, slaves to the relentless demands of the assembly line. Like the robot Maria, designed to suppress a workers' cult, the underground masses have become automata, driven only by the imperatives of machinery and efficiency. There is also a contrast in the film between the workers' factory workplace and their subterranean home, where Maria the preacher-prophet propagates values of the heart, affectivity and spirituality, in contrast to the dehumanizing forces of industry. This expresses an important theme, therefore, of technology effecting a kind of *disenchantment*; not only the erosion of something distinctively human, but the loss of some spiritual essence of human nature.

3 Technocracy

This is a third position, in which technologies are neutral instruments, merely means to an end. It is often allied to an unreconstructed futurism, in which technology solves our problems, grants us unlimited prosperity, guarantees democracy, fulfils our every desire, and is very pervasive in the media and other representations of popular science (Kaku, 1998; Kurzweil, 1999; Warwick, 2002).

In his book *Visions*, the Japanese-American physicist Michio Kaku predicts a world of microprocessors that will be so cheap to manufacture that we will treat them like so much scrap paper in 2020; there will be 'smart' machines that think and anticipate our needs; by 2050 there will be intelligent robots and by 2100 self-conscious, sentient artificial intelligence.

> By 2020, microprocessors will be as cheap and plentiful as scrap paper, scattered by the millions into the environment, allowing us to place intelligent systems everywhere. This will change every-thing around us, including the nature of commerce, the wealth of nations, and the way we communicate, work, play, and live. This will give us smart homes, cars, TVs, clothes, jewelry, and money. We will speak to our appliances, and they will speak back... The Internet will eventually become a 'Magic Mirror' that appears in fairy tales, able to speak with the wisdom of the human race.
>
> (Kaku, 1998, pp. 14–15)

Similarly, in describing his own (temporary) transformation from organic human to cyborg via the implantation of a silicon chip transmitter in his forearm, Kevin Warwick is expansive in his speculations about the potential of such technological enhancement. 'Might it be possible for humans to have extra capabilities, particularly mental attributes, and become super humans or, as some regard it, post humans [sic]?' (Warwick, 2002, p. 175). His enthusiasm encapsulates perfectly the vision of those who see the promise of cybernetic technologies as going beyond mere clinical benefits to embrace nothing less than an ontological transformation. Warwick sees no limit to the trans-cendence of normal physical and cognitive limitations, an achieve-ment that for him signals nothing less than a new phase in human evolution (Warwick, 2002, pp. 295–6).

However, I will return to the *political economy* of such a per-spective later on.

4 Evolution

For some, technologies promise the *evolution* of Homo sapiens from organic to silicon-based life. This perspective is sometimes known as 'transhumanism'. Transhumanists argue that, augmented and perfected by the latest innovations in artificial intelligence, genetic modifications, nanotechnology, cryonics, the human race will be liberated from the chains of poverty, disease and ignorance, to ascend to a better, higher, more superior state: the 'posthuman' condition. With the aid of technological enhancements, human beings can guarantee themselves immortality and omnipotence (Regis, 1990; More, 1998). Machinic evolution will complete the process of natural selection.

The apotheosis of the transhumanist ethos is to be found in a group known as the 'Extropians', their name encapsulating their quest to defy entropy as expressed in human bodily deterioration such as disease and ageing. The transhumanist spirit of technological and evolutionary inevitability expels defeatism and negativity, qualities that have no place in the Extropian world. One of their leading gurus, Max More, puts it this way: 'No mysteries are sacrosanct, no limits unquestionable; the unknown will yield to the ingenious mind. The practice of progress challenges us to understand the universe, not to cower before mystery. It invites us to learn and grow and enjoy our lives ever more' (More, 1998).

Yet this is not a human distinctiveness grounded in embodiment or even rational mind per se so much as a set of abstract qualities enshrined in a human 'spirit' of inventiveness and self-actualization: 'It is not our human shape or the details of our current human biology that define what is valuable about us, but rather our aspirations and ideals, our experiences and the kinds of lives we live. To a transhumanist, progress is when more people become more able to deliberately shape themselves, their lives, and the ways they relate to others, in accordance with their own deepest values' (Bostrom, 2003, p. 6).

While many of the transhumanists' proposed technological developments are yet to be realized, it may be more appropriate to regard transhumanism, like all other posthuman thinking, as another kind of thought experiment, which, like fictional representations of technologized humanity, serve to illuminate and refract deeper hopes and fears. What makes transhumanism such a vivid example of posthuman thinking is the way in which it articulates a particular set of humanist ideals and transposes them into the technological sphere. Transhumanists deliberately harness the aspirations of Enlightenment humanism and individualism as a philosophical underpinning for their endeavours. In its endorsement of human self-actualization unconstrained by fear, tradition or superstition, transhumanism exhibits a secular scepticism towards theologically grounded values, arguing that these serve to rationalize passivity and resignation in the face of human mortality and suffering.

As to technology, I think we can see how this tendency regards it not as threat but promise. Implants and prostheses, artificial intelligence, smart drugs, genetic therapies and other technological fixes will compensate for our physical limitations, overcoming even the existential challenge of mortality. Technology thus furnishes humanity with the means to complete the next phase of evolution, from Homo sapiens to 'Techno sapiens' (Jackelén, 2002).

5 Re-enchantment, transcendence

Contrary to popular assumptions concerning the antipathy between science and religion, discussion of new technologies discloses a surprising number of allusions to and celebrations of religion and spirituality. There are perhaps two main facets to this:

First, excitement at the opportunities opened up by new communications media (such as the internet) for the exchange and propagation of information. Established religions can present themselves to a truly global audience; the worldwide web can lodge an infinite repository of sacred texts; seekers after truth can sample at will with no obligation; new forms of spiritual expression can flourish unhindered (Brasher, 2001). It may be worth noting, however, that the fault-lines of suspicion and celebration of new technologies are evident here too: just as there are those who extol the potential for creating virtual faith communities 'online', so there are others who argue that this represents a diminishment, even a parody, of collective religious experience. Freed from physical community or temporal location, such cyber-spirituality does nothing to correct but merely exacerbates the rootlessness and anomie of Western society.

Second, there are those who regard technology as 'instruments of deliverance' (Noble, 1999): vehicles of ascent to higher planes, the harnessing of elemental powers, affording the power to transport their users into a sacred realm of 'transcendence', free of the encumbrances of the flesh. This perplexing re-emergence of what Noble calls 'the Religion of Technology', articulates the idea that advanced technologies hold the potential to 're-enchant' the world.

Indeed, some commentators liken cyberspace to a kind of sacred space, extolling the numinous quality of virtual reality. The codes and bytes of digital information are the material manifestations of a higher realm (Ziguras, 1997). Michael Benedikt deploys the biblical language of the 'Heavenly City' of Revelation, which in all its 'weightlessness, radiance, numerological complexity ... utter cleanliness, transcendence of nature and of crude beginnings' is the epitome of human longings for enlightenment, perfectibility and immortality (Benedikt, 2001). Similarly, Erik Davis speculates that these cybernauts are latter day exponents of Gnosticism and hermetism (Davis, 1998).

But note how 'religion' is being invoked here; it is equated with knowledge of or ascent towards a dispassionate 'transcendent' disembodied immutable God: and being religious is, of course, about desiring to be just like that kind of God. Yet this assumes that this particular model of transcendence is the genuine article, and that advanced technologies are the expression of a sort of eternal religious aspiration. But whose version of religion, and of 'transcendence', is being taken as exemplary and normative? Is it really the case that to be made in the image of God involves the emulation of such qualities of omnipotence, immortality and invulnerability?

In whose image?

These questions lie behind my decision to draw a distinction in my work between the 'posthuman' and 'post/human' (Graham, 2002). A pedantic point, you may think, but that 'slash' represents precisely my argument: that talk of the posthuman all too easily assumes a logical process of advancement, technocracy and progress that is assumed to be axiomatic but in fact underpins and justifies sectional and selective interests.

For me, therefore, the 'post-slash-human' is not so much a condition, as an *interrogation*; and this terminology is designed to reflect not so much a narrative inexorability as a questioning of whose exemplary model of what it means to be human is being privileged within technological design and technological development. For technologies not only reflect social and cultural values but actually shape and constitute choices. So the 'oblique' in post/human (Badmington, 2003) is intended precisely to alert us to the political choices inherent in the use of all technologies, to the values beneath the choices that get made, and who gets included and who gets excluded by 'the posthuman condition' – and last but not least, to the implicit spirituality and theological anthropology behind many of the technological desires and anxieties in Western culture.

Whether it is expressed in its secular (transhumanism) or religious (techno-transcendence) form, therefore, these narratives of salvation through technology implicitly act out a number of particular themes:

1 Posthuman as superhuman

In their elevation of individualism and self-improvement, and in the rejection of external authority or interference, transhumanism upholds some fairly unreconstructed libertarian principles. It is descended from the unalloyed faith in the primacy of the Enlightenment subject – rational, autonomous, self-determining. Indeed, More's 'Extropian Principles 3.0' cite Eric Drexler, Hans Moravec, Richard Dawkins, Friedrich Hayek and Karl Popper, all champions of a neo-liberal, rationalist, secular humanism: the posthuman as *superhuman?* We are confronted with the contrast between alternative representations of possible post/human futures, however, when we compare such rhetoric with a very different perspective.

Yet in that respect transhumanism represents something of a paradox, in that to become posthuman – to be radically dependent on technology for future evolution and survival – actually entails the erosion of the very categories of bodily integrity, autonomy and personal subjectivity that define liberal 'human nature'. Furthermore, in its 'realized eschatology' of immortality and escape from biological contingency, transhumanism embraces a dualistic – one might say Cartesian – anthropology, in that the continuity of individuals and the human species is equated with the continuation of consciousness rather than any notion of embodied selfhood. Theologically, as Brent Waters has argued, Christian doctrine has envisaged that the griefs and limitations of the human condition take place not via a denial of death but via its embrace, but ultimate defeat, through cross and resurrection. In other words, the betterment or perfection of humanity does not occur by the negation of the body but by embracing and redeeming corporeal humanity (Waters, 2006).

2 The political economy of the post/human

Let us now return to the technocratic futurism espoused by Michio Kaku and others. By 2020, Kaku predicts a 'planetary civilization' encompassing a global culture with a steady economic growth rate, embraced by a worldwide net of interactive communication (Kaku, 1998). In the process, Kaku accepts as inevitable the loss of 90 per cent of living human languages, and the triumph of multinational corporate interests, although he does concede that 'not everyone may find a planetary culture to their taste' (Kaku, 1998, p. 337).

Yet implicitly, questions of equity and distribution become pressing once we begin to ask what models of being human are being celebrated or upheld in these various futuristic visions. Who is the 'we' to whom this vision is addressed? Who will benefit from the advances being envisaged? What priorities are being articulated? What is unspoken in what Kaku is saying? Who doesn't get represented in the future world order of Kaku's posthuman technocratic vision? It is important to note that access to such opportunities – and therefore the potential to benefit from such technologies – are hugely skewed towards the West and away from the two-thirds world.

While pundits such as Michio Kaku and Kevin Warwick make headlines with their predictions of sophisticated new technologies by 2020 and beyond, others have very different priorities. The United Nations Human Development Programme has established targets for global development by 2015. These include goals to combat illiteracy, reduce child mortality, eradicate poverty and to promote primary health care (Jolly, 1999). This exposes, I think, the mismatch between scientific popularizers and those concerned with questions of distribution, access and equity in relation to new technologies.

Such considerations are starkly illuminated by the priorities of the UNHDP report:

> In mid-1998 industrial countries – home to less than 15% of people – had 88% of internet users. North America alone – with less than 5% of people – had more than 50% of internet users. By contrast, South Asia is home to over 20% of all people but had less than 1% of the world's internet users . . . Thailand has more cellular phones than the whole of Africa. There are more internet hosts in Bulgaria than in sub-Saharan Africa (excluding South Africa). The United States has more computers than the rest of the world combined, and more computers per capita than any other country. Just 55 countries account for 99% of global spending on information technology.
>
> (Jolly, 1999, p. 62)

It would seem that the desires of a minority of the world's population fuel the priorities of technoscientific innovation, yet in the context of cultural representations of the post/human, it is clear that they leave the interests of a significant minority *un*represented. In contrast to the prospect of smart houses, cheap microprocessors and gene therapies advanced by the technocratic futurists, the comparatively technologically rudimentary prospect of furnishing every man, woman and child on the planet with clean water goes unaddressed. There is nothing, except political will, stopping us achieving that goal immediately (cf. Norris, 2001).

3 Religion of technology

The quest to transcend bodily finitude via the seductions of artificial minds, prosthetic modifications and cyberspatial embodiments invokes a kind of 'technological sublime' that claims to be the latest expression of timeless human desires. I have already mentioned David Noble's evocation of 'the Religion of Technology', in which he argues that a quest for transcendence of the body, immortality of the flesh, omniscience, domination of nature, are fundamental human cravings, and actually constitute an essentially 'spiritual' drive towards scientific and technological innovation: 'Although today's technologists, in their sober pursuit of utility, power, and profit, seem to set society's standard for rationality, they are driven also by distant dreams, spiritual yearnings for supernatural redemption. However dazzling and daunting their display of worldly wisdom, their true inspiration lies elsewhere, in an *enduring, other-worldly* quest for transcendence and salvation' (Noble, 1999, p. 3, my italics).

Yet what we might call the *technological sublime* actually rests upon an unexamined identification of 'religion' with a flight from contingency and materialism, and a spirituality that seeks fulfilment in union with a 'transcendent' deity entirely removed from the immanence of this mortal world. The presumption is that the quest for technological advancement is at some level an expression of the *imago Dei*, and that this entails a necessary mastery over creation, heedless of the fragility and interdependence of life – ambitions that have in the past been used as rationalizations for dominion over non-human nature, and even colonized peoples. Its predilection for the qualities of detachment, omniscience, immutability and incorporeality promote disdain for embodied contingency and foster technologies that are obsessed with cheating death, vulnerability and finitude. To represent religion in this way, therefore, is to see it as providing the ideological underpinning for many of the dualisms that have fuelled modernity and technoscientific innovation (Jantzen, 1998; Carrette and King, 1998).

Yet there are alternative aspects of the notion of humanity as created in the image of God that serve as a vital theological corrective to all this. Certainly, an understanding of *human* creativity as participation in *divine* creativity affirms the goodness of our inventive abilities, and I would wish to celebrate that capacity to be 'builders of worlds', tool-makers and tool-users, and see this as part of what makes us distinctive as a species. Yet the materialist and incarnationalist nature of Christianity also teaches that the God in whose image we are made is not only transcendent but also immanent in the world, in history, in human affairs.

'Transcendence' is therefore not about God's absence from history, or God's antipathy to matter, as some of the quasignostic evocations of cyberspace as sacred space seem to suggest. Rather, it means that God is never reducible to this world, and is inviting creation into its final transformation that surpasses creation as it can presently be known; and this is a necessary reminder that our technologies are ultimately not our own, that our inventions, like the created order, only make sense when offered up as part of God's larger purposes. They cannot simply be reduced to the objects of human self-interest; and the 'divine horizon' of talk about God serves to orientate us to the view that humans are part of a wider web of creation and relatedness that is not, ultimately, of their making. Creation – including human participation in its transformation – is gift and grace, guarding against the hubris of too much power, of our seeking to 'play God', of remaking the world in the image of our own desires at the expense of other members of the human community or the rest of (non-human) nature.

So while theology affirms the dignity of humanity's role as *(co)-creators*, it also recalls us, crucially, to human *creatureliness*; to a dependence on the ultimate reality we call God and an interdependence with the rest of the created order of which we are a part.

In thinking about the future of human nature in a technological age, therefore, it may be more appropriate to acknowledge that humans are capable of building and inhabiting all kinds of worlds – some material, others virtual – but that they are all bound by the relations of their production, albeit working according to different conventions. Who and what 'we' are or become is thus intimately linked to the conditions under which we engage with technologies, and to what end. Neither the 'deification' nor the 'reification' of technologies, in the form of dreams of the technological sublime or fears of humanity's disenchantment, fully captures the necessarily complex, reflexive and hybrid nature of post/human experience.

And although the prospect of (post)humans being all mixed up with other parts of creation – nature, machines, non-human animals – may seem disturbing, it is, I believe, simply a reflection of the fact that human beings have always, as it were, 'co-evolved' with their environments, tools and technologies. By that I mean that to be human is already to be in a web of relationships, where our humanity can only be articulated – realized – in and through our environment, our tools, our artefacts, and the networks of human and non-human life around us.

It also means, I think, that we do not need to be afraid of our complicity with technologies, or fear our hybridity, or assume that proper knowledge of and access to God can only come through a withdrawal from these activities of world-building. What it means to be human, what is happening to the material world, are not matters that divert us from the true task of spiritual reflection and Christian living, but their very preconditions.

Conclusion: representing the post/human

New technologies promise to enhance lives, relieve suffering and extend capabilities. Yet they are often also perceived as threatening bodily integrity, undermining feelings of uniqueness, evoking feelings of growing dependency and encroaching on privacy. Whether advanced technologies are to be regarded as essentially bringing enslavement or liberation (Cooper, 1995), however, will be shaped by implicit philosophical and theological convictions about what it means to be human, what the purpose of humanity is, what will contribute to human flourishing, what threatens human integrity, and so on.

The various representations of the post/human are a tribute to humanity's propensity for constructing new technological worlds, but reveal also our tendency to invent other worlds of imagination, meaning and value, and to invest these creations with diverse hopes, fears and aspirations. For embedded in the various representations implicit in new technologies are crucial issues of identity, community and spirituality: what it means to be human, who counts as being fully human, who gets excluded and included in definitions of the post/human; and in our understandings of the nature of the God in whose image we have been formed. How we conceive of God will, even in a supposedly secular age, still impinge on the kinds of normative and exemplary models of divine nature and human destiny that fuel our technological dreams.

Exercising some control over the post/human future will necessitate not just ethical debate but, I contend, a theological orientation also. That is because, in thinking about the values embodied in these representations, we are effectively asking a theological question: in a digital and biotechnological age, what choices, destinies – and ideologies – has Western culture chosen to elevate as its objects of worship?

Notes

1 In the broader research from which this paper has emerged I am interested in the technologies emerging from two key scientific discoveries of the mid-twentieth century, namely the identification of DNA and the invention of the computer. But for purposes of clarity I am going to talk mainly about digital and information technologies and computer-assisted communications of various kinds, and leave the biotechnologies to one side (cf. Graham, 2002).

2 Although I have always regarded the latter as a parody of this tendency.

References

Film

eXistenZ, directed by David Cronenberg, 1999.
Johnny Mnemonic, directed by Robert Longo, 1995.
Metropolis, directed by Fritz Lang, 1927.
The Matrix, directed by Andy and Larry Wachowski, 1999.
Robocop, directed by Paul Verheoven, 1987.
Strange Days, directed by Katherine Bigelow, 1995.
Terminator, directed by James Cameron, 1984.
Total Recall, directed by Paul Verheoven, 1990.

Literature

Atzori, P. and Woolford, K., 'Extended-Body: Interview with Stelarc', *Ctheory*, (online), 6 September 1995, available at <http://www.ctheory.com/a29extended_body.html> 6 pp. [accessed 14 July 1999].

Badmington, N., 'Review of E. Graham, *Representations of the Post/Human* (2002)', *Textual Practice*. 2003, pp. 146–9.

Benedikt, M., 'Cyberspace: First Steps', in Bell, D. and Kennedy, B. M. (eds), *The Cybercultures Reader*. Routledge, London, 2001, pp. 29–44.

Bostrom, N. et al., 'The Transhumanist FAQ', 13 May 1999, available at <http://www.transhumanist.org> [accessed 20 August 2000].

Brasher, B. E., *Give me that Online Religion*. Jossey-Bass, San Francisco, 2001.

Brown, R. A. and Wesson, A. J., 'Technology and Theology: Co-operation or Conflict?' *Modern Churchman*. New Series, Vol. XXII, No. 5, 1991, pp. 16–23.

Bukatman, S., *Terminal Identity: the Virtual Subject in Post-Modern Science Fiction*. Duke University Press, Durham, NC., 1993.

Carrette, J. R. and King, R., 'Giving "Birth" to Theory: Critical perspectives on religion and the body', *Scottish Journal of Religious Studies*. Special Edition, 'Beginning with Birth', 19:1, 1998, pp. 123–43.

Clynes, M. E. and Kline, N. S., 'Cyborgs and Space', in Gray, C. H. (ed.), *The Cyborg Handbook*. Routledge, London, 1995, pp. 29–34.

Cooper, D. E., 'Technology: Liberation or Enslavement?', in Fellows, R. (ed.), *Philosophy and Technology*. Cambridge University Press, Cambridge, 1995, pp. 7–18.

Davis, E., *Techgnosis: Myth, Magic and Mysticism in the Age of Information*. Serpent's Tail, London, 1998.

Graham, E. L., *Representations of the Post/Human: Monsters, Aliens and Others*. Manchester University Press, Manchester, 2002.

Gray, C. H. (ed.), *The Cyborg Handbook*. Routledge, London, 1995.

Haraway, D., 'A Cyborg Manifesto: Science, Technology, and Socialist-Feminism in the Late Twentieth Century', in *Simians, Cyborgs and Women: The Reinvention of Nature*. Free Association Books, London, 1991, pp. 149–81.

Haraway, D., 'When Man™ is on the Menu', in Crary, J. and Kwinter, S. (eds), *Incorporations*. Zone Books, London, 1992, pp. 38–43.

Haraway, D., *Modest Witness@Second_Millennium.FemaleMan©_Meets_OncoMouse™*. Routledge, London, 1997.

Hayles, N. K., *How we became posthuman: virtual bodies in cybernetics, literature, and informatics*. University of Chicago Press, Chicago, 1999.

Hefner, P., *Technology and Human Becoming*. Fortress, Minneapolis, 2003.

Herzfeld, N., *In Our Image: Artificial Intelligence and the Human Spirit*. Fortress, Minneapolis, 2002.

Jackelén, A., 'The Image of God as *Techno Sapiens*', *Zygon*. 37:2, 2002, pp. 289–302.

Jantzen, G. M., *Becoming Divine: Towards a Feminist Philosophy of Religion*. Manchester University Press, Manchester, 1998.

Jolly, R. (ed.), *United Nations Human Development Report 1999*. Oxford University Press, Oxford, 1999.

Kaku, M., *Visions: How Science will Revolutionize the 21st Century and Beyond*. Oxford University Press, Oxford, 1998.

Kurzweil, R., *The Age of Spiritual Machines*. Orion, London, 1999.

Monsanto™ Corporation, 'Frankenstein Food? Take Another Look', 1999, (online), available at <http://www.searchmonsanto.com/monsanto-uk/frankensteinfoods.html> 2pp. [accessed 23 November 1999].

More, M., 'The Extropian Principles: A Transhumanist Declaration, Version 3.0', 1998. (online), available at <http://extropy.org.extprn.html> 13 pp. [accessed 19 March 1999].

Newton, P., Brown, D. and Clover, C., 'Alarm over "Frankenstein Foods"', *Daily Telegraph*. 12 February 1999, pp. 1–2.

Noble, D., *The Religion of Technology* (2nd edn). Penguin, Harmondsworth, 1999.

Norris, P., *Digital Divide: Civic Engagement, Information Poverty, and the Internet Worldwide*. Cambridge University Press, Cambridge, 2001.

Pepperell, R., *The Posthuman Condition*. Intellect, Bristol, 1995.

Poster, M., 'Postmodern virtualities', in Robertson, G., Mash, M., Tickner, L., Bird, J., Curtis, B. and Putnam T. (eds), *FutureNatural: Nature/Science/Culture*. Routledge, London, 1996, pp. 183–202.

Regis, E., *Great Mambo Chicken and the Transhuman Condition: Science Slightly over the Edge*. Addison-Wesley, Reading, MA, 1990.

Warwick, K., *I, Cyborg*. Century, London, 2002.

Waters, B., *From Human to Posthuman: Christian Theology and Technology in a Postmodern World*. Ashgate, London, 2006.

Wood, V. B., 'It's not nice to fool Mother Nature', *The Austin Chronicle* (online). 9 August, 1999, available at <http://www.weeklywire.com/ww/08-09-99/austin_food_featuref.html> 6pp. [accessed 23 November 1999].

Ziguras, C., 'The Technologization of the Sacred: Virtual Reality and the New Age', in Holmes, D. (ed.), *Virtual Politics: Identity and Community in Cyberspace*. Sage, London, 1997, pp. 197–211.

8

The womb and the tomb: health and flourishing in medieval mystical literature

GRACE JANTZEN

———◆———

It is with a mixture of sadness and gratitude that the following chapter, first delivered as the 2004 Hildegard Lecture, goes to print. Grace Jantzen's death on 2 May 2006 was a great loss to those who knew her personally, and to scholarship generally – as is evident in this chapter.

Here Jantzen explores the tensional relationship between necrophilia and natality in the anchoritic spirituality of medieval mystical literature – with a particular emphasis on Julian of Norwich. Her chapter can be read as a literary-historical investigation and as the ambivalent legacy of our spiritual forefathers and foremothers. However, by presenting the difference between necrophilia and natality in this way, Jantzen also provides us with a useful model for discerning the currents of necrophilia or natality within our own cultural symbolics – including, potentially, that of the Christian healing ministry.

* * *

The tension between necrophilia and natality is nowhere clearer in medieval Christendom than in the lives of anchorites and anchoresses, and the writings by them and for them. In English anchoritic spirituality can be found simultaneously an emphasis on life, healing and flourishing, and a morbid preoccupation with death, its practices and paraphernalia. This may in part be due to differences of religiosity during the centuries when anchoritic spirituality was a prominent part of the religious life of Western Christendom (Watson, 1987, pp. 132–53).

149

However, the tensions do not occur only over time, but can be seen also within the writings of individuals, as they struggled for a spirituality appropriate to their situation. In this chapter I wish to trace out some aspects of the gendered necrophilia of anchoritic spirituality, but also show how the categories of death could not contain the vibrant newness of life and wholeness that was celebrated by recluses, especially Julian of Norwich, and that subverted even the most insistent necrophilia.

Before the religious turbulence initiated in England by Henry VIII, the vocation to the solitary life was a significant ingredient in social and religious culture. This might take the form either of the life of a hermit or of that of anchorite/anchoress: the rough distinction between the two was that hermits were allowed – indeed expected – to come out of their hermitages to engage in such activities as preaching, building roads, or maintaining bridges, while those in anchorholds were expected to remain strictly enclosed. Their chief duties were prayers for themselves, their patrons, and the needs of the world; as well as counselling those who came seeking their wisdom (Clay, 1914; Darwin, 1944; Warren, 1985). They were in one sense a taken-for-granted element of medieval society: ordinary and yet extraordinary, 'a commonplace daily presence and a likely heavenly dweller' (Warren, 1985, p. 279). While their prayers and counsel were much relied upon by society as a whole, and in that sense not thought unusual, it was also held that such prayers were particularly effectual because the solitary was deemed especially holy, occupying the same status in the spiritual hierarchy as the martyrs and the Desert Mothers and Fathers in whose steps they were thought to follow (Watson, 1991, pp. 9–15). Since, therefore, the anchoress and anchorite occupied the highest form of the spiritual life in the medieval symbolic, it is particularly fascinating to trace the gendered workings of necrophilia and natality in their lives and writings.

1 Enclosure

From the day of her enclosure in an anchorhold, neither the anchoress herself nor any who participated in the ritual of her enclosure could be in any doubt about the centrality of death to her spirituality. Procedures varied, but according to some usages, the rite for the enclosure of an anchoress would begin in the church with a sung requiem mass. When the mass was over, the priests, anchoress and people would go in solemn procession to the anchorhold in much the same way as a funeral cortège would process from church to cemetery, the anchoress taking the place of the coffin. The anchoress would be led inside the anchorhold, and the place would be blessed as a grave might be blessed: indeed, her coffin might be placed in prominent view in the anchorhold. She was then given the sacrament of extreme unction, dust was scattered on her and on the anchorhold, and she was shut inside. After the officiant had come out, the door was (symbolically) blocked on the outside, possibly with earth. Then priests and people would return to the church, leaving the anchoress entombed. She was considered dead to the world, never again to return to it (Clay, 1914, Appendix A pp. 193–8; Darwin, 1944, ch. 6; Warren, 1985, pp. 98–100).

However, it was not only their own death or their own soul's destiny with which anchoresses and anchorites were concerned but also the death and destiny of others. Their work of prayer was considered indispensable for the eternal well-being of the souls of those who supported them. As Ann Warren has documented, solitaries were dependent for their support on patronage: royal and aristocratic, clerical and lay. The gifts of money and materials, often given as a regular annual grant, were intended to secure the prayers of the recluse for the donor, most especially prayers for their souls after death. Thus for example William Lord Roos of Helmsley, making his will in 1412, left a 'bequest of four hundred pounds to pay for ten chaplains to say daily masses . . . for a period of eight years for his soul and the souls of his relatives' and additional amounts for recluses to pray for them as well (Warren, 1985, p. 197). It is not far-fetched to see anchoresses and anchorites as the spiritual employees of their patrons, with responsibility for their souls after death, just as other servants and employees would be responsible for aspects of their material well-being during their lives. It is even possible that anxiety about death prompted additional patronage and almsgiving to recluses: Warren suggests, for instance, that in the case of King Henry II 'there was a direct relationship between his concern about death (which he may have felt was imminent) and his seeking of the goodwill and prayers of anchorites and others' in the making of his will (Warren, 1985, p. 147). The symbolism of death enacted in the ritual of enclosure was appropriate to a key part of the social function of the anchoress, namely prayers for the souls of the deceased. The preoccupation with death could hardly be clearer.

Although the anchorhold was associated with the tomb, however, its actual physical structure might be modestly comfortable. The anchoress might have more than one room, with a servant or two to fetch and carry, and perhaps a garden in which she could take some air (Warren, 1985, p. 31). Yet this was not always so. In the case of Christina of Markyate, an anchoress in the twelfth century, the early years of her enclosure were tomb-like in the extreme. Against her will, Christina had been betrothed; and her family as well as her prospective husband were searching for her, determined not to let her escape the duties of marriage. She was therefore hidden by the hermit Roger in a tiny cell adjoining his hermitage. Her biographer exclaims, 'And so, thus confined, the handmaid of Christ sat on a hard stone until Roger's death, that is, four years and more, concealed even from those who dwelt together with Roger. O what trials she had to bear of cold and heat, hunger and thirst, daily fasting! The confined space would not allow her to wear even the necessary clothing when it was cold. The airless little enclosure became stifling when she was hot' (Talbot (ed.), 1959, p. 103). The biographer goes on to tell in painful detail of the privations she suffered and of the physical ailments that, unsurprisingly, developed as a result of such a deathly existence. Although the case of Christina is extreme, it was only taking to its logical conclusion the enactment of death that was part of every anchoritic life, even though in most cases the physical hardship was much more moderate.

The symbolism of death and burial, thus enacted in her enclosure, was to be characteristic of the whole of the anchoress's subsequent life; and she was to take good care that this was no empty show. Thus for example Walter Hilton, writing for an anchoress, says at the very beginning of his book, 'Since you have forsaken the world and turned wholly to God, you are symbolically dead in the eyes of men; therefore let your heart be dead to all earthly affections and concerns and wholly dedicated to our Lord Jesus Christ' (Hilton, 1957, p. 1). Hilton is entirely realistic about this process: the ritual of enclosure, dramatic as it is, is the easy part: 'I do not say that you can be converted immediately, and possess all virtues in the same way as you can enclose yourself in a cell; but you should bear in mind that the purpose of your present bodily enclosure is to enable you more readily to attain spiritual enclosure' (Hilton, 1957, p. 1).

But what is this 'spiritual enclosure'? Surely it is precisely the devotion to Christ that Hilton has already referred to; and in the rest of his book that devotion is characterized as contemplative union with Christ and its relation to the virtuous life. There is a tension in his book between denial of this life in favour of the next, on the one hand, and on the other hand denial of distorted or diminished *forms* of this life, not so much to attain another life after death as to find life and flourishing in its fullness here and now. This is a tension that runs through the whole of anchoritic spirituality, sometimes weighted more heavily to one side or the other; and it is the focus of my exploration in this chapter.

The author of the *Ancrene Wisse*, a thirteenth-century book of instructions for anchoresses, draws vividly on the symbolism of death to pour sarcasm on frivolous and proud anchoresses delighting in luxury. 'Such things would be unfitting for a lady of a castle; it is a contemptible and unreasonable thing that an anointed anchoress, and an anchoress buried – for what is an anchorhouse but her grave? – wishes to be more graciously regarded than the lady of a house' (Savage and Watson (tr.), 1991, p. 88). Like Hilton, moreover, the author of *Ancrene Wisse* intends that this symbolic death shall effect much spiritual good. He speaks of three kinds of people: pilgrims, the dead, and those hung with Christ on the cross; and compares the anchoress with all three, though the last group are to be her highest aspiration. The dead, he says, are better than those who are still pilgrims, 'For many things still trouble the pilgrim; to the dead it is of no importance if he lies unburied and rotting above the earth – praise him, blame him, do shameful things to him, say shameful things to him, it is all the same to him. This is a blessed death which takes a living man or a living woman like this, away from the world' (Savage and Watson (tr.), 1991, p. 177). Yet once again, the object is not death but life; for the author goes on at once, 'But certainly, whoever is dead like this to herself, God lives in her heart.' And again the question arises as it does in Hilton: is this new life a present reality, or is this present life being denied in favour of some heavenly attainment? Or is this, indeed, a false contrast, a misunderstanding of the life/death of anchoritic spirituality?

For if the metaphor of the tomb and its deathly associations has a large place in anchoritic spirituality, it is to some degree subverted by a quite different metaphor. The anchorhold may be a tomb; but it is also a womb: a womb in which Christ comes to new birth in the anchoress. If she is dead, she is also fully alive, reborn. Moreover, not only is the anchorhold itself a womb, but the anchoress, herself reborn, is reborn through her own gestation of Christ: she is simultaneously mother and foetus. Such convoluted imagery arises in the *Ancrene Wisse* out of the strong Marian devotion of the anchoress and her self-identification with Mary, while at the same time she seeks to identify with Christ who was born of Mary (and, symbolically, of herself). The following passage shows the tensions: it begins as a meditation on the three Marys coming to anoint Jesus' body in his tomb, and at the beginning of the quotation the anchoress is positioned among them.

> They are coming to anoint our Lord ... who stretches himself toward us as one who is anointed, and makes himself smooth and soft to touch. And was he not himself a recluse in Mary's womb? These two things belong to the anchoress: narrowness and bitterness. For the womb is a narrow dwelling, where our Lord was a recluse; and this word 'Mary', as I have often said, means 'bitterness.' If you then suffer bitterness in a narrow place, you are his fellows, recluse as he was in Mary's womb. Are you imprisoned within your four wide walls? – And he in a narrow cradle, nailed on the cross, enclosed tight in a stone tomb. Mary's womb and this tomb were his anchorhouses.
>
> (Savage and Watson (tr.), 1991, p. 186)

Nor is the contrast between womb and tomb as sharply drawn as modern sensibilities might expect, since both are taken as the place from which one emerges to new life.

It would not do, therefore, to see the two metaphors as unambiguously symbolic of necrophilia and natality. The tensions are not just between the two metaphors of womb and tomb, but within each of them. I have already indicated how even in the emphasis on death, the object is not death but life. And in the above quotation, where the metaphor of the womb might be thought to be a clear indication of a symbolic of natality, it turns out that birth – emergence from the womb – is actually death. The author concludes the passage just quoted with the assurance to the anchoress that she, like Christ, will emerge from her present place. As Christ emerged from both the womb and the tomb, so will she depart from her two anchorhouses, that is, from her body and from the anchorhold in which she is housed, leaving them both whole. If the metaphor of the womb offers the potential to subvert the necrophilia of anchoritic spirituality, that potential is quickly contained by the author of *Ancrene Wisse* in his insistence that the rebirth in question is to a life after death, an other-worldly flourishing that will recompense the narrowness and bitterness of the anchoress's life here. The body born of a woman, and the life of this earth, are supplanted by a 'new birth' and a life that, even in this world, looks away from it to a heavenly world beyond.

2 Marian devotion

The high and late Middle Ages were characterized by their emphasis on Mary; and it is only to be expected that such an emphasis would be congenial to anchoresses and taken up by them in a particular way. We have already noted, for instance, how the author of the *Ancrene Wisse* makes an identification between Mary and the anchoress, even if he soon shies away from it. At first sight it might seem that Marian devotion, taking its point of departure from her willingness to give birth to Christ, would naturally lead away from preoccupation with death. Things are not that simple, however. As we saw in the case of the *Ancrene Wisse*, the womb, even when venerated, is quickly assimilated to the tomb: the Mary who gives birth to Jesus also anoints his dead body. Nevertheless, the identification of the anchoress with Mary opened up for her some possibilities of natality which were specifically gender related. This stands out with particular clarity in the writings of Julian of Norwich.

A comparison of the Short and Long Texts of Julian's visions, written perhaps 20 years apart, shows her increasing confidence as a woman visionary. In the early Short Text Julian struggles with what she feels as a contradiction between her gender (she describes herself as a 'wretched worm' (Julian, 1978, p. 113)) and her sense that she must write her visions for the help and comfort of others: 'But God forbid that you should say or assume that I am a teacher, for that is not and never was my intention; for I am a woman, ignorant, weak and frail . . . But because I am a woman, ought I therefore to believe that I should not tell you of the goodness of God, when I saw at the same time that it is his will that it be known?' (Julian, 1978, p. 135). By the time she wrote the Long Text, however, much of this struggle and self-deprecation had fallen away, and been replaced with profound spiritual teaching for *all* her 'even Christians', women as well as men.[1] What made the difference?

The answer, no doubt, is complex, and most of it inaccessible from this historical position. I suggest, however, that one significant strand is Julian's meditation on, and identification with, Mary, whom she had several times seen in her visions. Although Mary is only infrequently at the centre of Julian's revelations, she plays a quiet but persistent part. When Julian first describes her, in her account of the first revelation, she says,

> I saw her spiritually in her bodily likeness, a simple, humble maiden, young in years, grown a little taller than a child, of the stature which she had when she conceived. Also God showed me part of the wisdom and the truth of her soul, and in this I understood the reverent contemplation with which she beheld her God, who is her Creator, marvelling with great reverence that he was willing to be born of her who was a simple creature created by him. And this wisdom and truth, this knowledge of her Creator's greatness and her own created littleness, made her say very meekly to Gabriel: Behold me here, God's handmaiden.
>
> (Julian, 1978, p. 182)

This description of Mary echoes some of Julian's own self-description. After her listing of the revelations in chapter one of the Long Text, Julian's first phrase of the text proper is, 'this revelation was made to a simple, unlettered creature' (Julian, 1978, p. 177), a woman, that is, who is like the 'simple, humble maiden' to whom Gabriel appeared. To be sure, Julian was considerably older than she took Mary to have been, since she was 'thirty and a half years old' at the time of the revelations (Julian, 1978, p. 179). But Julian writes of her own reverent contemplation, paralleling the 'reverent contemplation with which [Mary] beheld her God', and her wonder 'that he who is so to be revered and feared would be so familiar [ms. "homely"] with a sinful creature...' (Julian, 1978, p. 181). Like Mary, Julian too made herself available to bring the revelation of Jesus to the world, 'her Creator's greatness' shown through 'her own created littleness', the willing handmaiden of the Lord.

Julian was, of course, not the only woman writer of the medieval period to identify with Mary, or to take over the so-called 'modesty formula' (Tugwell, 1984, p. 188). Already in the twelfth century, Hildegard of Bingen had protested that because the male religious leaders were corrupt, God had turned to her, a woman, the lowest of the low, to convey the divine message to the world – as indeed God had also done with Mary (Hildegard, 1990, p. 59). Such identifications with Mary occurred repeatedly as medieval women visionaries sought to claim religious authority in a male-dominated ecclesiastical context.

The particular form that these reflections take in Julian's writings, situated as she is in the anchorhold, is a profound meditation on motherhood, famously on the Motherhood of God, and of what our natality comes to in the light of this. I shall discuss some aspects of this natality in a moment, but first I wish to note how important Mary is for Julian's theology of God as Mother. Julian approaches the subject from her discussion of our two aspects, substance and sensuality (not to be confused with body and soul) which, she holds, were joined together by Christ in Mary's womb. The consequence is that since Mary is the mother of Christ, her motherhood extends to all who are Christ's: 'So our Lady is our mother, in whom we are all enclosed and born of her in Christ, for she who is mother of our saviour is mother of all who are saved in our saviour; and our saviour is our true Mother, in whom we are endlessly born and out of whom we shall never come' (Julian, 1978, p. 292). It is from this discussion of Mary as our Mother that Julian expands her reflection on divine motherhood (cf. Jantzen, 1987, pp. 115–24).

But what does it mean, for a woman living in the womb/tomb of an anchorhold and who identifies herself with Mary, to say that in this Motherhood of our saviour 'we are endlessly born'? There is here a striking contrast to the imagery of

Ancrene Wisse. In that book, although the anchorhold was thought of as both womb and tomb, the ardent expectation was that in due time the anchoress would burst forth into new life, a life born out of her bodily death. She would not stay in the womb/tomb forever. In Julian, however, the imagery works differently. On the one hand we are 'endlessly born' in a natality that is about this present life, not simply about life in another world after our death in this one. But on the other hand, we are *continually* enfolded in the womb of Christ, 'out of whom we shall never come'. Natality, even while it is about new beginnings and growth and flourishing, does not mean separation from the enfolding love and protection of Christ. These different uses of the imagery of the womb should not be overstated: they can be made compatible. The *Ancrene Wisse*, too, talks about new life that is nevertheless continually protected by divine love. And Julian, for her part, makes much of heaven and escape from the 'prison' of this life (Julian, 1978, p. 331), as I shall discuss more fully below. Yet the accent falls differently. The *Ancrene Wisse* is much more preoccupied with death and all its ways, while Julian is opening her heart to natality.

3 Mortification

This difference of accent can also be seen quite strikingly in the contrasting attitudes toward asceticism and mortification of the flesh. Asceticism was, of course, central to all anchoritic spirituality, and had long and tangled historical roots. From at least the time of the Desert Mothers and Fathers, heroic asceticism had been part and parcel of Christian spirituality. This asceticism had as one of its sources a Platonic identification of the body with the maternal: chaotic, changing, filled with demanding passions and desires. The soul, by contrast, was conceptually linked with reason, the male, the divine. Spiritual progress therefore entailed progressive liberation of the soul from the body, a process that would be completed only at death when the soul would at last be released. Yet even in this life one should work toward such liberation as much as possible by the mortification (literally: putting to death) of the flesh, most particularly of its sexual desires. For the highest spiritual life, chastity was obligatory.

This story has often been told; and there are of course many qualifications and nuances that must be added to its broad outlines. For example, Caroline Walker Bynum has argued convincingly that medieval women mystics found the practices of asceticism transformative and liberating rather than stifling, because these practices enabled them to make an identification between their suffering bodies and the suffering body of Jesus (Bynum, 1987). Such qualifications notwithstanding, however, it is clear that the idea of mortification of the flesh is an old one in Western spirituality, and that in its particular preoccupation with sex, coupled with the medieval notion that women are sexually insatiable and are the cause of male sexual temptation, this mortification is clearly tied to gender. It is therefore fascinating to contrast the writings of male advisors in anchoritic spirituality with the lives and writings of female anchoresses, who, I suggest, were at least in some cases subverting the necrophilia of the tradition.

Many of the male writers of advice to anchoresses are overwhelmingly preoccupied with chastity, and are inclined to see all aspects of the mortification of the flesh as intended chiefly toward its preservation. The author of *Holy Maidenhood*, for example, places himself in a long tradition of extolling virginity, and chooses to do so by a virulent attack on sexual intercourse and marriage that ranges from the pornographic to the comic. He has plenty to say about 'that stinking and ugly act full of filth' (Savage and Watson (tr.), 1991, p. 228); and expatiates on the result for a woman when her life turns into the 'slavery' of marriage and looking after children: 'what life is like for the woman who, when she comes in, hears her children screaming, sees the cat at the bacon and the dog at the rind, her cake burning on the hearth and her calf sucking spilt milk, the pot boiling over in the fire – and the lout [her husband] grumbles away . . .' (Savage and Watson, 1991, p. 239). Any fate would be better than this one, it is suggested; and if quite heroic efforts are necessary to preserve virginity, they are well worth it!

To be fair, the author of *Holy Maidenhood* also sees positive reasons for preserving chastity (and sees positive aspects to marriage): the virgin is not just to avoid the miseries of wedlock but to be the spouse of Christ. In this he is at one with Aelred, who in his 'Rule of Life for a Recluse' similarly placed great emphasis on chastity (Aelred, 1971). *Ancrene Wisse* refers to Aelred, and confirms his view that chastity can only be preserved with 'mortification of the flesh, with fasts, with vigils, with disciplines, with rough clothing, a rough shelter, with illness, with heavy labours': these are the basis for the development of virtues of 'devotion, compassion, right love, humility' and the like (Savage and Watson, 1991, p. 183). To those who he thinks might object to such stringent measures he replies,

> In the middle of delights and ease and fleshly comfort, who was ever chaste? Who ever fed a fire within her and did not burn? Will not a violently boiling pot spill over unless cold water is poured in it and brands taken from underneath it? The belly, a pot that boils with food and drink, is so near a neighbour to that ill-disciplined part that it shares with it the burning of its heat. But many, more's the pity, are so concerned with their bodies, and so excessively frightened that their heads ache, lest their bodies become too weak, and guard their health so carefully that their spirits weaken, and sicken in sin; and those who should only be tending to their souls with contrition of heart and fleshly mortification, degenerate into physicians and healers of the body. (Savage and Watson, 1991, p. 183)

In this passage and many others like it, the author of the *Ancrene Wisse* proceeds as though body and soul are enemies; the welfare of one is the detriment of the other. We have here the necrophilia of the Western tradition presented in very stark terms indeed.

There are, however, other passages in which the author mitigates this stridency and urges sensible moderation. The advice that he gives about the anchoresses' daily life is, he emphasizes, only the 'outer rule', of importance only as an aid to keep the inner rule of prayer (Savage and Watson, 1991, p. 199). Added to this qualification that the outer rule is only a means to an end, and that the rules can be changed 'whenever you want for better ones', he is at pains to stress moderation, often giving a rule but then urging that the anchoresses be sensible in its application: for instance, 'You must not eat meat or fat, except in the case of great illness, or unless someone is very weak. Eat vegetable stew willingly, and accustom yourselves to little drink. Nevertheless, dear sisters, your food and drink have often seemed less to me than I would want you to have' (Savage and Watson,

1991, p. 199). Yet in all this the imagery of death is always near. The author warns that an anchoress must never take her meals with guests, because she 'is dead to all the world. One hears often of the dead speaking with the living – but eating with the living? I have never heard of it' (Savage and Watson, 1991, p. 200).

Regulations about food arise at least in part out of the pre-occupation with chastity, as already mentioned, controlling the body in order to help control its 'near neighbour': anatomical considerations suggest that although the writer is addressing himself to women, he is working out of a male imaginary. Sometimes more stringent methods than the regulation of food is necessary. The account of the twelfth-century anchorite, Wulfric of Haselbury, is full of the severe mortifications he imposed upon himself in order to escape the 'temptations of the flesh'. He wore a hair shirt with a coat of chain mail over it; he immersed himself in tubs of cold water, he deprived himself of sleep and when he did sleep it was on a bed 'made by himself by intertwining rough branches, a place of torment for his tortured body' (Bell, 1933, p. li). The editor of Wulfric's biography paraphrases the medieval author's description:

> It is only natural that a man who lives very much alone should be attacked severely by temptations against the virtue of chastity. In order to be on his guard against moments of weakness St Wulfric, as was the practice of the time, would scourge himself till the blood flowed freely, saying the *Miserere* and begging God to keep him from consent to the suggestions of the flesh. This was the reason for his fasts and his frequent genuflections, his deprivation of sleep, of food, and of drink, his iron shirt and his taciturnity.　　　　　　　　　　　　　(Bell, 1933, p. lii)

No wonder he was taciturn!

Writings for and about women are considerably more moderate in their recommendations for mortification; though even here the practices could be harsh. Although presented as a counsel of moderation, the following advice from the author of the *Ancrene Wisse* actually suggests considerable severity:

> Let no one belt herself with any kind of belt next to the body, except with her confessor's leave, nor wear any iron or hair, or hedgehog skins; let her not beat herself with them, nor with a leaded scourge, with holly or briars, nor draw blood from herself

without her confessor's leave; let her not sting herself with nettles anywhere, nor beat herself in front, nor cut herself, nor impose on herself too many severe disciplines to quench temptations at one time. (Savage and Watson, 1991, p. 202)

While this is presented as – and by comparison with Wulfric of Haselbury it certainly was – much less harsh than were some other ascetical regimes of the time, it still assumes that the confessors *will* sometimes give leave, and that self-discipline (i.e. flagellation) is an ordinary remedy against sexual temptation – only not 'too many' at a time. Nevertheless, the author sees this as moderate.

In spirit, the author of the *Ancrene Wisse* is in this respect close to the author of *The Cloud of Unknowing*, also written for a solitary, who said, 'Insofar as you can, never be the cause of your physical weakness. For it is true what I say: this work demands a great tranquillity, and a clean bill of health as well in body as in soul. So for the love of God, govern yourself wisely in body and soul, and keep in good health as much as possible' (Walsh (ed.), 1981, p. 199; cf. Hilton, 1957, p. 94). Walter Hilton, likewise, is much more concerned about the development of charity and humility than about the mortification of the flesh (and indeed is far less preoccupied with issues of sexuality and chastity). He says, 'It is no achievement to watch and fast until your head aches and your body sickens, nor to go to Rome and Jerusalem on your bare feet, nor to rush about preaching as though you expected to convert everybody ... But it is a great achievement for a man [sic] to be able to love his fellow Christian in charity ...' (Hilton, 1957, p. 78).

Yet the very fact that all these writers find it necessary to counsel moderation (even if what counts as moderation seems austere by our own standards) bespeaks the severity of the asceticism that was taken for granted as a normal part of anchoritic spirituality. And this asceticism was born out of a deep suspicion of the gendered body and a tendency to identify sexuality with sinfulness, a tendency that each of these writers reinforces even while urging moderation in the methods of dealing with it. Such exhortation to the mortification of the flesh is thus part of the necrophilia of Christendom, brought to sharp focus in the writings of anchoritic spirituality.

Yet always there is a space for resistance, a tension that allows this necrophilia to be subverted. Each of the writers cited is more or less explicit that the point of mortification is to increase in spiritual virtues: Walter Hilton especially makes much of this. Even the Wulfric of Haselbury stories are told – if rather in a backhanded fashion – to show his compassion for the smallest of God's creatures.

We are told that, upon looking round his cell, he saw that his cape had been nibbled by a mouse. 'Perish that mouse', he said, and straightway the mouse ran out of the wall and fell at his feet dead. Sending for a priest he confessed his fault, and met with little material comfort, for his confessor expressed the wish that he would use a like anathema to get rid of all the mice of that countryside (Bell, 1933, p. lvii).

Such compassion for all the created world was often recounted of anchorites and anchoresses. In the very early life of Guthlac, an anchorite of Crowland in the late seventh century, his biographer writes of Guthlac's communion with animals and birds. 'For the grace of his excellent charity abounded to all creatures, so that even the birds of the untamed wilderness and the wandering fishes of the muddy marshes would come flying or swimming swiftly to his call as if to a shepherd; and they were even accustomed to take from his hand such food as the nature of each demanded' (Colgrave (tr.), 1956, p. 121). And of each of these anchorites there are many stories of their compassion for their fellow human beings, ministering healing to them in body and mind, offering wise counsel, and sharing whatever they had. In the account of Roger, mentor of Christina of Markyate, the rigorous asceticism and the compassion for others are brought into deliberate juxtaposition: 'Who could have been more cruel to his own flesh? He allowed himself no pleasure. His whole endeavour was to progress more and more in the service of God. His compassion on the afflicted and their wretchedness was such that he could not have borne their miseries so hardly if they had been inflicted on himself' (Talbot (ed.), 1959, p. 83). There is therefore an opening for a different sort of approach, one that lays the stress on natality and flourishing in this life rather than focusing on death and salvation beyond the grave.

In Julian of Norwich this opening is probed, with the result that her book resonates with quite different attitudes to the body and how it should be treated than we find in even the most moderate of the male writers. The contrast must immediately be qualified: Julian is after all part of the tradition of medieval Christendom and inevitably adopts its necrophilia to a considerable extent: some aspects of this will become apparent below. Nevertheless, Julian takes seriously her teaching that in the Motherhood of God 'we are endlessly born', and, remarkably, that this applies to body as well as to soul. This understanding of ourselves as natals leads her to teachings about the body that would be unthinkable in the male writings of anchoritic spirituality.

Central to Julian's teaching is her insistence that we are enfolded in divine love, that God our Mother has 'enclosed us all in himself' (Julian, 1978, p. 186) as in a divine womb: the gender bending achieved by moving between God as Mother and the male pronouns is itself subversive. The enclosure applies in Julian not just to the soul but also to the body: 'For as the body is clad in the cloth, and the flesh in the skin, and the bones in the flesh, and the heart in the trunk, so are we, soul and body, clad and enclosed in the goodness of God' (Julian, 1978, p. 186). It is rather a different picture from that of Walter Hilton's suggestion that the anchoress may 'realize that you are as full of sin as a hide is of meat' (Hilton, 1957, p. 106) – even though he then counsels her not to be discouraged.

Julian emphasizes her insistence on the loving care of God for our bodies by an example that is startling even in our own times and must have been scandalous as spiritual writing in the fourteenth century: the example of bodily evacuation.

> A man [sic] walks upright, and the food in his body is shut in as if in a well-made purse. When the time of his necessity comes, the purse is opened and then shut again, in most seemly fashion. And it is God who does this, as it is shown when he says that he comes down to us in our humblest needs. For he does not despise what he has made, nor does he disdain to serve us in the simplest natural functions of our body, for love of the soul which he created in his own likeness.
>
> (Julian, 1978, p. 186)

With this sort of example as an illustration of the love of God, it is not surprising that we find in Julian none of the obsessive suspicion of the body and especially of sexuality that is commonplace in other writers of anchoritic spirituality. She never speaks of fasting or vigils; disciplines and hair shirts make no appearance in her writings. And there is total silence about chastity, a silence that in the context of anchoritic spirituality with its devotion to Mary the virgin is deafening. Yet Julian's appreciation of the body follows from her acceptance that, soul and body, we are enclosed and gestated in divine love.

Nevertheless, Julian's writing is not without tension in its portrayal of the body. She thinks much about death, as is unsurprising given that her visions occurred when she was severely ill and thought that she was about to die. Her desire, natural enough in that situation, is to be taken out of pain. 'And in this time I saw a body lying on the earth, which appeared oppressive and fearsome and without shape or form, as it were a devouring pit of stinking mud; and suddenly out of this body there sprang a most beautiful creature, a little child, fully shaped and formed, swift and lively and whiter than the lily, which quickly glided up to heaven' (Julian, 1978, p. 306). This seems a beautiful portrayal of natality; yet its focus is on *escaping* from this body and this earth; and the 'swift and lively' little child glides immediately to heaven. Moreover, Julian continues, 'The pit which was the body signifies the great wretchedness of our mortal flesh; and the smallness of the child signifies the cleanness and the purity of our soul. And I thought: In this body there remains none of the child's beauty, and in this child there remains none of the body's foulness ... Therefore this is a supreme comfort and a blessed contemplation for a longing soul, that we shall be taken out of pain' (Julian, 1978, pp. 306–7).

Yet while this passage seems to revert to body–soul dualism and to denigration of the body, that impression must be qualified at least to some extent by the recognition that Julian is not speaking of the body per se as 'a devouring pit of stinking mud' but rather of a body that is mortally ill and in great pain. It would be wrong to conclude from this passage that Julian subscribed to the view, common enough in her time, that the body itself is foul, let alone evil: the body she sees in this vision is a *particular* body, a body in mortal agony. When we consider the illnesses of the fourteenth century, especially the Black Death, and the general lack of medical facilities and even sanitation, the stench and loathsomeness she describes is only to be expected. What is perhaps much more surprising is that even against such a background, Julian on the whole has a strongly positive view of the body, enclosed in divine love.

4 Other worlds

Nevertheless in this vision and elsewhere Julian places great emphasis on heaven, to which she sees the little child ascend. I have argued that one of the central features of necrophilia is its focus on other worlds, in religious terms the 'world to come', heaven and hell. To this aspect of necrophilia anchoritic spirituality heartily contributes, both in relation to the anchorite or anchoress and in relation to their patrons. I shall suggest, however, that once again there is a considerable pull away from this focus, a pull that becomes especially insistent in Julian. At least some of the time she refuses the usual ideas of heaven and hell, and is deeply concerned with this life and this world, not just as a preparation for the next.

For the author of the *Ancrene Wisse*, the focus on heaven is crucial to his understanding of what the anchoress is about: she shuts herself into the womb/tomb of the anchorhold so that death for her will be rebirth into the life of heaven. This also is the motivation for all the strenuous ascetical efforts. He says, 'Let everyone now choose one of these two, earthly comfort or heavenly, whichever she wants to keep – because she must let go the other' (Savage and Watson (tr.), 1991, p. 197). Sometimes the author speaks of punishments for sin, especially the damnation that can follow if the anchoress succumbs to sexual temptation. Sometimes, however, he speaks of the special rewards to which she can look forward because of her special privations here.

> For so the righteous God has decreed: that the reward of each person there will be according to the work and according to the trouble that they have suffered humbly for his love here . . . All in heaven will be as swift as human thought is now, as is the sun's ray glancing from the east into the west in the twinkling of an eye. But anchoresses, shut in here, will be – if any can be – both lighter and swifter there, and play in the meadows of heaven in such loose chains, as they say, that the body will be wherever it wants to go in a moment.   (Savage and Watson, 1991, p. 83)

The body, note, does get to heaven; but it is purified by its austerities on earth, and the greater the austerities, the greater its heavenly freedom from the constraints that are experienced on earth.

Walter Hilton's expectations of the after-life are bound up with his ideas of the conflict between body and soul, about which he has a good deal to say. Although on the one hand he advocates moderation in ascetical practices, as we have seen, on the other hand he holds that it will only be by severe control of the body that the soul will be liberated, its final liberation not coming until after bodily death.

The soul cannot experience true inward joy until the body has been largely deprived of sensual pleasures, writes Hilton (Hilton, 1957, p. 94). The soul is 'beautiful by nature, made in the likeness of God,' but it is 'frail as a woman in your body because of original sin' (Hilton, 1957, p. 97). The five bodily senses Hilton compares to windows, perhaps in an allusion to the windows of the anchorhold (at which an anchoress should not be gazing outwards); and they are a source of danger: 'Death comes in at the windows' (Hilton, 1957, p. 96). 'These windows are the five senses, through which your soul, contrary to its true nature, goes out and seeks its pleasure and support in earthly things . . . So you must close and shutter these windows, and only open them when necessary. This would not be very difficult once you clearly understood the nature of your soul and its potential beauty were it not stifled under the black influence of this vile image' (Hilton, 1957, p. 96).

From this passage and many like it, it would appear that body and soul are straightforwardly in conflict with one another in a fourteenth-century version of Manichaeism. But of course things are far more complicated. For one thing, Hilton accepts the standard Christian teaching that we have already noted in the *Ancrene Wisse* that the body will be saved: yet that is a prospect only for another world, a world after death, not for this world. 'The soul of man will then be fully restored . . . Man's body also will be glorified, for it will receive the precious gift of immortality with all its blessings. Both soul and body will receive more blessings than I can describe, but this will be in heaven, and not in this life' (Hilton, 1957, p. 120).

For another, not only is the body redeemable, but the soul itself is corrupted by sin. Again this is standard Christian teaching, though sometimes so strongly overlaid with Platonism that it is obscured. The dualism of Hilton is similar to the dualism of much of the Christian tradition, in which, while both soul and body are sinful and both will be redeemed, yet the soul, being non-material, is higher in the scale of being than the body, which, born of woman, is material and gross and must be carefully regulated or mortified so as not to get in the way of the soul's progress. Some writers in the tradition are much more virulent than is Hilton in their denigration of the body; while Julian, as we have seen, takes a rather more positive view.

The point here, however, is that although on the one hand Hilton says that the salvation of this body can come only in the next life, on the other he places great stress on its active engagement in works of charity in *this* life. We have already noted that charity is, according to Hilton, a greater achievement than fasting 'until your head aches and your body sickens' (Hilton, 1957, p. 78). In this passage he is arguably talking about an attitude rather than an activity; but his book is full of counsel on the importance of charitable work. If someone comes to see the anchoress, for example, she is to be as 'ready and glad' to see them as 'if an angel came from heaven to speak to you', and 'if he comes to tell you his troubles and receive comfort, give him a ready hearing and allow him to say what he wishes to ease his heart' (Hilton, 1957, p. 101). It is known that anchorites and anchoresses were much sought after as counsellors in medieval society, their clientele ranging from kings to commoners (Clay, 1914, pp. 146–66; Warren, 1985, pp. 110–13). The anchoress's role as counsellor and intercessor is meant as the polar opposite of a life of selfish absorption with her own soul. Solitary she may be, but medieval society sees her as making a great contribution not only in her prayers for the dead but in her counsel to the living, a counsel whose wisdom and compassion will be in direct proportion to the depth of her prayer. Hilton exhorts the women to whom he writes: 'And although you may be at prayer and reluctant to abandon it, thinking that it is not proper to leave God in order to speak to man, I do not think that you would be right in this instance, for if you are wise, you will not leave God by so doing. You will find him, possess him, and see him as fully in your fellow-man as in prayer, but it will be in a different way' (Hilton, 1957, p. 101).

It would thus not be accurate to characterize Hilton, or indeed anchoritic spirituality more generally, as focused only on other worlds: there is far too insistent a concern for activities of mercy and compassion. Moreover it should be noted that this was as true of their patrons as of the recluses themselves: Warren in her study of anchorites and their supporters shows that those who made bequests for recluses also often left gifts that show concern and compassion for the poor, including debtors, lepers, or those without adequate clothing or shoes (Warren, 1985, pp. 255–6). Yet often even in compassionate activity there is an undercurrent suggesting that these activities are undertaken not out of simple regard for the other's need but with one eye also on the self-reflexive possibility of the recluse's eternal reward. As Warren shows, although the philanthropy of those leaving bequests to the poor was real, it could also be seen as advantageous for the soul of the benefactor. 'A pattern of accretion emerges here – if one charity was good, more were better. Many roads to heaven were surer than few. Piety and charity merged with anxiety' (Warren, 1985, p. 255). And Walter Hilton exhorts the anchoress to whom he writes, 'Humility and charity will fashion you to the likeness of Jesus in his Humanity, and will at length transform you to the true likeness of Jesus in his Godhead. You will have only a glimmering of it here in contemplation, but in the bliss of heaven it will be yours in the fullness of reality' (Hilton, 1957, p. 109).

Even in so moderate a writer as Hilton, the concern for the other world can seem to override engagement with this one. And of course in a climate where heaven and hell are constantly emphasized and death is very much present to everyone's mind, such preoccupation with an other world is hardly surprising. It is no more than an expression of the generalized necrophilia of Christendom, much more moderate in Hilton than in many other writers.

Yet in this regard once again the accent in Julian falls differently. Though she is part of a necrophilic culture, and participates in and contributes to it, there is also much in her writings which subverts it. From the first pages of her book the tensions are obvious. She writes that in her youth she prayed three prayers, the second of which she recognized as highly unusual: 'a bodily sickness. I wished that sickness to be so severe that it might seem mortal, so that I might in it receive all the rites which Holy Church has to give me, whilst I myself should think that I was dying, and everyone who saw me would think the same . . . I wanted to have every kind of pain, bodily and spiritual, which I should have had if I had died . . .' (Julian, 1978, p. 178). On the face of it, this desire for mortal illness seems to participate directly in the all-too-familiar emphasis on death as the means of ridding oneself of the flesh with its passions and desires, and in that context one would expect Julian to go on to pray that she might thus enter heaven and be worthy of an eternal reward.

But she does not. Her prayer, in fact, is not that she would actually die but that she would be so ill that she would *think* she was dying. And why? 'I intended this because I wanted to be purged by God's mercy, and afterwards live more to his glory because of that sickness' (Julian, 1978, p. 178). The prayer was in fact about how she should live *this* life, how she might as a result of her experience of suffering and her recognition of mortality deepen in compassion and in the purification of her desire. It was the sort of encounter with death that Heidegger would characterize as enabling authenticity, the death that gives me my life. In that sense the focus is held in tension: while it is only in the recognition of mortality that life can be authentic, nevertheless the motive for the focus is not a glorification of death but the emergence of a new quality of life. And for Julian this new quality of life is directly related to her desire to live 'more to [God's] glory' in compassionate charity to her 'even Christians'.

Yet the tension is still more convoluted. For while it is true that Julian's desire is to live rather than to die, her eye is nevertheless on her eternal reward. Immediately after her statement that she wished to live more to God's glory as a result of her illness, she continues, 'because I hoped that this would be to my reward when I should die, because I desired soon to be with my God and my Creator' (Julian, 1978, p. 178). Throughout her writings Julian refers frequently to heavenly rewards, and to their correlation with earthly suffering. She takes for granted that the pain and trouble of this life contrasts with the peace and fulfilment of heaven, and speaks often of its joy and bliss, as well as of the fullness of the knowledge that it will bring. Thus for instance in her discussion of the contemplation of God's love, even while recognizing our perpetual sinfulness, she says, 'But our good Lord always wants us to remain much more in the contemplation of the higher, and not to forsake the knowledge of the lower, until the time that we are brought up above, where we shall have our Lord Jesus for our reward, and be filled full of joy and bliss without end' (Julian, 1978, p. 339). In dozens of other passages she speaks similarly of the eternal joys of heaven; her whole approach is saturated with an awareness of this life as preparatory to another one.

So it would be ridiculous not to read Julian as deeply invested in the medieval necrophilic symbolic. Nevertheless, while this is beyond doubt the symbolic structure within which she operates, there are also to be found in her works resistances to and reinterpretations of this symbolic of death which effectively subvert it in the direction of a symbolic of natality. This is most clearly seen in her reinterpretation of hell and of heaven; and I shall discuss these briefly in turn.

Julian notoriously questions the very existence of hell. Hell is by definition the place where the sinner is due to experience endless divine wrath; yet in all her revelations Julian insists that she saw no wrath in God (Julian, 1978, p. 257). So how can there be hell? Julian struggles with the conflict between the teaching of the Church, to which she is committed, and the revelation she has received which, since she holds that it comes directly from God, would override even ecclesiastical dogma.

> Our faith is founded on God's word, and it belongs to our faith that we believe that God's word will be preserved in all things. And one article of our faith is that many creatures will be damned, such as the angels who fell out of heaven because of pride, who now are devils, and many men upon earth who die out of the faith of Holy Church, that is to say those who are pagans and many who have received baptism and who live unchristian lives and so die out of God's love. All these will be eternally condemned to hell, as Holy Church teaches me to believe.
>
> (Julian, 1978, p. 233)

But she immediately continues, 'And all this being so, it seemed to me that it was impossible that every kind of thing should be well, as our Lord revealed at this time' (Julian, 1978, p. 233).

She turns this conflict over in her mind, evidently in some anguish, and suggests several possibilities. The first is to appeal to a 'great deed' that God will do that nobody can know in advance, but that will make all things well. Second, Julian suggests that hell, rather than a place of endless torment, might simply be annihilation: 'every creature who is of the devil's condition in this life and so dies is no more mentioned before God' (Julian, 1978, p. 234). Since it is God's loving attention that preserves all things in being, this amounts to saying that creatures 'no more mentioned before God' no longer exist. Julian also finally appeals, as Christians have done for centuries, to the inscrutable mysteries of God. Yet although she retains all of these suggestions, none of them fully satisfies her: it is not without cause that she has been taken by some as pointing the way to universalism (cf. Llewellyn, 1982; Llewellyn (ed.), 1985).

I suggest, however, that the really radical subversion of necrophilia in Julian consists, not so much in this resistance to the idea of hell as endless punishment, important as that resistance is, but in a fundamental reinterpretation of hell into this-worldly rather than other-worldly terms, a reinterpretation that parallels her radical notions of heaven, as we shall see below. Julian says that, seen aright, sin itself is hell. There is nothing worse or more terrible, in this life or the next. 'For if it were laid in front of us, all the pain there is in hell and in purgatory and on earth, death and all the rest, we should choose all that pain rather than sin . . . And no more cruel hell than sin was revealed to me, for a loving soul hates no pain but sin; for everything is good except sin, and nothing is evil except sin' (Julian, 1978, p. 247).

This is not, of course, denial of hell after death. However, if sin is the cruellest hell, 'the sharpest scourge with which any chosen soul can be struck' (Julian, 1978, p. 244), then the central meaning of hell is brought squarely into *this* life, *this* world, not left for some other world beyond. Since, inevitably, we sin frequently, we are all too often in hellish pain if we are spiritually sensitive. 'And therefore it often seems to us as if we were in danger of death and in some part of hell, because of the sorrow and pain which sin is to us, and so for that time we are dead to the true sight of our blessed life' (Julian, 1978, p. 320).

This hell is not eternal damnation, since God's love and forgiveness restores a sinful person; but it is according to Julian a recognition of the worst that can be experienced. In her estimation, that worst is a feature of our present lives, not another world beyond death that inspires us with fear and dread. Indeed it would be consistent with Julian's thinking to hold that too much anxiety about such an other world could actually be detrimental to the life of compassion and charity that should rightly engage us here. In the necrophilic symbolic of her time, such a revision of the concept of hell is breathtaking.

Equally significant is Julian's reinterpretation of heaven. This first occurs in dramatic fashion in the context of a vision. She is gazing at the crucified Jesus, like herself at the point of death, when the suggestion is made to her to 'look up to heaven to his Father' (Julian, 1978, p. 211). It was a reasonable suggestion, since she presumably believed herself about to expire. But she had a choice, and she made it wisely. She says, 'Here I must look up or else answer. I answered inwardly with all the power of my soul, and said: No, I cannot, for you are my heaven... So I was taught to choose Jesus for my heaven, whom I saw only in pain at that time... And that has taught me that I should always do so, to choose only Jesus to be my heaven, in well-being and in woe' (Julian, 1978, pp. 211–12).

No more than Julian's reinterpretation of hell should this be taken as a denial of heaven as an eternal state after bodily death. Yet as Julian comes to understand it, heaven is this-worldly. Just as sin is hell, so Jesus is heaven. Toward the end of her book Julian reinforces this theme: '... for our Lord intends this to be an endless joy, that he who will be our bliss when we are there is our protector whilst we are here, our way and our heaven in true love and faithful trust. And he gave understanding of this in everything, and especially in the revelation of his Passion, where he made me to choose him with all my strength for my heaven' (Julian, 1978, p. 331). Nor should it be forgotten that the Jesus whom she chooses for her heaven is precisely the Jesus who is giving himself in compassionate care for humanity.

5 The case of Christina of Markyate

In the life of Christina of Markyate, an anchoress near St Albans in the mid twelfth century, many of these themes come together. Throughout her biography, themes of birth and death, this world and the other, Marian devotion and mortification, gender-bending and compassion are woven together. At Christina's own birth, we are told, there was a sign that 'showed that she would be taught by the example and strengthened by the protection of Blessed Mary, ever a virgin, and be holy both in mind and body; detaching herself from the things of the world and finding peace in the contemplation of the things that are above' (Talbot (ed. and tr.), 1959, p. 35). This Marian devotion was significant throughout her life; and since for her a central strand of the Marian symbolic was that Mary was queen of heaven, Marian devotion and desire for heaven were intermingled. Thus, for example, in her adult life in an account of one of her visions these themes come together: 'For once when she was at prayer and was shedding tears through her longing for heaven, she was suddenly rapt above the clouds even to heaven, where she saw the queen of heaven sitting on a throne and angels in brightness seated about her' (Talbot, 1959, p. 109). Christina is then bidden to ask whatever she chooses; and requests, and is granted, succession to Roger's anchorhold after his death.

We have already noted how tomb-like her enclosure was while Roger was still alive. She had, however, been preparing for such a living death from her youth. Her teacher at that time was a canon, Sueno, who made great point of emphasizing virginity. Through his teaching, we are told, 'she made such progress . . . that she accounted all the things of this world as but a fleeting shadow'. While her family and friends amused themselves, 'she imagined herself lying on her deathbed (as if the future were already present) and reflected that after life had departed from the body no one could foretell the abode of the freed spirit' (Talbot, 1959, p. 39). This preoccupation with death was continued when she came under the direct influence of Roger: 'He taught her things about heavenly secrets which are hardly credible, and acted as if he were on earth only in body, whilst his mind was fixed on heaven' (Talbot, 1959, p. 105).

It was this desire for heaven that led Christina to reject the marriage that was planned for her; and the first part of her biography contains many a story of her near escapes from her prospective bridegroom. However, once she achieved her goal of becoming an anchoress, and some time after Roger's death, she found herself beset after all with sexual desire, a desire strongly reciprocated by a cleric with whom she had had considerable spiritual conversation. Increasingly, he importuned her, but she resisted, in terms that her biographer describes in gender-bending categories:

> And though she herself was struggling with this wretched passion, she wisely pretended that she was untouched by it. Whence he sometimes said that she was more like a man than a woman, though she, with her more masculine qualities, might more justifiably have called him a woman.
> Would you like to know how manfully she behaved in so imminent a danger? She violently resisted the desires of the flesh, lest her own members should become the agents of wickedness against her. Long fastings, little food, and that only of raw herbs, a measure of water to drink, nights spent without sleep, harsh scourgings . . .   (Talbot, 1959, p. 115)

It would appear that we have here all the classical ingredients of necrophilia: dread of the body, especially of sexuality, which is conceptually linked with the female; heroic 'manful' mortification; desire to escape this world and the need to preserve chastity in order that heaven might be attained. Yet even here, the necrophilia is subverted by one of the loveliest images of natality in medieval spiritual writing. After Christina had struggled with much prayer and mortification to be freed from sexual temptation,

> Then the Son of the Virgin looked kindly upon the low estate of His handmaid and granted her the consolation of an unheard-of grace. For in the guise of a small child he came to the arms of his sorely tried spouse and remained with her a whole day, not only being felt but also seen. So the maiden took Him in her hands, gave thanks, and pressed Him to her bosom. And with immeasurable delight she held Him at one moment to her virginal breast, at another she felt His presence within her

even through the barrier of her flesh. Who shall describe the abounding sweetness with which the servant was filled by this condescension of her creator? From that moment the fire of lust was so completely extinguished that never afterwards could it be revived. (Talbot, 1959, p. 119)

This event seems to mark a turning point in her biography. From this time forward her life is described more in terms of its compassion for others, her active care for her friends and concern for the church, and the serenity of her life of prayer. There is joy in her life, a joy not focused on death. Even when she herself becomes ill one Christmastime, and is confined to her bed, her vision is not of death but of birth: 'And as she heard the anthem proper to the feast, *Christ is born*, she understood that she had been invited to the joy of His birth. Her illness disappeared and she was filled with such spiritual happiness that her mind could dwell on nothing but divine things...' (Talbot, 1959, p. 187).

The last part of her biography is lost; and it is impossible to know what the writer would have said about her closing years and death. Nor, of course, is it possible to know to what extent the emphases in her biography are accurate to Christina and to what extent they reflect the preoccupations of the (presumably male) biographer. Yet even in this account, which at first seems unremittingly preoccupied with death and other worlds, the movement is toward an increasingly delighted acceptance of life and birth, a subversion of the necrophilia of anchoritic spirituality.

Note

1 I have explored this change in Julian's self-perception in Jantzen, 1995, pp. 176–80, but without fully recognizing the significance of her Marian devotion for this change.

References

Aelred of Riveaux, 'Rule of Life for a Recluse' in *Treatises and the Pastoral Prayer*. MacPherson, M. P. (tr.), Cistercian Fathers Series 2, Kalamazoo, MI, 1971.

Bell, M., 'Introduction' to *Wulfric of Haselbury*, by John, Abbot of Ford. Somerset Record Society Vol. XLVII, 1933.

Bynum, C. W., *Holy Feast and Holy Fast: The Religious Significance of Food to Medieval Women.* University of California Press, Berkeley and London, 1987.

Clay, M. R., *The Hermits and Anchorites of England.* Methuen, London, 1914.

Colgrave, B. (tr.), *Felix's Life of St Guthlac.* Cambridge University Press, Cambridge, 1956.

Darwin, S., *The English Medieval Recluse.* SPCK, London, 1944.

Hildegard of Bingen, *Scivias.* Hart, C. (tr.), Paulist Press, New York, 1990.

Hilton, W., *The Ladder of Perfection.* Sherley-Price, L. (tr.), Penguin, Harmondsworth, 1957.

Jantzen, G. M., *Julian of Norwich: Mystic and Theologian.* SPCK, London, 1987.

Jantzen, G. M., *Power and Gender in Christian Mysticism.* Cambridge University Press, Cambridge, 1995.

Julian of Norwich, *Showings.* Colledge, E. and Walsh, J. (tr.), Classics of Western Spirituality. Paulist Press, New York, and SPCK, London, 1978.

Llewellyn, R., *With Pity, not With Blame.* Darton, Longman & Todd, London, 1982.

Llewellyn, R. (ed.), *Julian, Woman of our Day.* Darton, Longman & Todd, London, 1985.

Savage, A. and Watson, N. (tr.), 'Ancrene Wisse' and 'Holy Maidenhood', in *Anchoritic Spirituality.* Classics of Western Spirituality. Paulist Press, New York, 1991.

Talbot, C. H. (ed. and tr.), *The Life of Christina of Markyate, a Twelfth Century Recluse.* Clarendon Press, Oxford, 1959.

Tugwell, S., *Ways of Imperfection.* Darton, Longman & Todd, London, 1984.

Walsh, J. (ed.), *The Cloud of Unknowing.* Classics of Western Spirituality. Paulist Press, New York, and SPCK, London, 1981.

Warren, A. K., *Anchorites and Their Patrons in Medieval England.* University of California Press, Berkeley and London, 1985.

Watson, N., 'The Methods and Objectives of Thirteenth-Century Anchoritic Devotion', in Glasscoe, M. (ed.), *The Medieval Mystical Tradition in England.* Exeter Symposium IV. D. S. Brewer, Cambridge, 1987.

Watson, N., *Richard Rolle and the Invention of Authority.* Cambridge University Press, Cambridge, 1991.

9

Envisioning God and our well-being

PAUL AVIS

Paul Avis makes two claims that pertain to human well-being. The first is that 'for true happiness or blessedness we need to cherish our life with God'. The second is that 'the human imagination, above all else, enables us to know God and to know where our well-being lies'. These two points are fleshed out with reference to both the scriptural tradition and the writings of the English Romantics. This leads Avis to reflect upon the nature of Christian sacramentality through the 'indivisible trinity' of beauty, truth and goodness. While Avis' primary concern is to define Christian well-being, this chapter also raises the question of what we mean by a 'good death'. And it is to this question that Avis finally turns.

*   *   *

When I was a sixth-former I read a book by Billy Graham called *Peace with God*. Billy Graham said that he had written it virtually on his knees. Naturally, it culminated in the invitation to accept Christ as Lord and saviour and it quoted Frances Ridley Havergal's hymn, 'Just as I am, without one plea'. The book was a distillation of Graham's preaching and much of it probably had been preached. Looked at sympathetically, it was simple, heartfelt, biblical, personal, and Christ-centred. Or, taking an unduly cynical view, one could say it was simplistic, sentimental, fundamentalist, individualistic – but still Christ-centred. No one can take the centrality of Christ away from Billy Graham's ministry, or the centrality of the cross of Christ. He could say with Paul: 'God forbid that I should glory, save in the cross of our Lord Jesus Christ, by whom the world is crucified unto me and I unto the world' (Galatians 6.14).

'In the cross of Christ I glory, towering o'er the wrecks of time.' When Graham held his first London Crusade in 1954, during Winston Churchill's second premiership, Churchill, who was 80 that year, asked the evangelist to come and see him at Number 10. There was still much hardship at home and Britain was on its knees economically. The Cold War was intensifying. The euphoria of liberation in 1945 had turned to ashes in much of Europe, behind what Churchill himself had dubbed the 'Iron Curtain' of the Soviet police state. The atomic mushroom cloud now loomed apocalyptically over the world. 'Do you see any hope, young man?', Churchill growled. 'Mr Prime Minister,' the youthful evangelist replied, 'my heart is filled with hope.' Billy Graham's basic message was one of peace of mind for the individual and hope for humankind. He wrote in that book, I recall, that in his mind's eye he sometimes saw New York City reduced to radioactive rubble. But he preached a kingdom that cannot be shaken. It is easy to find fault with Billy Graham's ministry, though it seems to me a lot more palatable and enlightened than much that goes on now, even in the Church of England. But he put his finger on the crucial thing: human well-being flowing from knowing God. The evangelistic message of that book partly explains who I am 40 years later and what I am doing with my life today – and I am not ashamed to say so. As the Apostle Paul put it with powerful understatement: 'I am not ashamed of the gospel, for it is the power of God for salvation to everyone who has faith' (Romans 1.16).

Billy Graham's message had the heart of the matter in it. Another book of his (though I never read it) is called *The Secret of Happiness*. Our true happiness and our relationship to God are bound up together. The two – happiness and God – are intertwined and inseparable. Ultimately, they are the same thing. This is perhaps the deepest truth of all religions (unquestionably of all theistic religions) and is something that links them together. The third volume of Keith Ward's ambitious four-volume study of comparative theology deals with 'Religion and Human Nature'. In his conclusion, he observes that 'the differences between religious traditions are nowhere clearer than in their views of human nature'. But Ward goes on immediately to say that it is not implausible to suggest that common features can be identified within diverse religious views (he has been discussing Hinduism, Buddhism, Judaism and Christianity, so his observations are not confined to theistic religions).

> They all see the material world, as it is now constituted, as inherently unsatisfactory. They all propose some better, or truer, form of existence, which can be attained through religious practice. And they all construe that practice in terms of a rather ascetic or disciplined attitude to the material world, and the cultivation of conscious states of bliss, wisdom and compassion. They all seek liberation from selfish greed, and experience of a self-less and blissful state or condition... They thus consider that such experience can be attained, and that its attainment is the highest human goal. (Ward, 1998, p. 324)[1]

Whatever our religious background, our deepest spiritual instincts tell us that in our present condition there is something fundamentally missing, something gone wrong, and we identify this as a divine blank in our lives. The need can be met, what is amiss and awry can be put right, the yawning gap can be filled, only by putting our lives in touch and in tune with what we call the sacred, the transcendent or the divine. The insight at the heart of the three unambiguously theistic faiths (Judaism, Christianity and Islam) is that our personal well-being is linked with knowing God. The most fulfilled, most perfect life is a life lived in tune with God. We know deep down that we were created for fellowship with God and that as that fellowship becomes closer our well-being grows stronger. The first thesis of this chapter is the broadly supported truth that for true happiness or blessedness we need to cherish our life with God.

The second thesis of this chapter probably does not have as much consensus and weight of traditions behind it: the thesis is that the human imagination, above all, enables us to know God and to know where our well-being lies. Both of these crucial areas of knowledge (God and our flourishing) are matters of vision, of perception, of spiritual and moral intuition. It is the work of the imagination to bring them before us, to hold them up to our longing gaze, to bring them into contact, and to fuse them together in unity. Therefore, for the sake of our well-being and literally for God's sake, we must cultivate the imagination, feed it, exercise it, respect it, not let it atrophy. My theological mentor Bishop Charles Gore (my mentor even though he died in 1932, because I wrote my doctoral thesis on him) once said: 'We know we ought to cultivate beauty' (cf. Avis, 1988; Carpenter, 1960). I have to confess that I have been too busy to put Gore's words consistently into practice, and I fear that he was too, but I am sure that he was right. To be a more rounded person, I need more beauty in my life.

Of course, as Gore would have been the first to admit, we should cultivate truth and goodness, as well as beauty. But beauty, truth and goodness are an indivisible trinity. It is questionable whether we can ever apprehend one without the others. 'There is a truth – a reality, an authenticity – about beauty and goodness. There is a goodness – a wholesomeness, a salutariness, a sacredness – about both beauty and truth. There is beauty in truth – in its self-evidence, its simplicity, its trans-parency – and in goodness, especially in the comeliness of moral character' (Avis, 1999, pp. 78–9). We all know that, famously for Keats, 'beauty is truth, truth beauty' (Palgrave (ed.), 1928 p. 332). The fact that the Greeks had two words for 'good' – the *agathon*, what is profitable, favourable, desirable; and the *kalon*, what is beautiful, the morally good – shows how closely these ideas are connected, because of course the beautiful and morally good is also desirable. We find these ideas fused christologically in the Johannine phrase 'the good shepherd' (*ho poimēn ho kalos*: 'the shepherd, the beautiful one').

We see the interpenetration of beauty, truth and goodness in the medieval scholastic analysis of beauty. Beauty consists, first, in proportion or harmony; second, in unity or integrity; and third, in radiance or clarity. When we open ourselves to beauty we receive something of its harmonious, unifying and clarifying power. These three impart themselves to those who humbly allow them to do so. Experience of beauty can make a person beautiful. Exposure to truth can make a person truthful. And experience of goodness can make us good in response. (Though none of that is automatic or guaranteed.) Imagination – that is to say imaginative or creative insight, the whole person responding to what comes from outside us, yet touches a chord within – stretches out its hands to embrace what is given, whether beautiful, true or good, and knows it for what it is. Coleridge called imagination 'this beautiful and beauty-making power' (Coleridge, 1969, p. 365). The biblical wisdom tradition sees beauty, truth and goodness as inseparable attributes of divine wisdom; in seeking them we seek God, in seeking God we find wisdom. 'Wisdom is radiant and unfading, and she is easily discerned by those who love her, and found by those who seek her' (The Wisdom of Solomon 6.12).[2]

Beauty, truth and goodness – they all radiate from God and can be paths back to God, provided they pass through Calvary where, in the cross, we see a transcendent beauty, truth and goodness revealed – but revealed and discerned amid their opposites: ugliness and deformity, falsehood and intellectual darkness, iniquity and perversity. Our deepest well-being consists in letting our lives be conformed to the forms of beauty, truth and goodness – and that means being transformed into the likeness of Jesus Christ. As Paul says in Romans 12.1: 'Do not be conformed to this age, but be transformed by the renewal of the mind, so that you may discern what is the will of God, the good and acceptable and complete.'[3]

There are still waters, as well as surging torrents, in the realm of the imagination. The human psyche is often compared to a pool that reflects the image of those who look into it. This sounds narcissistic, but it is not derogatory, for as we say: 'still waters run deep'. The sea, whether calm or troubled, is a recognized image of the unconscious. It fills the horizon, is unfathomable in some of its depths and always seems brim-full. To be near it in any of its moods has a soothing effect on us. 'Deep calleth unto deep . . . all thy waves and thy billows are gone over me' (Psalm 42.7). On his voyage to die of consumption in Italy, John Keats compared the stillness and steadiness of the evening star with the ceaseless motion of the waves in the poem 'Bright Star'. 'Bright Star, would I were steadfast as thou art.' He envisaged the universal action of the sea: 'the moving waters at their priestlike task of pure ablution round earth's human shores'. He longed for an end to his suffering, to find peace, to lay his head on the breast of his beloved Fanny and 'to feel for ever its soft fall and swell' – like the gentle motion of the sea. Here we have the poetic imagination, 'the ocean of being', in tune with its most potent symbol, the infinite sea (Palgrave (ed.), pp. 228–9).

To continue the aquatic imagery, take the two most powerful and capacious minds of the English Romantic Movement: Wordsworth and Coleridge. Coleridge said of Wordsworth that his soul was a rock with torrents roaring. The rock and the river

are central biblical images. When Moses struck the rock at God's
command, water gushed out (Exodus 17.1–7). In some rabbinic
exegesis, apparently invoked by Paul in 1 Corinthians 10.1–4, the
rock accompanied the Israelites in their wilderness wanderings,
along with the pillar of fire and cloud, to provide their needs.
They were baptized into Moses (as we are baptized into Christ),
in the cloud and in the sea. Their spiritual food was the manna
and their spiritual drink the living water from the rock, as ours
is the bread and wine of the Eucharist. These were their sacraments, not merely by analogy, as though they were *like* the
sacraments of the Church and bore an uncanny similarity to
them, or even were types of them, but in a realist sense, for they
were sacraments of Christ and conveyed participation in him.
Nothing less than that is being affirmed. Their food and drink
was 'spiritual', that is to say, as always in Paul, 'of the Holy Spirit'.
'They all drank from the spiritual rock that followed them, and
the rock was Christ.' The pre-existent Christ, the eternal wisdom
of God, guided and sustained them. Through the ever-present
Holy Spirit, the Israelites of old were incorporated sacramentally
into Christ, by passing through the sea and by partaking of the
manna and the water, as types of baptism and the Eucharist. As
Calvin says, in the manna and the water flowing from the rock
'there was a sacrament' (Calvin, 1960, p. 201).[4]

The Old Testament is rich in sacraments, 'an outward and
visible sign of an inward and spiritual grace': Moses' staff, the
Passover meal, the bronze serpent that healed snake bites, the
waters of the Jordan that cleansed Naaman's leprosy, above all
circumcision. The life of faith is a sacramental continuum, under
both covenants, for we are sacramental beings, comprised of
material stuff and indefinable spiritual essence united together
by God's act of creation (cf. Genesis 2.7). The world is full of
sacraments for the Christian and is indeed a sacrament itself ('a
sacramental universe'), not merely because of fanciful analogies,
but because 'heaven and earth are full of God's glory'. I understand
the point of the medieval and Reformation debates about the
number of the sacraments – seven or two or three or some
other number – but in a sense it was (and is) futile. Australian
Aborigines apparently can't actually count; they know only
singular and plural; Christian sacramentalism is both singular
and plural: for us there is one supreme and definitive sacrament

of the gospel and that is Jesus Christ, as Luther[5] and Schillebeeckx have said, but beyond that, you cannot have too many sacraments (Schillebeeckx, 1963).

Sacramentality and creativity belong together. God's creative power, infusing the cosmos, is the ground of sacramentality: it makes the world potentially sacramental, endowing matter with the potential to become a vehicle of divine presence for those with eyes to see. 'Ever since the creation of the world, [God's] eternal power and divine nature, invisible though they are, have been understood and seen through the things he has made' (Romans 1.20). As The Wisdom of Solomon puts it: 'the author of beauty created them. And . . . from the greatness and beauty of created things comes a corresponding perception of their Creator' (13.5).

By the same token, the God-given sacramental capacity of the physical world is the presupposition of human creativity, especially in painting, sculpture, architecture, the making of gardens, the culinary arts and in fact all forms of design and fashioning. The creator of infinite worlds has imparted to humankind the power to create in manifold ways, but the highest and best of these is the charisma of communicating God and articulating God's truth. 'In every generation', says The Wisdom of Solomon, divine wisdom 'passes into holy souls and makes them friends of God and prophets' (7.27). From the rock of God-like imagination, living waters of creativity ever flow. God continues to create or co-create in and through us. Our artistic creativity is a major part of our human affinity with God. This truth suggests that God is not only the source of the beauty, truth and goodness that impart meaning to our lives and enhance their enjoyment, but also our destiny, the ocean into which all experiences and expressions of goodness, truth and beauty flow: source, guide and end of all. The fountain of creativity wells up from the divine being, flows through creation to us and from us and our works of beauty back to God again. Through imaginative vision God the creator and redeemer enables us to apprehend our true good and final happiness in God, Father, Son, Holy Spirit.

The consciousness that our well-being depends on God, that God is the well-spring of our lives – 'the fountain of life' (Psalm 36.9) – breathes through the Hebrew Bible (the Christian Old Testament), but it is always coupled with its converse: warnings against false gods, that is to say, idolatry. When does an icon become an idol? Perhaps when it ceases to be a sacrament. Idolatry is the attempt to capture the infinite in finite form, to bring the creator down to the level of the creature and to pervert gift into possession. This is the other side of the coin when we are speaking about the divine energy at work in all forms of creativity: what is created can supplant its transcendent source in our minds and scale of values. The love of earthly beauty and of artistic beauty can be perverted into the worship of artefacts, when we look upon them, not through them to what they intimate of beyond. (This is presumably what William Blake meant when he spoke in 'The Everlasting Gospel' of those who 'see with not thro the Eye' (Blake, 1977, p. 860)). The Wisdom of Solomon, uniquely in the biblical literature, combines praise for God's beauty and the beauty of God's creation with scorn of idols and denunciation of those who manufacture and reverence them, and there is a clear logic in this juxtaposition.

The deepest human longings can be articulated only in poetry; as Romantics such as Keats and Keble said, poetry is a form of prayer: the moving spirit is the same. In the Psalter poetry and prayer are one, just as they are in the finest Christian hymnody, such as that of Charles Wesley. The Psalter is par excellence the book of human desire for God and the good things that God gives. Open the Book of Psalms anywhere and you find the psalmists abandoning themselves to God and to the mercy of God: seeking from God rescue from enemies, forgiveness of sins, peace of mind, healing of spirit and blessing on their homes, families and livelihoods. 'You show me the path of life. In your presence there is fullness of joy; at your right hand are pleasures for evermore' (Psalm 16.11). To 'walk in the presence of God in the light of life' is the psalmist's idea of the good life, a life lived before God; as Luther characteristically says: *coram deo* (Psalm 56.13). Compared with this, idols are trash.

The same consciousness and conviction also underpins the Torah (the law books or Pentateuch) and the message of the Old Testament prophets. The happiness, success and prosperity of Israel and of all its people depend on their turning away from the worship of false gods, the pursuit of spurious goals and of inferior goods and instead devoting themselves faithfully and obediently to the love and service of God. Second-Isaiah proclaims to all who thirst, 'come to the waters; and you that have no money, come, buy and eat.' Isaiah asks incredulously of the people: Why do you spend money on what is not bread and devote your labour to what cannot satisfy? (Isaiah 55.1–2). Jeremiah laments that the people have forsaken the Lord, 'the fountain of living waters', and have dug out cracked cisterns from which the water simply drains away (Jeremiah 2.13).

The same truth fills the pages of the New Testament. If we were to analyse what the Gospels and the Epistles are saying, it would amount to variations on the theme 'our relation to God and our own well-being are inextricably connected'; they are simply two sides of the one coin. In the Johannine literature (the fourth Gospel and the Epistles of John), human flourishing and fulfilment are spoken of as 'eternal life'. John's 'eternal life' is not about an endless existence in another place (heaven) that begins after death, but about the fullness of the life of God that dwelling in Christ imparts to the believer who is born anew (or 'from above') into this divine life through water and the Spirit, which signifies physical and spiritual baptism (John 3.3–8). 'Eternal life' is an eschatological concept: that is to say, it is tasted and experienced now, but will be brought to fruition and perfection when God's gracious purposes for the world that he loves (John 3.16) are fulfilled in the last times. But in the Johannine literature it is also a life kept pure from idolatry. 'This is eternal life, that they may know you, the only true God, and Jesus Christ whom you have sent' (John 17.3). The Book of Common Prayer puts it in a way faithful to the fourth Gospel in the Collect for Epiphany: 'Mercifully grant that we, which know thee now by faith, may after this life have the fruition of thy glorious Godhead.' The First Epistle of John echoes the Gospel: 'We know that the Son of God has come and has given us understanding, so that we may know him who is true.... He is the true God and eternal life' (1 John 5.20). And where John ends his letter with the punch-line, 'Little children, keep your-selves from idols' (1 John 5.21), the Book of Common Prayer prays in the same spirit for grace 'to withstand the temptations of the world, the flesh and the devil, and with pure hearts and minds to follow thee the only God' (Collect for the Eighteenth Sunday after Trinity). Eternal life is a qualitative, not simply a quantitative concept and refers to the life lived in the light of God that is now begun and is perfected in the age to come, when we shall know fully, even as we have been fully known (1 Corinthians 13.12).

The fundamental insight, that our health and happiness as whole persons is connected with and inseparable from our relationship with God as creator, redeemer and sanctifier, is a fundamental Christian truth, one that echoes down the centuries of theological reflection. Irenaeus in the late second century was no doubt driving at this insight in the intriguing and cryptic words that have haunted theologians ever since: 'The glory of God is man fully alive.'[6] Augustine of Hippo had famously cried out in his *Confessions*: 'You have made us for yourself and our hearts are restless until they find their rest in you.' St Thomas Aquinas is a theologian of happiness; he devotes five sections or '*Questiones*' of the *Summa Theologiae* to the subject. Happiness is the perfect good of man. In accordance with Thomas' theological axiom that God is the ultimate end or goal of all things, he argues that perfect happiness is to be realized in the vision of God (Aquinas, n.d., vol. 16: 1a 2ae, 1–5). By the same token, for Thomas, sinfulness, leading to alienation from God and the loss of true happiness, is caused by the perversion of desire from its proper end – a sophisticated concept of idolatry.

The same sentiments infuse Thomas à Kempis' *The Imitation of Christ*, written in the upsurge of devotion and spiritual seriousness that marked the immediate pre-Reformation period. Earthly things can never satisfy us, for we were not created for the enjoyment of these alone. The more we know ourselves, Thomas insists, the more aware we are of our wretchedness. All goodness and blessing reside in God and as we turn to him we experience divine peace and comfort (Thomas à Kempis, 1952).

What is pervasive in patristic and medieval Christianity is no less true of the Reformation. Like all the great theologians, John Calvin had a powerful grasp of our first thesis, that our true happiness depends on our relationship with God. Although Calvin's notion of happiness was profoundly moral and spiritual, rather than affective or sensual, this thesis was the hinge of his theology. He famously begins his *Institutes of the Christian Religion* (1536–59) by affirming that our true and sound wisdom consists almost entirely of two inter-related parts: knowing God and knowing ourselves. But which of these two comes first, Calvin continues, is not easy to decide. Do we begin by coming to know the truth of God and in that light start to understand ourselves, or do we begin with our own self-consciousness and self-knowledge and then become aware of God through that? Some thinkers, Newman particularly, have suggested that self-awareness can make us aware of God (cf. Boekraad and Tristram, 1961). Calvin appears to share this view. No one, he believes, can reflect on their own existence without their thoughts being turned towards God, in whom they live and move and have their being, since (he says) all the good things that we constantly enjoy lead us back to God, the infinite source of goodness. On the other hand, our experiences of unhappiness, arising out of ignorance, weakness, moral failure and a sense of futility, also point us to God. For in fallen humankind there exists, Calvin says, 'something like a world of misery', and there is no one who does not feel this. It is this divine discontent with our condition that spurs us to seek God. And as we begin to do this, he goes on, we find that we are being met and welcomed. Everyone, therefore, on coming to the knowledge of themselves, 'is not only urged to seek God, but is also led as by the hand to find him'. (Calvin, 1962, vol. 1, pp. 37–8 [I, i, 1])[7] (This is reminiscent of the Jansenist, i.e. quasi-Calvinist, Pascal explaining human longing in the *Pensées* in the next century: we only seek God because we have already found him (Pascal, 1966).)

Calvin speaks not simply as a sixteenth-century Reformer but – in the accents of his time – as a representative of the Christian tradition through the centuries. Calvin's words are shot through with a strong Augustinian emphasis on the all-pervasive sinfulness or depravity of fallen human nature. Today a good many Christians have misgivings about this way of speaking about the relationship between God and ourselves. They suspect that to stress in this way the extrinsic origin of anything good that we experience (as Matthew Arnold famously put it: 'a power, not ourselves, that makes for righteousness' (Arnold, 1873, p. 388)) is a form of false consciousness. It is lacking in authenticity because it projects out on to God what really belongs within our own selves. It appears to be blind to the fact that our lives are adversely affected by conditions, circumstances and relationships over which we have little control, especially in infancy and childhood, and that these early experiences can permanently shape our character for good or ill.

The classical view of Christian theology, of which Calvin is simply a particularly eloquent spokesman, is unenlightened by the insights of the social sciences and of depth psychology. The traditional Christian theology of human nature (theological anthropology) has been rewritten in the light of these discoveries about the many complex factors that contribute to the shaping of human selfhood.[8]

Taking seriously the contingent, external determinants of the way we turn out certainly does not simplify things. It does not make human behaviour any more explicable. On the contrary, it makes it more mysterious, less amenable to reasoned analysis, because we cannot trace the line that divides determination from within and determination from without. What this anthropological enlightenment does do is to accentuate the tragic element in existence, the area where we have a bias to go wrong yet, in ordinary circumstances, cannot claim 'diminished responsibility'. It is we who act, yet we are not sole makers of ourselves, but are pushed and pulled by forces that we neither fully understand nor can fully master, and only partly assimilate and come to terms with. This sounds to me not a million miles from the idea that we are rather nervous and coy about these days: the doctrine of original sin.

Self-knowledge involves accepting that we are divided beings; as Paul put it in Romans: 'I do not understand my own actions. But I do not do what I want, but I do the very thing I hate. . . . It is no longer I that do it, but sin that dwells within me. For I know that nothing good dwells within me, that is, in my flesh. I can will what is right, but I cannot do it. For I do not do the good I want, but the evil I do not want is what I do. Now if I do what I do not want, it is no longer I that do it, but sin that dwells within me. . . . Wretched man that I am' (Romans 7.15–20; see to the end of the chapter).

Someone called human beings 'forked creatures', and indeed we are, not simply because we stand on two legs, but because we contain both good and bad, light and dark, that we lead chequered lives, and are pulled apart by contrary forces. In our nature genuinely noble and altruistic aspirations are mixed up with culpable moral failure and tragic waywardness. We are fashioned out of what Kant (echoed more recently by Isaiah Berlin) called 'the crooked timber of humanity'.[9] Christian theology speaks, therefore, of our 'fallen nature', fallen from the perfection of the image of God and the purpose of our creator – like the runner on a marathon who has crashed to the ground beside the route, only to stagger to his feet and to stumble and sway as he tries to complete the race.

In his poem 'September 1, 1939', W. H. Auden described the denizens of New York City on the outbreak of World War II, and I think he meant all the children of modernity, as

> Lost in a haunted wood
> Children afraid of the night
> Who have never been happy or good.
> (Auden in Skelton (ed.), 1964, p. 282)

Happy or good; happy and good: can we be one without the other: happy but not good, good but not happy? A life could not be said to have turned out well if one or the other were lacking.[10] To establish the ultimate coincidence of goodness and happiness has been the Holy Grail of moral philosophy and of theological ethics, from Socrates and Aristotle to Augustine and Aquinas, to Kant and the modern moralists, as philosophers and theologians thought through Aristotle's dictum that the aim of human life is not merely to live, but to live well (Aristotle, 1995, pp. 7–12). Together happiness and goodness go a long way towards making up our well-being. Christianity is a religion that addresses the issue of human happiness as well as the question of human goodness, and that is because the Christian faith is about our truest and deepest well-being. It may be counter-intuitive to say so (if you stopped people in the street and asked them what Christianity is about, how many would say, 'Happiness'?), but the Scriptures and much of the tradition are clear. In her book *The Hope of Happiness*, Helen Oppenheimer, a consistently joyful Anglican theologian and moralist, puzzles over why dreary Christians are prone to suggest that happiness is not important. 'We seem to have lost the art of expressing our faith in a way that gives people anything to be happy about' (Oppenheimer, 1983, p. 1).

In Christian theology, the perfection or completion by grace of a human nature that is already God-given holds goodness and happiness together, for happiness and goodness are what we are made for. The eighteenth-century apologist and moralist

Bishop Joseph Butler said that in the vision of God, when human goodness is perfected, God himself will be our happiness (Butler, 'Sermons', Sermon XIV, para. 19, cited Oppenheimer, 1983, p. 166). The classical and medieval tradition saw that the perfection or completion of human life, in the coming together of happiness and goodness, meant that this goal or end could not be envisaged in an individualistic way. Although it is difficult enough to be happy on our own, for we were designed for fellowship, it is probably impossible to be good alone, because goodness needs an object, a recipient. Because of its inextricable connection with goodness, happiness is regarded by Aristotle, Aquinas etc. as an *activity*. It is the characteristic performance of the human person; an active, not a passive state. Thomas Aquinas pointed to God as the supreme common good as well as our ultimate bliss.[11]

This makes happiness a moral concept. But this is not how it is generally understood in our culture, which often reduces happiness to what feels good (*eudaemonism*), and that sort of 'good' is not the same as the 'good' of goodness. Both happiness and goodness must be a part of well-being. Merely to be happy is not to enjoy well-being. If we ask, are we at our best when all we are doing is pursuing good feelings, the answer must be no (Spaemann, 2000, p. 32). Short-term happiness may be experienced at the expense of others, or even at the cost of damaging our physical, mental or spiritual health. But simply to be good (if only!) is not to achieve it either. Being good in some circumstances may be so costly that it makes us wretched. To make a martyr of oneself is not the way to well-being.

Well-being, combining happiness and goodness – goodness as a condition of happiness; happiness as the outcome of goodness – belongs to us as whole beings, whole multidimensional persons, made up of body, mind and spirit. Well-being is meant for the whole person now and hereafter. Aquinas puts too much emphasis on the perfection of our rational or intellectual nature, because that was what was distinctive of human being for him, as for Aristotle. But both he and Aristotle recognized that there is a natural level of well-being too, one suited to our animal nature, our social nature and our political nature. We must conceive our lives as a whole and it as a whole that we attain well-being. Aquinas spoke of 'the common goal of the whole of human life' (cited Spaemann, 2000, p. 7). Every dimension of our complex being needs to find its fulfilment and can do so, as far as this earthly life is concerned, through the practice of the virtues in the structured communities that make up political society. To live the good life, that is human life in accordance with the virtues, is normally enjoyable.[12] Taking the rough with the smooth, we are happy when we are good; living the good life brings a sense of satisfaction because we are staying in tune with our conscience. To make shipwreck of conscience by giving way to misdirected passion brings mental anguish and damage all round, not happiness, perhaps never more poignantly evoked than in Tolstoy's *Anna Karenina* (Tolstoy, 1978).

However, no finite good can fulfil completely the human desire for happiness: only God's infinity can do that. On any reckoning, if this life is not all the life there is, a life that turns out well must turn out well beyond this life (Spaemann, 2000). So alongside the idea of the good life, we need to recover the old-fashioned-seeming idea of 'a good death'. The Heidelberg Catechism of 1563 asks: 'What is your only comfort in life and in death?' And the answer comes back: 'That I, with body and soul, both in life and in death, am not my own, but belong to my faithful Saviour Jesus Christ . . .' (Schaff (ed.), 1877, p. 307, slightly modernized).

John Buchan offers us an example of a good death. Buchan ended his distinguished career as Governor-General of Canada. Its mountains, valleys and wildernesses, though on a vaster scale, evoked his native Scotland. Almost the last thing Buchan wrote before his death in 1940 was *Sick Heart River*. Sir Edward Leithen, a Buchan hero familiar from earlier novels, is given only months to live. A last rescue mission takes him to the Canadian wilderness where he hears of Sick Heart River, rumoured to be an earthly paradise where all ills are cured. The spell and fascination of the place lure the ailing Leithen to it. This part of the book bears the epitaph from Psalm 46.4 in the Authorized Version (KJB): 'There is a river, the streams whereof shall make glad the city of God.' When Leithen eventually picks his way through precipitous cliffs into the hidden valley, he is rapt by its beauty, but troubled by an uncanny feeling that something is amiss. It hits him that no creatures stir in the undergrowth and no birds sing. There are no sudden flashes of fish darting in the river. There is no animate existence. The hidden valley is sterile, a place not of life but of death. There is no earthly paradise. Redemption is not by that route.

Leithen turns away, his heart's sickness unhealed. But as he travels back he comes across a tribe of Native Americans – Hare Indians – on a reservation, who are suffering a deadly epidemic and have given up the struggle, resigned to fate. Leithen knows he cannot pass by; he stays and ministers to the sick and dying. By his authority he inspires the Hares to organize for survival; they find new hope and begin to build for the future. They revere him as a man with the mark of death already on him. He does enough to rehabilitate the tribe before his own inevitable death from TB. But he has found peace and made his soul – with the help of the Bible, the surrounding snow-capped mountains and the company, though not the ministrations, of a Roman Catholic priest. The valley of death becomes what Keats called a 'vale of soul making' (Keats, 1954, p. 266).[13] Leithen's sickness of heart is healed in a good death with the hope of life beyond. And his grave is marked with a cross. A wounded healer indeed – but that is another subject (cf. Avis, 2003).

Notes

1 For a discussion of the first three volumes, which includes the volume quoted here, cf. Avis, 2000, pp. 181–9; and for a review of the later fourth volume cf. Avis, 2001, pp. 657–9.
2 Among the biblical literature, The Wisdom of Solomon in the Apocrypha has most to say about beauty. The attributes of beauty – harmony, clarity, purity, radiance, etc. together with the attributes of truth and goodness (that I have not expanded on) come together in wisdom: 'There is in her a spirit that is intelligent, holy, unique, manifold, subtle, mobile, clear, unpolluted, distinct, invulnerable, loving the good, keen, irresistible, beneficent, humane, steadfast, sure, free from anxiety, all-powerful, overseeing all, and penetrating through all spirits that are intelligent, pure, and altogether subtle' (7.22–23, but keep reading!).
3 On the translation and exegesis of this verse cf. Dunn, 1988, pp. 712–15.
4 Calvin believed that it was not that the rock rolled along behind the Israelites, but that the stream from the rock flowed beside them. For a thorough discussion of the critical and exegetical issues

Wounds that Heal

involved in this passage cf. Thiselton, 2000, pp. 722–30. Thiselton's emphasis, like Calvin's, is on the sacramental participation of the Israelites in Christ.

5 'The Holy Scriptures contain one sacrament only, which is the Lord Jesus Christ himself' (Luther, WA 6, 1883, p. 86).

6 A more conventional translation of the whole sentence is: 'Life in man is the glory of God; the life of man is the vision of God' ('Against Heresies' IV, 20, 5–7).

7 In the next section, Calvin develops the converse proposition, namely that 'man never attains to a true self-knowledge until he has previously contemplated the face of God, and come down after such contemplation to look into himself' (Calvin, 1962, vol. 1, p. 38 [I, i, 2]).

8 A notable example is Pannenberg, 1985. For exposition and analysis of the projectionist critique of Christian claims cf. Avis, 1995.

9 'Out of the crooked timber of humanity, no straight thing can ever be made' (Kant, I., *Gesammelte Schriften*, Berlin, 1912, vol. 8, p. 23, cited Berlin, 1981, p. 148).

10 'A life that turns out well' is Spaemann's paraphrase of 'blessedness', *eudaemonia* (Spaemann, 2000).

11 Thomas Aquinas, *Summa Contra Gentiles*, III, 17: 'the highest good which is God is the common good, since the good of all things taken together depends on him . . . all things are ordered to one good as their end, and that is God' (Bourke (tr.), 1956, p. 72; cf. Finnis, 1998, pp. 111–7; Kempshall, 1999; Hollenbach, 2002; and Porter, 2005, pp. 141–230).

12 The tradition of virtue ethics was rediscovered outside Thomism by Alastair MacIntyre in *After Virtue* (1985). A convenient modern discussion of the virtues is Peter Geach's *The Virtues* (1970).

13 'Call the world if you Please "The vale of Soul-making". Then you will find out the use of the world.'

References

Aquinas, T., *Summa Theologiae*. (Blackfriars edn), Eyre and Spottiswoode, London, n.d.

Aquinas, T., *Summa Contra Gentiles*. Bourke, V. (tr.), *On the Truth of the Catholic Faith*. Doubleday/Image Books, New York, 1956.

Aristotle, *Politics*. Barker, E. (tr.), Staley, R. F. (intr.), Oxford University Press, Oxford, 1995.

Arnold, M., *Literature and Dogma*. Macmillan, London, 1873.

Augustine of Hippo, *Confessions*. Pine-Coffin, R. S. (tr.), Penguin, Harmondsworth, 1961.

Avis, P., *Gore: Construction and Conflict*. Churchman Publishing, Worthing, 1988.

Avis, P., *Faith in the Fires of Criticism*. Darton, Longman & Todd, London, 1995; reprinted Wipf and Stock, Eugene, OR, 2006.

Avis, P., *God and the Creative Imagination: Metaphor, Symbol and Myth in Religion and Theology*. Routledge, London, 1999.

Avis, P., 'An Anglican *Magnum Opus*: The Comparative Theology of Keith Ward', *Anglican Theological Review*. 82:1, 2000.

Avis, P., *Anglican Theological Review*. 83:3, 2001.

Avis, P., *A Church Drawing Near: Spirituality and Mission in a Post-Christian Culture*. T&T Clark, Edinburgh, 2003, ch.2.

Berlin, I., *Against the Current: Essays in the History of Ideas*. Oxford University Press, Oxford, 1981.

Blake, W., *The Complete Poems*. Ostriker, A. (ed.), Penguin, Harmondsworth, 1977.

Boekraad, A. J. and Tristram, H., *The Argument from Conscience to the Existence of God, according to J. H. Newman*. Editions Nauwelaerts, Louvain, 1961.

Buchan, J., *Sick Heart River*. Hodder & Stoughton, London, 1941.

Calvin, J., *The First Epistle of Paul to the Corinthians*. Fraser, J. W. (tr.), The Saint Andrew Press, Edinburgh, 1960. (*Calvin's Commentaries*. Torrance, D. W. and Torrance, T. F. (eds))

Calvin, J., *Institutes of the Christian Religion*. Beveridge, H., (tr.), 2 vols, James Clarke, London, 1962.

Carpenter, J., *Gore: A Study in Liberal Catholic Thought*. Faith Press, London, 1960.

Coleridge, S. T., 'Dejection: An Ode', *Poetical Works*. Coleridge, E. H. (ed.), Oxford University Press, Oxford, 1969.

Dunn, J. D. G., 'Romans 9–16', *Word Biblical Commentary 38B*. Word Books, Dallas, TX, 1988.

Finnis, J., *Aquinas: Moral, Political and Legal Theory*. Oxford University Press, Oxford, 1998.

Geach, P., *The Virtues*. Cambridge University Press, Cambridge, 1977.

Hollenbach, D., *The Common Good and Christian Ethics*. Cambridge University Press, Cambridge, 2002.

Keats, J., *Letters of John Keats*. Page, F. (ed.), Oxford University Press, London, 1954.

Kempshall, M. S., *The Common Good in Late Medieval Political Thought*. Clarendon Press, Oxford, 1999.

Luther, M., *Luthers Werke*, Weimarer Ausgabe, Weimar, 1883.

MacIntyre, A., *After Virtue*. (2nd edn), Duckworth, London, 1985.

Oppenheimer, H., *The Hope of Happiness*. SCM Press, London, 1983.

Palgrave, F. (ed.), *The Golden Treasury*. (3rd edn), Macmillan, London, 1928.

Pannenberg, W., *Anthropology in Theological Perspective*. O'Connell, M. J. (tr.), T&T Clark, Edinburgh, 1985.

Pascal, B., *Pensées*. Krailsheimer, A. J. (tr.), Penguin, Harmondsworth, 1966.

Porter, J., *Nature as Reason: A Thomistic Theory of the Natural Law*. Eerdmans, Grand Rapids, Michigan, 2005.

Schaff, P. (ed.), *The Creeds of the Evangelical Protestant Churches*. Hodder & Stoughton, London, 1877.

Schillebeeckx, E., *Christ the Sacrament of the Encounter with God*. Sheed and Ward, London, 1963.

Skelton, R. (ed.), *Poetry of the Thirties*. Penguin, Harmondsworth, 1964.

Spaemann, R., *Happiness and Benevolence*. Alderberg, J. (tr.), T&T Clark, Edinburgh, 2000.

Thiselton, A. C., *The First Epistle to the Corinthians: New International Greek Testament Commentary*. Eerdmans, Grand Rapids, Michigan and Paternoster, Carlisle, 2000.

Thomas à Kempis, *The Imitation of Christ*, Shirley-Price, L. (tr.), Penguin, Harmondsworth, 1952.

Tolstoy, L., *Anna Karenina*. Edmunds, R. (tr.), Penguin, Harmondsworth, 1978.

Ward, K., *Religion and Human Nature*. Clarendon Press, Oxford, 1998.

10

The sacrament of unction

ELIZABETH STUART

———◆◆◆———

Developing the theme of sacramentality, Elizabeth Stuart explores the sacrament of unction. But if that is her theme there may be some surprises in store. Perhaps it would be more accurate to say that Stuart's theme is in fact the extravagance of God, and that Stuart uses the sacrament of unction as a way of re-imagining our contemporary and contracted understandings of God. In this way Stuart speaks of the 'ever-broken heart of God' and, by analogy, of our own human experiences of suffering, illness and death. In particular, Stuart addresses the question of human identity and argues that our constructed identities, including those of 'sickness' and 'the dead', are relativized and reoriented by God's 'extravagant grace'.

* * *

Are there any among you sick? They should call for the elders of the church and have them pray over them, anointing them with oil in the name of the Lord. The prayer of faith will save the sick, and the Lord will raise them up; and anyone who has committed sins will be forgiven. Therefore confess your sins to one another, and pray for one another, so that you may be healed. The prayer of the righteous is powerful and effective.

(James 5.14–16)

Extravagant re-membrance

The baptized person is one who has been initiated into the mystery of the pleroma of the divine life. The baptized is plunged into the depths of catholicity, which is the dynamic, extravagant life of God whose rhythm is always that of inclusion and expansion as well as focus. In the richness and diversity

197

of this life gender, sexual orientation and other forms of constructed identity are eclipsed and rendered non-ultimate. To be baptized is to have one's heart direction trained on the endlessness of God, to be pulled like a magnet into the ever-broken heart of God. It is to become part of a group mind, a corporate body, attempting to develop a singing, hospitable self that in mirror of the divine dynamic is constantly broken open to be expanded and enlarged. But to be baptized is also to be constantly tested and tempted; it is to be constantly driven into the wilderness to be tempted by Satan into contraction of the self into the confines of human constructions.

When he rode into Jerusalem on a donkey Jesus almost lost the struggle with Satan that began immediately after his baptism. For he almost yielded to the pressure to perform the dominant script of messiahship, a script that he had rejected after his baptism. The messiah was expected to come triumphant and victorious, humble and riding on a donkey into Jerusalem (Zechariah 9.9). What saved Jesus from temptation? Sometime during the subsequent days he rejected that script and reset his heart on the identity given him during his baptism, an identity that would lead to his being broken open on the cross. The author of the Gospel of Mark tells us that it was during that last week at the house of Simon the leper that a woman came and anointed Jesus with oil (Mark 14.3–9). It is common for scholars to root the sacrament of unction in Jesus' healing ministry or in the practice of the early Church attested to in the Letter of James. But in fact, just as the sacrament of baptism is rooted in Christ the one who was baptized, so the sacrament of unction is rooted in the experience of Christ the anointed one. Indeed, if Jesus is the Christ, the messiah, the anointed, it is this moment that focuses and actualizes that identity, in the process completely deconstructing the messiahship practised on the Sunday before his death.

The woman engages in a highly extravagant act: she breaks open an alabaster jar of costly ointment and pours it over Jesus' head. The extravagance of the act is noted by some present, who complain that the ointment could have been sold for a good sum and the money given to the poor. The extravagance of the act is significant, for the act re-members Jesus' baptism, the descent of the spirit like a dove, it re-members the ever expanding, never contracting nature of the divine life, it re-members the cosmic cross upon which God stretches himself for all eternity in an act of outrageous self-giving that is to become focused in Jesus. It is the extravagance of the act that jolts Jesus back into his baptismal identity. He is overwhelmed and overshadowed by the divine life, as he was at his baptism. He interprets her act as preparation for his death: 'she has anointed my body for burial' (Mark 14.8) and in the process understands that his life must be nothing less than an outpouring of the divine life in sacrifice. This realization precipitates Judas' betrayal, and the drama unfolds.

In the Gospels of Luke and John the anointing is also accompanied by foot washing, and John has Jesus perform a similar action on his disciples the night before he died (John 13.1–11). This illustrates again the expansive and inclusive nature of catholicity. Having been reminded of the exploding mystery of the divine life in which all constructed identities are eclipsed, Jesus passes that reminder on and indeed instructs his disciples to do likewise (John 13.14).

The sacrament of unction is possible because Jesus accepted the anointing of the woman. It is this anointing that enables him to overcome the temptation to be a different sort of saviour. He rejects the dominant script and this leads him to the cross and to the plunging of the divine and humanity together into the experience of death and resurrection. There is now no place where God is not and death is defeated.

The connection between the sacrament and this act is implicitly made in the Orthodox tradition, where it is customary for the faithful to be anointed on Holy Wednesday, the Wednesday before Easter, by tradition the day on which Judas betrayed Jesus. The Gospel reading for that service is the story of the woman anointing Jesus.

In the sacrament of unction the baptized are offered the extravagant grace of God, which reaches out to them when they have forgotten the nature of their belonging, when they have been seduced into behaving as if the dominant cultural scripts have ultimate status, when they have forgotten who they are. The sacrament of unction re-members the body of

Christ by flooding the baptized with the divine life, overwhelming with the mystery of catholicity, eclipsing all other forms of identity, and reorientating the soul's desire.

The contraction of pain

It would be a mistake to confine the administration of the sacrament of unction to those who are physically or mentally sick. The sacrament of unction is for those who need to be reconnected with the mystery of the divine life. It is a sacrament for those who are suffering from the contraction of existence. It is the sacrament for those who have been sorely tested beyond their ability to endure. It is the sacrament for those who are suffering from the melancholia diagnosed by the theorist Judith Butler, the unfinished and irresolvable grief upon which the subject is constructed in contemporary Western society. Yet this melancholia was wrongly attributed by Butler to the foreclosure of human love in the creation of sexual orientation and gender, which leaves us haunted by the love we cannot mourn (Butler, 1997, pp. 132–50). She failed to see that it was in fact the foreclosure of desire for the divine that is at the root of modern Western melancholia, and this was both expressed by and manifest in the turn of human desire on itself and the construction of the sexual relationship as the *telos* of desire. In other words, the sacrament of unction is a sacrament for all the baptized as they find their identity tested. Jesus was not sick when the woman anointed him with oil, he was tested.

However, the association of the sacrament with sickness is important. Sickness is both intensely personal and also a social construction. Mental illness, for example, is understood in some circles as a protest against dominant social structures, so that behaviour is then labelled in such a way by those dominant structures as to diminish the powers of protest. Paul Hollenbach has argued that this is the context in which to understand demon possession in first-century Palestine (Hollenbach, 1981, pp. 567–88). Jesus' exorcisms can be understood in this context as actions directed against the social order that inspired protest and then labelled it as demon possession. Such healing is an attack on the dominant order and an attempt to free those suffering from its oppressive structures. The possible connections here between unction, healing and identity are clear and are brought out by Robert Goss in his analysis of the healing of the boy in Mark 9.14–24 through the lens of gay and lesbian biblical criticism:

> For years the Christian church has labelled those who practiced their same-sex attractions as sinners. It rendered mute those men and women attracted to the same sex, like the boy in Mark 9.14–24, who was possessed by a spirit that rendered him dumb and threw him into fire and water to destroy him. Likewise, gay men and lesbians for a hundred years have been defined as pathological or clinically ill by psychiatrists... and have been portrayed in fundamentalist discursive practice as the 'demonised other'. (Goss, 1993, pp. 107–8)

The world of the sick is a world of contraction, whether that is the contraction of oppression or the contraction of pain. Suffering inevitably narrows our horizons and tends to define, constrict and dominate lives. Reality collapses into the limits of our own horizons. Ironically, this may be necessary for the purposes of immediate survival but for the baptized it cannot be allowed to become a long-term, stable identity because it is an identity antithetical to the catholicity of the Godhead into which they have been plunged and which they are called to live out. This applies to any identity built upon an experience of suffering and oppression.

In the sacrament of unction Christ, through his Church, touches the recipient with the outrageous, extravagant, ever-expanding life of the divine and thus once again the baptized re-member their salvation and rising up, as the Letter of James puts it, by a refreshment of that grace. It is the experience of salvation, of the enlargement of the soul and self that is also the experience of resurrection, bursting one out of the constraints of constructed identities by the sheer gifting of the identity as an adopted child of God.

In the sacrament of unction the Church saves 'the sick' and all those struggling with the testing of their baptismal identity and raises them up, it challenges and refuses to acknowledge other identities that contract the self and make it inhospitable. This is made very explicit in one of the prayers included in the pre-Vatican II rites of the Roman Catholic Church, which asks that the recipient will be raised up, strengthened and given back 'to your holy Church'. This is a clear recognition that there has been some sort of alienation from the group mind or body.

Re-membering baptism

It is appropriate, then, that much of the rite of unction recalls that of baptism. In most catholic rites the rite of unction begins with the sprinkling of the recipient with holy water. This immediately reconnects the recipient with their baptismal identity and also serves to cleanse the space, making it immediately a sacred space in which the work of liturgy is to take place and the presence of God is to be focused and manifest. Other elements that reprise baptism are the confession and absolution, the anointing with oil, the laying on of hands and, in some rites, the exorcism. This serves to remind the Church that the sacraments are not repetitions but extensions, re-membrances across time and place of the eternal outpouring of the divine, and each sacrament is a focusing of the primordial sacrament of Christ himself.

The reconnection with the ever-expansive, multi-layered nature of catholic life was also evident in the invocation of the angels that characterized all catholic rites of unction pre-Vatican II (they have been dropped from the post-Vatican II rites of anointing). The Archangel Raphael has long been associated in the Christian tradition with healing (Tobit 12.14), and is explicitly invoked in the Liberal Catholic rite. Indeed Leadbeater recommended that a green stole be used by a priest in the administration of the sacrament of unction, the colour associated with this archangel (Leadbeater, 1920, p. 249). By the invocation of the angels the recipients are plunged back into the multidimensional, enchanted world of mystery to which they belong.

The remote matter (the external sign) of the sacrament of unction is the holy olive oil usually blessed at the Chrism Mass by the bishop, and the proximate matter is the anointing of the person with that oil. Traditionally, the priest anointed the person's eyes, ears, nostrils, mouth, hands and feet. These were understood to be the apertures of the senses and therefore open channels into which both grace and evil could seep. Many of these channels were also anointed at baptism. In extremity the forehead only is signed, the head channel having been opened at baptism. The Liberal Catholic Church, following the Qabalistic notion of the body as the middle pillar of the tree of life, also recommends the anointing of the sacred centres of the sacral plexus (at the base of the spine; the nape of the neck may be anointed instead), the solar plexus, the heart, the pharyngeal plexus (at the front of the throat) and the crown of the head, and indeed will only anoint these when a recipient is seriously ill. The point is that the ever-flowing and rich grace of God, represented by and in the oil, flows into the recipient through the same cracks that make them vulnerable. The form of the rite is the prayer that accompanies the anointing.

The laying on of hands is not essential to the rite but is present in the contemporary Roman Catholic and Liberal Catholic rites of unction. In the laying of the hands on the head the priest acts as a channel of divine power, which flows into the person through the crown centre.

The normal minister of the sacrament of anointing is the priest acting on behalf of the bishop (who has blessed the oil). In the Western rites it is normally only one priest who administers the sacrament but in the East, following the instructions of the Letter of James to 'call for the elders', it is considered desirable for the sacrament to be administered by seven priests, the mystical number of completeness. Again this practice conveys something of the deep meaning of the sacrament: it is about healing inasmuch as it is about re-enchanting the recipient, restoring them to the mystery in which by virtue of their baptism they live and move. It is an action of relocation after dislocation.

The end of the beginning

It seems to have been in the Middle Ages that the sacrament of unction became closely associated with the last rites and thus became known as extreme unction. It thus became the means by which those who were dying were prepared for their deaths. Just as baptism, confirmation and the Eucharist initiated the recipient into the Church on earth, so penance, unction and the Eucharist came to be understood as initiating the recipient into the Church in heaven. For the baptized, death is a transition not a tragedy, for they have already died and risen with Christ. Hence the addition of the viaticum, food for the journey, to the sacrament of unction when the person is *in extremis.* The anointing that takes place in the context of extreme unction has a rather different purpose than normal use of the sacrament of unction. For Leadbeater it had the function of closing the centres that had been opened at baptism. This sealing of the corpse encourages the dead to move on in the spiritual body, of which St Paul spoke, and resist the temptation to remain somehow attached to the decomposing flesh.

Up until the second half of the twentieth century the thought of dying without the sacrament of extreme unction would have appalled most Catholics. The concept of a 'good death' was clearly defined as a death prepared for in which the dying person was conscious of his or her state and able to receive the fortifications of the Church through the sacrament of extreme unction. Death was an ecclesial event and it was an event, a departure not an ending. As a person went through the dying process the Church through its priest commended the departing soul to God, begged for mercy on behalf of the deceased, and summoned the saints and angels to meet the departing soul. Death was something to be done and done correctly. But at the beginning of the twenty-first century in Britain, at least, the last rites are no longer considered essential to a good (Catholic) death. Death has become largely invisible, as Phillipe Ariès has noted (Ariès, 1991). Most of us will die in hospital, alone, and drugged into unconsciousness. A good death in contemporary British culture would be generally understood to be a quick and unconscious one. As a culture we have lost sight of eschatological horizons and so death is understood to be a natural end to life, a closing down, a turning off that is tragic when it happens to the young and sad when it takes our beloved elderly, but not something to spend one's life contemplating or planning for.

The Church, having lost confidence of its own knowledge of other worlds, other bodies and different layers of reality, no longer seems to operate with clear eschatological horizons either. Few theologians now feel comfortable dealing with life after death because it takes them into the realm of the imagination and therefore out of the realm of social-scientific models of academic credibility. With the exception of the Orthodox funeral rite, contemporary funeral liturgies tend to be full of rather vague hope with, in practice, the primary focus on the life of the deceased and the grief of the bereaved, rather than the dead body in the coffin. The dead can be an embarrassing presence at their own funerals, in some crematoria literally pushed to one side out of the way. Before the terrible void of death we place screens so that we do not have to face the mystery, we resort to easy banality to keep our eyes from straying on to the transcendent and we bury ourselves in our own grief to avoid the obvious questions about mortality.

Yet we will all die, and the Church continues to teach through its creeds and tradition the clear belief that life is not ended, but changed at death. As the woman anointed the body of Jesus in preparation for his death, so the Church, his body, anoints its own for the next stage in the journey into the mystery of God. A properly theological approach to death understands it not as an end but, as Ladislaus Boros put it, a 'metaphysical process' (Boros, 1962, p. 1). For Boros, the moment of death, which is in reality simultaneously the last moment of dying and the first moment after death, is the moment of truth,

> Man's deepest being comes rushing towards him. With it comes all at once and all together the universe he has always borne hidden within himself, the universe with which he was already most intimately united, and which, in one way or another, was always being produced with him.... Being flows towards him like a boundless stream of things, meanings, persons and happenings, ready to convey him right into the Godhead. Yes; God himself stretches out his hand for him. (Boros, 1962, pp. viii–ix)

For Boros, death presents the moment of truth in which the individual has the opportunity to plunge into the mystery of the divine life or to stand on the edge of true existence. The divine and the universe rush towards us like a tidal wave, but we have the freedom to step aside. Boros is clear that this rush of the universe is absolutely inclusive; none are excluded from it. Death is in a real sense sacramental because it involves a real encounter with the Christ for all without exception. Following Boros's thought it is then easy to understand why premodern Christians worried about their death-bed and spent much of their life preparing for it. If the life of the baptized is a constantly tested one, then the death bed was understood to be a moment of supreme testing. In the fifteenth century, *Ars Moriendi* taught that at death the Christian would be haunted by five temptations: the temptation to abandon faith, the temptation to despair, the temptation to be impatient, the temptation to spiritual pride and the temptation to avarice. Antidotes to these temptations were also articulated in the form of faith, hope, patience, humility and generosity. This was the final moment of testing, the moment of truth, the moment for which the baptized had been practising, failing, and recovering all their lives; it was the ultimate test of their identity as people who had already died and risen with Christ.

It is now common to regard our foreparents' ability to live with and confront the reality of death as morbid. The prayers for a happy and good death, the thinking upon the last things as one drifted into sleep, the practice adopted by some religious of sleeping in their shrouds or coffins, the keeping of candles to light at one's death bed are all now regarded as rather unhealthy. We may think that in those days people had to deal with death because it was closer and more common than it is for us (in the contemporary West). But the fact is that we all die, we are all dying, we all reach our *telos* in the divine, and the baptized should know this, embrace it and prepare for it in their lives.

The sacrament of extreme unction fortifies the dying and prepares them for the rush of the cosmos. It does this by reminding them of and sacramentally re-membering their baptismal identity, supplying the food for the journey that is the very life of Christ himself, and by entreating the divine to 'bring it on', to meet the dying. Just as traditionally the vast majority are baptized without their consent because as babies they are incapable of giving it, so traditionally most of those on the point of death in receipt of the sacrament of extreme unction would be passive participants. But that is proper because the self of the baptized is a corporate, not an atomistic self, a self intimately bound up with that of others, part of the group mind, the body of Christ and a self ultimately utterly dependent upon divine grace. This is something Boros failed to emphasize, being rather existentialist in his approach. The final decision we make is not an individual one but a corporate one; we do not make it alone, we make it as members of a body, and it is the whole body that makes the decision in the individual and vice-versa. This is why the body speaks for the child and speaks for the dying.

It is hard to imagine anybody able to resist the rush of the cosmos and therefore it is hard to imagine that anyone will be lost to the life of the divine that encompasses and infuses all that it has made. The baptized, through participation in the sacraments, experience this rush of the divine throughout their lives and hence should be well prepared for the moment of death. The reality of it, one can speculate, will be less of a shock for those who have experienced it in life, and hence the onward journey into the endless of the divine may be in some way different in terms of pace or direction for those who have not had such experiences. But one can speculate that all will go through a purification/purgation in which the white heat of divine love burns off all that may restrict, disorientate or hinder the pilgrim of the heart of God.

In his novel *Easter*, Michael Arditti writes movingly of the death of a young gay man from AIDS from the perspective of all who are gathered around his death bed. In describing the dying man's experiences of the last rites Arditti has him entering into a world that would be highly familiar to Leadbeater and others who are conscious of different layers of reality, a world of auras and colours and music rather than just words:

> The thrill of transformation banishes his fear. His mind is as peaceful as the dove which flutters over him, fanning him with his wings. He has broken all ties with the present. His last words lie sealed against his lips. The people he leaves behind will be coming with him. Nothing is lost . . . Death is the apex of existence. It is the prism for the cosmic radiance which is refracting through his body. It is the forge of the molten stars which are streaming through his blood. He is returning to . . . he is part of . . . he is God. . . . Julian feels the oil spin around him like silk. He watches the words fly about the room like humming birds. His mortal mind makes a final attempt to define . . . to confine his senses as he swept up on the wings of a vast embrace. He has solved the mystery of creation. He is love. He is power. He is.
>
> (Arditti, 2000, pp. 246–53)

Arditti has the dove hover over the dying man as it hovered over Jesus at his baptism. This is a moment at which the dying's identity as a child of God is confirmed, eclipsing and relativizing all other forms of identity. Like Boros, Arditti constructs death as the moment of truth because it is the moment of absorption into the divine mystery. 'Nothing is lost' and hence melancholia no longer has any force. Death is the experience of that which the sacraments mediate, the fullness of the endlessness of the divine life.

The sacrament of extreme unction gives a shape, a form, an art to dying. It helps a person to die and it makes dying a corporate rather than an individual event. Dying is an event about identity, a time, perhaps, of supreme testing when the ties of constructed identity pull particularly tight, when what is required is a surrender to the identity of one sealed with the cross, a surrender to the mystery.

Journeys of any sort always involve risk. The most serious risk of the journey is the risk of getting lost. The risk of the journey of faith is the risk experienced by Jesus, the risk of the loss of a God-given identity in the mire of constructed identities through which we have to tread. Jesus' descent into hell signifies the end of the risk of the permanent loss of such identity, but a temporary loss is a real risk for the individual and for the corporate body, and this is the frightening aspect of discipleship. We may in fact not know when we are lost. We may feel at our most confident when we have strayed furthest from the track. The body as a whole of which we are a part may be temporally lost. Our maps are never entirely accurate. The terrifying realization of the Christian is that this world is both good, a reflection of its creator, the matter through which the Spirit courses, and also the matter in which we can actually lose ourselves and our track of the divine. The sacraments are designed to keep us on track and put us back on that track by reminding us who we really are and reconnecting us to the life of the cosmos. Those in receipt of the sacraments, particularly the sacrament of extreme unction, are right to be confident that when the rush of the universe sweeps over them the discovery of who they really are will not be such a shock as to be a moment of judgement on their lives. For that element of judgement comes with every participation in the sacraments, but for those who die suddenly and unprepared, for those who die without the fortification of the sacraments, there must be an element of unease that must be acknowledged in the funeral rites and not smothered by the cloak of bland hope. In addition, death is fearful because it seems to be what we are entreated to believe it is not: the absolute negation of our existence and the loss of those we love, sometimes in tragic and unfathomable circumstances. There is nothing more dead than a corpse. And whatever we might believe and however powerfully we may believe it, it is still a belief and not certainty, a belief that has to be maintained in the face of the evidence of the eye and heart. The death of another also brings us face to face with our own mortality and that of all that lives and the apparent meaninglessness of existence. Most contemporary funeral liturgies are rightfully (though banally) hopeful but woefully inadequate when it comes to dealing with these other dimensions of death. The exceptions to this trend are the Orthodox Churches, which continue to express in their funeral rites confidence tinged with a fear of being lost. The fear of that loss is particularly focused in the separation of the soul from the body in Orthodox Rites. What is faced is the disintegration of what is commonly supposed to constitute humanity:

> Alas! What an agony the soul endures when from the body it is parting; how many are her tears for weeping, but there is none that will show compassion: unto the angels she turns with downcast eyes; useless are her supplications; and unto men she extends her imploring hands, but finds none to bring her rescue. Thus, my beloved brethren, let us all ponder well how brief is the span of our life; and peaceful rest for him [her] that now is gone. . . . Terror truly past compare is by the mystery of death inspired; now the soul and the body part, disjoined by resistless might, and their concord is broken; and the bond of nature which made them live and grow as one, now by the edict of God is rest in twain. Wherefore now we implore Your aid grant that Your servant now gone to rest where the just that are Yours abide, Life-bestower and Friend of Mankind.
> (<http://www.goarch.org/en/Chapel/liturgical_texts/funeral2.asp>)

In the separation of soul and body we face the fear of loss of identity, as Newman put it so powerfully in *The Dream of Gerontius*:

I can no more; for now it comes again,
That sense of ruin, which is worse than pain,
That masterful negation and collapse
Of all that makes me man; as though I bent
Over the dizzy brink
Of some sheer infinite descent;
(Newman, *The Dream of Gerontius*, 1865)

The Orthodox funeral service manages to hold together and express a sense of that fear with a clear hope in a resurrection in which identity does not rest in earthly constructions. The dead him/herself pleads with the congregation for their prayers as they stand before the judge, 'where no person is valued for his [her] earthly station: Yea, slave and master together stand before Him, king and soldier, rich man and poor man, all accounted of equal rank' (<http://www.goarch.org/en/Chapel/liturgical_texts/funeral2.asp>).

The baptized must die. They must face the test of apparent dissolution. In this sense they are locked into the endless repetition of humanity: we are born, we live and we die, whether that process takes a few minutes or over a century. Death shadows our lives from the moment we are born. In Philip Pullman's *His Dark Materials* trilogy (2001), each person's death is depicted as following them throughout life, ready to step forward and take the person by the hand when it is time for them to cross over. A wise person will face their death and make friends with it in order that when the time comes, the sudden appearance of their death will not be a shock and an opportunity will be given to make it meaningful to oneself and those we leave behind. It is an opportunity to witness to the nature of divine life.

Judith Butler, writing about gender and the way in which gender scripts are written on to our bodies through repetition, noted: 'the task is not whether to repeat, but how to repeat' (Butler, 1990, p. 148). Repetition with critical difference, the essence of parody and camp, is the key to unravelling the scripts, 'queering' the whole construction, which we cannot just step out of. The baptized should die with critical difference. The difference being that they know that death has been defeated. God has embraced death and thereby defeated it. Hell is harrowed into non-existence. As St John Chrysostom put it:

Hell was in an uproar because it was done away with.
It was in an uproar because it is mocked.
It was in an uproar, for it is destroyed.
It is in an uproar, for it is annihilated.
It is in an uproar, for it is now made captive.

Hell took a body, and discovered God.
It took earth, and encountered Heaven.
It took what it saw, and was overcome by what it did not see.

(St John Chrysostom, Easter Sermon, c. 400 CE)

Whatever death now involves it does not herald the absence of God, the source of life, for there is now no place where God is not. Death is not in dualistic relationship to life any more than male is to female; in fact both death and life are deconstructed in the blaze of resurrection. In the resurrection, God overwhelms death with life, but he does so as a mortal human being. We all know that there is something about death that is sticky, the death of one recalls the death of another, and as we move through life the ball of grief gets larger, a heavy weight upon our souls. To Christ attached the stickiness of all human death, grief and sin. It was not just that God defeated death but that God did so in human flesh, and this has profound implications for flesh itself. It bursts from the tomb, the same but different, a flesh no longer meant for oblivion. Christians die, their bodies wear out or fall vulnerable to disease or violence, but a Christian death is a death with critical difference. For the Christian, death no longer promises or threatens oblivion, the absence of God, it does not even threaten the end of bodiliness, but rather death becomes a physical experience/encounter with the divine.

The baptized die but that is all they do for death; they are not consumed by death, they die to enter life. Hence the baffling longing of figures such as Ignatius of Antioch and countless martyrs through the ages for death. In embracing death martyrs queered it, performing it subversively in order to point to its defeat. This queer performance begins at the resurrection and reverberates across the cosmos. With the end of the dualism between life and death comes the end of the dualisms of gender and sexual orientation, the dualisms of race and class. The Church is mandated as the body of Christ to live out this new reality in the midst of a world still being born into it.

The Christian performance of death

How Christians perform death is therefore important as a witness against the dominant constructions of death. An understanding of dying as a moment of radical transition that has some risk attached to it should result in a dying/deceased-oriented approach to death. We would again prepare for death as we do for the other sacraments and transitions in our lives, and we would seek to do so consciously and deliberately. The sacrament of unction/extreme unction would be sought to assist the dying, the eucharistic experience of the heavenly liturgy would be embraced as a foretaste of what is to come. Funerals would be about the dead, not the pain of the living, and be a conscious effort on behalf of the body of Christ to assist its members in their movement from one stage of Christian life to another. This is made clear in the Liberal Catholic Burial of the Dead, where Leadbeater charged the congregation to 'think not of ourselves but of him/her', and prayed that, 'Our loving thought shall follow and surround him/her; O take thou this our gift of thought, imperfect though it may be and touch it with the eternal fire of thy love, so that it may become for him/her a guardian angel to help him/her on his/her upward way' (Leadbeater, 1983, pp. 343; 348). The last rites and funeral would be understood as a great ecclesial work of committal and commendation, a work of witness on behalf of the body for one of its members to aid him/her on their journey. The dead are not dead to the Church, they remain part of the living body on a different stage of the journey. The baptized follow the same pattern as the Christ: in baptism they die and rise again, they then continue on their journey of ascension towards the endlessness of God. They are never out of our reach and never closer to us than in the celebration of the heavenly liturgy of the Eucharist.

Catholic Christianity has always prayed for the dead. The rationale for such prayer eventually developed into a complicated system of post-mortem satisfaction that the Reformation rightly critiqued. But that critique was itself flawed in that it led to a hard distinction and barrier being drawn between the living and the dead and a flattening out of the Christian pilgrimage into earthly life alone. Catholic Christianity has constructed the onward journeying of the dead in terms of a time of purgation sometimes represented in terms of fire, sometimes, as in the *Dream of Gerontius*, as waters, sometimes, as in Dante's *Divine Comedy*, as a green, jovial ascent of healing, of recovery of one's true identity as a child of God through a purgation of that which masks it (Dante, 1974). In that sense purgatory is a continuation of the sacrament of unction and part of the journey into the divine life, not to be feared, but anticipated with hope and joy. And therefore it is appropriate that those in that state should be sustained, encouraged and nourished by the prayers of the Church as they have been throughout their pilgrimage thus far. Between the dead and the living, there is no between.

In *Brideshead Revisited*, Evelyn Waugh describes the deathbed of Lord Marchmain and the struggle that goes on in the minds of his family and in his own person over reception of the last rites. Some object to 'witchcraft and hypocrisy' and the dying first sends the priest away in anger. Charles Ryder, the narrator of the story, remarks to the doctor that Marchmain has a wonderful will to live. The doctor counters that he has, rather, a great fear of death, a fear that is wearing him out (Waugh, 1962, p. 316). But in the end the priest is brought to him and asks the now unconscious Marchmain for a sign of his repentance. The atheist Ryder finds himself praying to a God he does not believe in for the forgiveness of the man's sins and for a sign from the man himself that he has accepted that forgiveness. The priest anoints with oil and Marchmain makes the sign of the cross, 'Then I knew that the sign I had asked for was not a little thing, not a pass nod of recognition, and a phrase came back to me from my childhood of the veil of the temple being rent from top to bottom' (Waugh, 1962, p. 322).

What Ryder had witnessed was the power of the sacrament of unction, in this case *in extremis*, to enable the baptized to recover their true identity even when it appeared to have been overwritten by a lifetime of alternative scripts. Marchmain makes the sign of the cross. Death and resurrection are written onto the bodies of Christians because their bodies have been incorporated into and are shaped by that drama. It is because of that drama that death is not the last but the first thing for a Christian, and dying is not consumption but a birth into a changed life. The radical discontinuity that is at the root of all fear of death has already been experienced in baptism, and the identity that emerges from this *aporia* is constantly tested, perhaps especially in illness and in dying. The sacrament of unction re-members the recipient's baptism and reorients them as the woman reoriented Christ in the last week of his life. Like all the sacraments, it provides an experience of the rush of the divine life into which we are plunged at death, its very extravagance re-enchanting our lives and relativizing all other forms of identity.

References

Arditti, M., *Easter*. Arcadia Books, London, 2000.

Ariès, P., *The Hour of Our Death*. Oxford University Press, Oxford, 1991.

Boros, L., *The Moment of Truth: Mysterium Mortis*. Burns and Oates, London, 1962.

Butler, J., *Gender Trouble: Feminism and the Subversion of Identity*. Routledge, New York, 1990.

Butler, J., *The Psychic Life of Power*. Stanford University Press, Stanford, 1997.

Dante, A., *Divine Comedy*. Vols 1–3. Penguin, Harmondsworth, 1974.

Goss, R., *Jesus Acted Up: A Gay and Lesbian Manifesto*. HarperSanFrancisco, San Francisco, 1993.

Hollenbach, P., 'Jesus, Demoniacs, and Public Authorities: A Socio-Historical Study', *Journal of the American Academy of Religion*. 49, Oxford University Press, Oxford, 1981, pp. 567–88.

Leadbeater, C. W., *The Science of the Sacraments*. The Theosophical Publishing House, Adyar, 1920.

Leadbeater, C. W., *The Liturgy of the Liberal Catholic Church*. (5th edn), St Alban Press, London, 1983.

Newman, J. H., *The Dream of Gerontius*, 1865. Available at <http://www.newmanreader.org/works/verses/gerontius.html>.

Pullman, P., *His Dark Materials Trilogy*. Scholastic Press, London, 2001.

St John Chrysostom, *Easter Sermon*. c. 400 CE. Available at <http://www.fordham.edu/halsall/source/chrysostom-easter.html>.

Waugh, E., *Brideshead Revisited*. Penguin, Harmondsworth, 1962.

11

Spiritual intelligence and the person-centred therapist

BRIAN THORNE

————◾◆◾————

Echoing the 'mystical' theme of Elizabeth Stuart's chapter, but exploring it from the perspective of person-centred therapy, Brian Thorne develops the notion of 'spiritual intelligence' and its relevance for both secular and Christian healing ministries. Thorne brings this definition to life by weaving Zohar's and Marshall's reflections on 'spiritual intelligence' with his early childhood experiences during World War II. He follows this with a critique of current trends within contemporary counselling and psychotherapy, and contrasts these with his own understanding of person-centred therapy as a 'spiritual discipline'. Ultimately, Thorne argues for a therapeutic approach that acknowledges the 'primacy of love' as a transformative power within the world.

* * *

Holy Rood House, with which it is my privilege to have been associated for many years, is a place where I have always experienced a freedom of mind and spirit that is rare for a practising person-centred therapist who is also a committed member of an institutional church. All too often I have found myself caught in the cross-fire between traditional Christians on the one hand and secular, church-hating humanistic therapists on the other. At Holy Rood it has been possible to breathe a different air where psychology and theology, therapy and pastoral care, experiential knowledge and empirical research embrace each other in the impassioned quest for new forms of healing for wounded souls. In what follows, as I explore the concept of Spiritual Intelligence, I am conscious that those who work at Holy Rood House and those who stay there will have little difficulty in recognizing its relevance to all that takes place within the nurturing environment that this remarkable sanctuary provides.

It was in 2000 that the term 'spiritual intelligence' first captured the popular imagination with the appearance of a book of that title by Danah Zohar and Ian Marshall. Zohar was already well-known as the author of *The Quantum Self*, but this new book broke fresh ground. At the beginning of the new millennium Zohar and Marshall purported to show that a formidable array of recent but largely undigested scientific data powerfully suggested that there was a third 'Q' to complete the trinity of intellectual intelligence and the more recently discovered emotional intelligence popularized by Daniel Goleman (Goleman, 1996). Emotional intelligence, you will remember, gives us an awareness of our own and other people's feelings. In some ways it is the fundamental pragmatic intelligence of the person-centred therapist for it gives us empathy, deep compassion and the motivational capacity to respond appropriately to pain or pleasure. What's more, as Goleman pointed out, emotional intelligence is an essential requirement for the proper use of IQ. Neuroscientists and psychologists had demonstrated that if the brain areas with which we *feel* are damaged or impaired, we think much less clearly and effectively. Now, however, Zohar and Marshall make the claim that the full picture of human intelligence needs to be completed by the third 'Q' – spiritual intelligence. In the introduction to their book they offer a succinct definition of this third intelligence. It is, they claim,

> the intelligence with which we address and solve problems of meaning and value, the intelligence with which we can place our actions and our lives in a wider, richer, meaning-giving context, the intelligence with which we can assess that one course of action or one life-path is more meaningful than another. SQ is the necessary foundation for the effective functioning of both IQ and EQ. It is our ultimate intelligence.
>
> (Zohar and Marshall, 2000, pp. 3–4)

A little later in their introductory chapter, Zohar and Marshall spell out the characteristics of a person who has a highly developed spiritual intelligence, and as I list these characteristics you might like to recall Carl Rogers' famous characteristics of the 'Person of Tomorrow' (cf. Rogers, 1989).

The indications of a highly developed spiritual intelligence include, then

- the capacity to be flexible (actively and spontaneously adaptive)
- a high degree of self-awareness
- a capacity to face and use suffering
- a capacity to face and transcend pain
- the quality of being inspired by vision and values
- a reluctance to cause unnecessary harm
- a tendency to see the connections between diverse things (being 'holistic')
- a marked tendency to ask 'Why?' or 'What if?' questions and to seek 'fundamental' answers
- being what psychologists call 'field-independent' – possessing a facility for working against convention
  A person high in SQ is also likely to be a servant leader – someone who is responsible for bringing higher vision and value to others and showing them how to use it, in other words a person who inspires others.

(Zohar and Marshall, 2000, pp. 15–16)

Before I launch out on my own autobiographical experience let me tell you something more about Danah Zohar. Halfway through the book, Zohar, while acknowledging how painful and risky it is, shares personal material from which her work is drawn. She describes her 'annus horribilis' during which, despite her already established fame as a writer and lecturer, she descends into a pit of despair and alcohol abuse. She is on the verge of disintegration when she finally consults a therapist. She undertakes a painful exploration of her family history, its oppressive conditions of worth and episodes of violence and drug abuse. More particularly she confronts the relationship with her father who had left the family when she was five and had become the family 'shadow', to be repressed and forgotten. The details of Zohar's personal odyssey are perhaps unimportant. What matters is her struggle with pain and potential disintegration, her work in therapy and her eventual emergence into hope and new life. After a particularly telling dream she writes: '[I was] left with a visceral sense of deep spontaneity, a deep sense that there was an active centre within that bestowed grace.' And a little later, as she reflects on her pilgrimage through pain: 'When we are using our spiritual intelligence we are seeing things from the centre. We are putting feelings and events in an ever wider context, relating things that had seemed separate, seeing and creating relationships and patterns' (Zohar and Marshall, 2000, p. 191).

It does not take much imagination for a person-centred therapist to see in this account the gradual reconnection with the actualizing tendency and the establishment of a locus of evaluation that is thoroughly internalized and has become the firm reference point for establishing meaning and integrity. What is new is the description of this process as a spiritual journey and the portrayal of spiritual intelligence as the faculty which, once enlivened, can heal the wounds that cut us off from the deep centre of ourselves through fragmentation, one-sidedness, pain or obstruction and then cast an inner light that illuminates the path to wholeness and meaning. Perhaps it is not surprising that later in their book Zohar and Marshall speak of Carl Rogers with deep respect and appreciation. But more of that anon.

I want now to come at our theme from a different angle – namely from that of my own experience. I am currently trying to write my own life-story – the result of an invitation from an intrepid publisher who seems to believe that there are enough people out there wanting to know about the life of Brian to make this a commercially viable venture. It is not an undertaking I would recommend. Since last autumn I have been in a state of almost permanent self-analysis, and although this has its joyful, even ecstatic moments, there are many other memories that stir up old pains and conflicts. One thing, however, is clear, and that is the singular importance of the interweaving of experiences in my early childhood during World War II in Bristol. It is to those that I now wish to turn as I give you an extract from the first draft of Chapter One of my work in progress.

> Chappells grocer's shop, as I remember it, was a rather dark place although the assistants were always friendly and, despite the wartime shortages, my mother usually managed to find what she needed. It was also something of a community centre and the women of the district would congregate there to exchange gossip. A little later on in the war, when the American servicemen had arrived on the scene, Chappells also became the place for swapping scandal about illicit amorous activities in the neighbour-hood. My mother was to have her own contribution to make to

these stories when our home became the temporary refuge for a series of American soldiers. Victor, of Italian descent, seemed to attract many of the prettiest young women, most of whom my mother feigned to despise. I recall with most pleasure a fat, red-faced sergeant who seemed to have an endless supply of large bars of dark, delicious chocolate with which he quickly won my affection. The day I saw her, however, preceded the arrival of the Americans and I can only imagine that the subject of my mother's conversation at that time was of insufficient interest to capture the imagination of a four and a half year old. My attention was elsewhere and I was staring at the glass-panelled door of the shop, perhaps to see if it had begun to snow again.

What happened next has remained imprinted on my memory for sixty-two years. I do not know if it was 'real', 'imagined', a 'fantasy', a 'dream', an 'hallucination'. All I do know is that I remember it still and that it entered the core of my being and lodged there. It was and is a milestone in the journey of a soul.

As I stared at the shop door I became gradually aware of a figure standing outside. At first there seemed nothing exceptional about this occurrence and, in any case, I could not see clearly because of condensation on the glass. Nonetheless my gaze remained fixed on the door as if some sixth sense compelled me to keep watching. Whether the condensation cleared I do not know but, within a minute or two, the figure outside became increasingly visible. Framed in the glass panel, almost like a photographic model, there stood a little girl dressed in a white coat with a fluffy hat perched somewhat jauntily on her head. Her beauty was spell-binding and the feelings I experienced in that moment can never be expressed for no adequate words were available to a child of four and a half. Certainly I was transfixed, unable to move, unable to speak. My adult mind tells me that if I had died in that moment I should not have noticed for I was already in heaven. Much later I was to study the poetry of William Wordsworth and knew what he meant when he wrote that 'Heaven lies about us in our infancy'. And then the little girl smiled at me and waved. As if awoken from a trance, I tugged at my mother's arm and pleaded with her to stop her chatter and come home. Reluctantly she allowed herself to be dragged to the door and as she opened it I ran out into the street. The little girl was nowhere to be seen. Only her smile continued to accompany me as we made our way home beneath a threatening sky. I never saw her again.

Dante met Beatrice when he was nine and she remained a source of inspiration throughout his life and, if we are to believe him, into eternity. My little girl with the fluffy hat is, I suppose, my Beatrice.

And then, second, a brief extract from the Introduction to *Behold The Man*, which was published in 1991. The terrible World War II had only recently ended – a time when for me as a child there had always been the possibility of instant death as a result of the incessant air raids on my home city of Bristol.

> Good Friday 1946 found me playing cricket in a Bristol park which was still full of air-raid shelters and all the bric-a-brac of war. Suddenly there appeared in the street at the side of the park a procession of witness headed by a crucifer, candle bearers and a thurifer swinging a censer. The effect on me was instantaneous. I left my friends, ran all the way home and shut myself in my bedroom and sobbed for what seemed like hours. In the midst of this overwhelming distress I encountered the living Jesus and from that day until this I have had an unshakeable conviction that love is the primary force in the universe no matter how great the evidence may seem to the contrary. Looking back on it, the events of that Good Friday afternoon probably determined the direction of my life because they impinged on me at so many different levels. In the first place the initial incident was visually stupendous: the contrast between the solemn beauty of the procession and the barrenness of the park still ravaged by war could not have been greater. Secondly, the experience established in a moment an order of values. I suppose I felt mildly guilty that I was playing cricket on Good Friday but the main feeling was one of quite overwhelming gratitude that I could be so incredibly loved. In that moment I knew that in the last analysis all that matters is loving and being loved. I also knew that the love I had experienced brought with it a sense of being fully and profoundly understood. It followed therefore that to love in this way must involve the deepest commitment to understanding. I have since discovered that love devoid of understanding, although it can bring comfort and solace, can never heal. Thirdly, the incident endowed me with an intoxicating sense of my own unique value. At a wholly conscious level I knew that something special had happened to me which I would never be able to deny or eradicate.
>
> (Thorne, 1991, pp. 5–6)

I shall return to these two pivotal incidents later, but first a comment on the appearance of Carl Rogers in Zohar's and Marshall's book. In the thirteenth chapter they explore six paths towards greater spiritual intelligence and make the point that during a lifetime an individual's main spiritual path may change according to personality, circumstances or the ageing process. All six paths may therefore have their contribution to make to an individual's spiritual development but it is likely that one will have the primacy for at least a good part of the journey. The second path Zohar and Marshall identify is that of the 'Path of Nurturing'. This path is 'about loving, nurturing, protecting and making fertile', and those who follow it, Zohar and Marshall inform us, 'are likely to include therapists, counsellors, social workers and saints'. To the spiritual aspirant on this path Zohar and Marshall have this to say:

> To become more spiritually intelligent on the path of nurturing we must be more open to the person or people with whom we are in a caring relationship. We must learn to be receptive and to listen well with our true selves. We must be willing to be open, to be exposed, to take the risk of self-disclosure to others.
>
> (Zohar and Marshall, 2000, p. 237)

And then, less than a page later, Carl Rogers is introduced as providing a powerful example of precisely this kind of spiritual intelligence. The point is made with a telling quotation from *On Becoming a Person*.

> How can I provide a relationship which this person may use for his own personal growth? No approach which relies upon knowledge, upon training, upon the acceptance of something that is *taught*, is of any use. The more that I can be genuine in the relationship, the more helpful it will be. It is only by providing the genuine reality which is in me, that the other person can successfully seek for the reality in him. The relationship is significant to the extent that I feel a continuing desire to understand. There is also a complete freedom from any type of moral or diagnostic evaluation.   (Rogers, cited Zohar and Marshall, 2000, p. 238)

The fact that Rogers is seen as so exemplary a representative of the spiritual seeker would perhaps have surprised him at the time that he wrote *On Becoming a Person*, for during that period he was keenly embracing the role of the psychologist and empirical scientist and, if we are to believe those close to him, was unwilling to discuss religion or spiritual matters at all, presumably because they stirred up for him too many painful memories of his Christian upbringing and subsequent exploration of Christian ministry. With the appearance in 1980, however, of *A Way of Being*, we find Rogers prepared to use words such as 'spiritual, mystical and transcendent' of his experiences with individuals and in groups and, as I recall the man with whom I had lengthy conversations in 1979, I do not believe that by then he would have found it altogether inappropriate or puzzling to be quoted in a book on spiritual intelligence. Indeed, it could justifiably be claimed that much of the content of *A Way of Being* is directly concerned with spiritual reality.

If Zohar and Marshall unhesitatingly claim Rogers as a spiritual traveller this is perhaps provocative enough, but they do not stop there. The passage from *On Becoming a Person* is followed by a startling statement: 'Rogers' vision is a secular version of St Paul's famous definition of love in the New Testament.' And we are then given a direct quotation from the famous passage in 1 Corinthians 13 so much beloved by men and women on their wedding day throughout the centuries:

> And though I bestow all my goods to feed the poor, and though I give my body to be burned, and have not love, it profits me nothing.
> Love suffers long, and is kind: love envies not; love vaunts not itself, is not puffed up.
> Doth not behave itself unseemly, seeks not her own, is not easily provoked, thinks no evil;
> Rejoices not in iniquity, but rejoices in the truth;
> Love bears all things, believes all things, hopes all things, endures all things.
> Love never fails.
> (1 Corinthians 13.4–8; cited Zohar and Marshall, 2000, p. 238)

Zohar and Marshall are not as far as I know psychotherapists. Their concern was to write a book about spiritual intelligence and yet in their chapter on the Six Spiritual Paths, Rogers is the only psychotherapist to be quoted – interestingly the transpersonal therapists do not get a look in and even Jung gets only a passing mention. I believe that Zohar and Marshall have – perhaps unwittingly – put their finger on the essential truth about both the originator of person-centred therapy and the practice of that therapy as I have come to know it.

This leads immediately to reflections about the current state of counselling and psychotherapy in Britain. In brief, I am disenchanted. I perceive power-struggles, rampant competitiveness and many vested interests. Of course, much has happened in recent years to improve the quality of training, to enhance the capacities of therapists, to raise standards of professional and ethical practice. All of that is wholly admirable, but sadly it would seem that we are now caught in the conflicting interests of government departments, not least in so far as financial underpinning is concerned. And we are trapped in a culture that in its obsession with accountability, attaching blame and avoiding risk makes it increasingly difficult for therapists to have the confidence to be creative and to respond to the deepest needs of many of their clients. The fear of over-involvement, for example, has led in many instances to a culpable underinvolvement. Much the same can be said of other caring professions where practitioners, as well as being deprived of the essential core of the work to which they felt originally called, are increasingly burdened with regulations, administrative procedures and unrealistic outcome requirements. The fallout from the teaching, social work and medical professions in recent years, for example, has been nothing short of disastrous, and even the ranks of the clergy have been depleted by burn-out, breakdown and premature retirement. I am not for one moment suggesting that there are not still many committed and deeply caring therapists in the ranks of all the therapeutic orientations but, for me, it becomes increasingly evident that the recent development of our profession and the historical context in which we find ourselves do not bode well for the emergence of therapists who can respond to the needs of a desperate and broken world.

In what I am about to say I am very conscious that not all person-centred practitioners would construe the challenges facing our orientation in the same way. At the level of professional credibility and survival there is for many of them the challenge of how to position ourselves in what one might term the battle of the orientations or, viewed from another angle, how to be loved by those who hold the purse-strings. The temptation here is to capitulate to the contemporary Zeitgeist and to attempt to play the cognitive behavioural therapists at their own game – to show that we can do all the things they do and perhaps do them even better. We can devise treatment plans, achieve goals, provide short-term therapy with the best of them and through our research and practice show government that we are just as worthy of their respect and funding as the most effective cognitive behaviourist. The irony of this temptation is that there is a sense in which we can succumb to it with integrity. We are not by definition opposed to setting goals if that is what the client wishes; we can certainly do excellent short-term work if, again, the client is wanting that; research strongly suggests that person-centred therapy is admirably effective with anxiety and depressive states and even with psychotic episodes – we can, if you like, rival cognitive behavioural therapy and come through with flying colours. But is that what we really wish to do? Perhaps our survival as an orientation demands such a strategy and I have great sympathy with those who embrace it and expend enormous energy marketing our approach in this way. I fully commend, too, those throughout Europe who are endeavouring to undertake research that will convince the faceless ones for whom so-called empirically validated approaches are the only ones for which they are prepared to open the state coffers. My great fear, however, is that in this attempt to 'play them at their own game' where 'them' means behavioural approaches, medical approaches or funding bodies, we lose our own souls and in the process deny prospective clients the essence of our approach. The legacy we have been left is an approach that majors in respect for the individual and his or her experience, in the centrality of relationship and perhaps above all in a way of being that acknowledges the interconnectedness of all things. It is – put somewhat differently – a functional philosophy that offers meaning and purpose and is based on the primacy of love in the evolution of the human person and of our global heritage. For better or worse that is the kind of mast to which I have attempted to nail my colours for at least the last decade. What is more, I believe that the time is approaching when the yearning for such an approach – couched in precisely these terms – will become almost universal. As I have watched and often been involved in the development of counselling and psychotherapy in our own country, I have seen the insidious advance of professionalization in a culture that threatens to stifle creativity and could well lead

eventually to a craven sterility, a fear of risk-taking and a protect-
ive self-interest masquerading as a concern for the well-being
of clients. I may, of course, be quite wrong and in some ways I
hope I am, but the signs for me are ominous. If I am right, then
counselling and psychotherapy will gradually die because they
will manifestly no longer meet the needs of a twenty-first century
that has much greater and more desperate concerns – namely
how to remain human and how to know what it means to be
fully alive in a world poised on the brink of disaster.

For me, then, the task is not how to convince others that
person-centred therapy warrants state approval (although, of
course, it does) but how to respond to the challenge Carl
Rogers' later work has left us. How to be a force *in the world*
not only in our consulting rooms but on the broader canvas?
And what does it mean to acknowledge that person-centred
therapy is essentially a spiritual discipline that gives access to
the transcendent? How can I be more fully present to myself and
to others so that miracles of transformation can occur? How can
I have confidence in my own way of being in the world without succumbing to arrogance or self-deception? These are the
questions with which I wrestle and they have engendered many
different developments in my own life and practice.

The conceptualization of person-centred therapy as a spiritual
discipline has led me to take with the utmost seriousness what
it means as a therapist to be spiritually disciplined. More particularly it has led me to focus on what it means to be truly self-
loving as opposed to self-centred, what it means to love the other
whether client, friend, lover or stranger in the street, what it
entails to cherish the created order of which I am a part and
what it means to believe in a God, a Higher Power or in the benevolence of the Cosmos. Clearly for me, as a life-long Christian,
this exploration of the therapist's spiritual discipline has meant
an ever-deepening understanding of my own religion and
spiritual tradition and how this nourishes – or impedes – my
task as a therapist. None of this work has been easy and indeed
in some instances it has proved costly and painful. In church
and theological circles I have sometimes been bitterly attacked
as some kind of dangerous heretic, and in the therapeutic world
I have been accused of irresponsibility and foolhardiness and an
inability to live in the real world.

So let me end by returning to those two pivotal experiences from my childhood. Perhaps the implications of the Good Friday episode in 1946 are the more obvious. So much suffering and anguish in the world, I am convinced, spring from self-loathing and self-denigration. It is well-nigh impossible for the person who hates or even simply dislikes himself or herself to be truly affirming of others or to respond to the world with hope let alone with joy. The person-centred approach majors in the subjective world of the client and most particularly in the creation of a climate where the client can begin to experience himself or herself as a person of value who is deeply worthy of respect. In brief, person-centred therapy offers a path along which the client can travel from self-denigration to self-affirmation, from despair to hope. Such a path has universal application. We person-centred therapists are the guardians of a process through which men and women can discover their essential wonder and belovedness – and so often we forget the transformational potency of the treasure we possess.

The story of my meeting with my Beatrice, the little girl in the fluffy hat is, I believe, more complex in its hidden meaning and it is only in the writing of this chapter that I believe I have stumbled on its full significance. I have been aided by recently re-reading some of the work of the extraordinary priest–scientist, Father Pierre Teilhard de Chardin, one of Carl Rogers' heroes, who is enjoying something of a comeback after being a vogue figure in the 1960s. In a book entitled *Toward the Future*, published in 1973 nearly 20 years after his death, Teilhard has a remarkable essay on 'The Evolution of Chastity'. In it he talks about the transformation of love and says, disarmingly, that theoretically the transformation of love is quite possible. All that is needed, he suggests, is that the pull of the divine centre be felt with sufficient force to dominate the natural biological and sexual attraction that tends to cause pairs of human monads to rush prematurely into each other's arms and into each other's beds. Almost immediately he acknowledges that 90 per cent of his readers will perceive this idea as wildly absurd. Surely, he says wryly, universal experience has shown conclusively that spiritual loves have always ended in grossness. I have heard just such comments whenever I have suggested that in therapy – and particularly in person-centred therapy – a relationship can develop where the deepest love is experienced between therapist and client, which transcends the physical and the sexual and moves on to a plane where healing forces of great potency are released and the interconnectedness of all things is experienced. Such talk seems far removed from the notion of therapy as a science until we remember, of course, that the boundaries of scientific knowledge have been extended beyond all expectation in recent years, not least by the new physics, as Rogers correctly predicted they would be. Why should the transformation of love not be susceptible to scientific enquiry and scientific understanding? Carl Rogers the mystic and empirical scientist would surely have rejoiced to see the day on which that became possible.

Back to my Beatrice in the fluffy hat. I am suggesting that somehow that early childhood experience with all its intensity and yearning pointed to the possibility of a transformational love that can irradiate the world. What nonsense, I can hear some readers say – Thorne has now gone completely over the top or descended into farcical fantasy. And then Teilhard de Chardin – who incidentally was beset by a great deal of anxiety, questioning and self-doubt – comes to my rescue. Let me conclude with his words:

> Surely universal experience has shown conclusively that spiritual loves have always ended in grossness? The human being is made to walk with feet on the ground. Has anyone ever had the idea of flying?
>
> Yes, I shall answer: some mad people have had such a dream, and that is why we have today conquered the skies. What paralyses life is lack of faith and lack of audacity. The difficulty lies not in solving problems but in identifying them. And so we cannot avoid this conclusion: it is biologically evident that to gain control of passion and so make it serve spirit must be a condition of progress. Sooner or later then, the world will brush aside our incredulity and take this step: because whatever is the more true comes out into the open, and whatever is better is ultimately realised.
>
> The day will come when, after harnessing the ether, the winds, the tides, gravitation, we shall harness for God the energies of love. And, on that day, for the second time in the history of the world, human beings will have discovered fire.
>
> (Teilhard de Chardin, 1973, pp. 85–7)

It is my hope and my belief that person-centred therapy points along the road to that discovery and that therein lies its true significance at this time in the history of humankind.

References

Goleman, D., *Emotional Intelligence*. Bloomsbury, London, 1996.

Rogers, C., *On Becoming a Person*. Houghton Mifflin, Boston, 1961.

Rogers, C., *A Way of Being*. Houghton Mifflin, Boston, 1980.

Rogers, C., *Carl Rogers – Dialogues: Conversations with Martin Buber, Paul Tillich, B. F. Skinner, Gregory Bateson, Michael Polanyi, Rollo May, and others*. H. Kirkschenbaum and V. L. Henderson (eds), Houghton Mifflin, Boston, 1989.

Teilhard de Chardin, P., *Toward the Future*. William Collins Sons and Co. Ltd., London, 1975.

Thorne, B., *Behold The Man*. Darton, Longman & Todd, London, 1991.

Zohar, D., *The Quantum Self*. Flamingo/HarperCollins, London, 1990.

Zohar, D. and Marshall, I., *Spiritual Intelligence: The Ultimate Intelligence*. Bloomsbury, London, 2000.

This is an abridged and amended version of the Mary Kilborn Memorial Lecture originally given in the University of Strathclyde in May, 2004. Thanks are extended to the Lecture's organizing committee for permission to reproduce it here and particularly to Professor Dave Mearns, formerly Director of the Counselling Unit at Strathclyde. Mary Kilborn was a prominent and much-loved person-centred therapist who died in 2000.

12

The wounds that sing: music as transformation

JUNE BOYCE-TILLMAN

'Words divide but sounds unite.' That is the challenge of June Boyce-Tillman as she explores the healing power of music in our lives. This she does by outlining a 'dynamic model of self in society', where healing is defined as the restoration of wholeness and where the flow between dualities – 'disembodiment/embodiment', 'unity/diversity', 'public/private', 'challenge/nurture', 'community/individualism' – is 'restored to fluidity and dynamism'. Taking each duality in turn, Boyce-Tillman shows how music can be used to rebalance our society, including our understanding of theology and health, and so create 'the possibility of transformed and strengthened living'.

* * *

Introduction

Inside all of us, there is a musician trying to get out. That musician is our own healer and potentially, through us, a healer of others. It is a crucial player in the game of divine redemption that takes place within each of us. One of the central strands in Christian theology is redemption. The crucifixion/resurrection story tells us that the greatest damage that human beings can inflict can ultimately be transformed.

This chapter will set out a model of disease as imbalance – within society, within the self, within the wider cosmos. Many theologians, including medieval figures such as Hildegard of Bingen, have seen redemption as the restoration of right relationship between the different parts of the cosmos. Pain can be regarded as cracks in a fabric that needs a right relatedness. The disjunctions are the wounds – personal, cultural and cosmic.

Splits in Western society – disembodiment/embodiment

Western society is plagued by dualisms, and many of these can be traced to the development of Christian theology. The body/soul split developed with such figures as Augustine, drawing on the Greek philosophies of figures like Plato, and it is frequently addressed by feminist theologians. The Enlightenment added a third element that could be split off – the mind or intellect. Few other human societies have achieved such an effective split between these elements. And yet the result of the flow among these three elements is true wisdom; indeed, it is the essence of incarnational theology – that at the heart of Christianity is a God who can become human.

The consequences for life in Western cultures have been considerable, and these have been inflicted on cultures to whom they are absolutely foreign. Manual labour is now split from white and blue collar labour. One uses the bodies of people as if they had no minds, the other the mind as if it had no body. The excesses of asceticism are to be found in the stories of many medieval mystics and are now counterbalanced by the pornographic concern with the body (now minus mind and spirit) of the secular world.[1] However, the development of Protestantism undoubtedly helped to widen the split further. As the sensuousness of Roman Catholicism with its visual images, its sweet-smelling incense, its array of bodily gestures and variety of musics was systematically dismantled, the experience of God came to be located purely in the mind, and spirit and worship became denuded of symbols that involved the rest of the body.

This has caused some feminist thinkers to rethink notions of transcendence or disembodiment. Jantzen retains a notion of transcendence to prevent 'reduction' of an embodied God into mere physiology (Jantzen, 1995, p. 127), while Heyward argues for a notion of relationality rather than metaphysical distance by using the 'trans' of transcendence as a movement 'across' rather than 'out of' (Heyward, 1989).

Music offers a great possibility for the uniting of body and soul. It is a physical, mental and spiritual activity (Boyce-Tillman, 2001-a). Brendan Doyle describes the physical effects of singing the chants of Hildegard of Bingen; when they are sung, the control of the breath required to manage the long phrases is seen as a meditation associated with the Holy Spirit (Doyle, in Fox (ed.), 1987, p. 364).

It is in the alliance of music and dance that we see a clear example of the blend of body and soul. In traditional societies the close relationship of dance to music-making has meant that the bodily aspects of music-making are more self-evident. The circle dance has become popular as a way of cementing group cohesion in liturgies such as those practised at Holy Rood House.

The rediscovery of drumming has also helped people to rediscover the embodiment of performance. A student from a largely Western classical background after a concert of African drumming said to me, 'At first I hated it. I found it strange, different and fought the power of the drums. Eventually, I yielded to their power and I found my whole body taken over by the drums so that they seemed to play my body. Then I never wanted them to stop.'[2]

Transcendence in the sense of connection to the divine or spiritual was present in the thinking of the earliest Western philosophers of music. In the hands of the philosophers of the Enlightenment the link between music and the spiritual became weakened and the search for the spiritual that had characterized the musical tradition for hundreds of years became an essentially human search (Argyle, 2000). The notion of transcendence as part of self-actualization leads people to regard the musical experience as the last remaining place for the spiritual in Western society (Hay, 1982). Now transcendence is often dissociated from a religious tradition or a spiritual frame and linked with the stuff of the universe that links it with theologians like Hildegard:

> No one knows what music is. It is performed, listened to, composed, and talked about; but its essential reality is as little understood as that of its cousin, electricity. We know it detaches the understanding, enabling thoughts to turn inward upon themselves and clarify; we know that it releases the human spirit

into some solitude of meditation where the creative process can freely act; we know that it can soothe pain, relieve anxiety, comfort distress, exhilarate health, confirm courage, inspire clear and bold thinking, ennoble the will, refine taste, uplift the heart, stimulate intellect, and do many another interesting and beautiful thing. And yet, when all is said and done, no one knows what music is. Perhaps the explanation is that music is the very stuff of creation itself.

(Lucien Price, cited Exley, 1991, no page numbers)

Ways of knowing

The discussion of the resolution of this crucial dualism, which at its best incarnational theology resolves, starts to explore the philosophies that underpin this chapter. The thesis that underpins my argument is that of the social construction of knowledge based on such theorists as Foucault (Foucault/Gordon, 1980). In an increasing movement in the early twenty-first century, the West is endeavouring to restore a rift that has developed in its intensely rationalistic culture. Gooch (1972) defines two systems of thought, both of which co-exist in the human personality and have the potential for development. The favoured characteristics of one system (System A) are

- activity leading to products
- objectivity
- impersonal logic
- thinking and thought
- detachment
- discrete categories of knowledge that is based on proof and scientific evidence.

The other system (System B) favours

- being
- subjectivity
- personal feeling
- emotion
- magic
- involvement
- associative ways of knowing
- belief and non-causal knowledge.

Gooch suggests that the Western world has chosen the first of these value systems. The second has therefore become devalued. I have called the ways of knowing that characterize System B 'subjugated ways of knowing' (Boyce-Tillman, 2000-a).

There is an inextricable relationship between the individual and the society in which s/he lives. Theories of personality like the inventory of the Myers-Briggs Type Indicator (Myers and McCaulley, 1985; Myers, 1980/1993) classifies personalities in terms of types and shows that it is possible to identify certain individuals as Type A, that is, those who are happy acting on logic and scientific reasoning, which are part of System A. Others can be called Type B and will favour System B, acting intuitively and valuing belief and magic. It is clear that the Type A people will feel more at ease than Type B in Western society. Type B people are more likely to exhibit signs of disease and, indeed, to be classified as 'abnormal' by the surrounding society than Type A. However, Type A people will also have the Type B characteristics within themselves and these will require exploration to achieve a fully rounded humanity. Similarly, Type B people can use the prevailing values in the culture to develop the less favoured aspects of their personality. This serves to highlight the relationship between the individual personality and society and the roots of some human dis-eases.

Western society has embraced one set of values. Other value systems exist that are reflected in other cultures. These are sub-jugated within Western culture (Foucault/Gordon, 1980). Indi-viduals also have a preference for a particular way of knowing, although all the ways of knowing exist within the human psyche. In a society where the individual's way of knowing is in tune with that of the wider society, the person is more likely to be seen as well-adjusted and will suffer less stress and dis-ease.

Healing as balance

From the literature on creativity and therapy certain themes emerge, and it is from these that I have drawn the list of 16 polarities that make up the dynamic model of the self in society as shown in the following model (see Figure 1).

These polarities are drawn as having a constant flow between them. Redemption/healing is defined as being when that flow

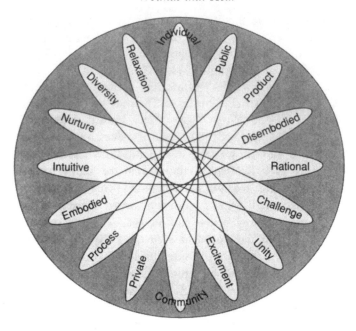

Figure 1 The dynamic model of the self in society

is restored to fluidity and dynamism. The subjugated and dominant knowings have to be in dialogue with one another to achieve a wholeness. The dominant culture will validate one of the poles more highly than the other so effort will be required to keep the flow moving to the subjugated way of knowing. When the balance is achieved, the self or the society will have developed the new paradigm of self and society searched for by such writers as Donna Haraway (1992), Chela Sandoval (2000) and Chris Clarke (2002). In the following sections I shall examine what happens when this dynamism is broken and how music might restore it.

This is a theory based on Hildegard's theology of virtue (Boyce-Tillman, 2000-b). Hildegard sees virtue and vice inextricably linked, the vice being a twisted form of the virtue. So we have a theology of music and healing based on a right relationship between dominant and subjugated values – the establishment of a creative flow. This, for me, is part of the process of redemption for the self and the culture, and the following sections will deal with both as they are intertwined. For the purposes of this chapter, I shall only deal with some of the polarities seen in the above model, and it might be worth bearing in mind that I have already dealt with Disembodiment/ Embodiment in my introduction.

1 Effecting transformation – Unity/Diversity

'Behold I am making all things new', says God in the Book of Revelation (21.5), and this is picked up in Christian notions of redemption. All descriptions of creativity, and in particular its processes, include a measure of chaos or darkness – a time when the whole appears to fragment before it re-establishes itself again in a different configuration (cf. Wallas, in Vernon (ed.), 1970). So the flow between these two polarities produces creativity.

The Cartesian view of the unified, separated self has been central to the project of Western rationalism. It was attached to a notion of a steady march towards wholeness that was often equated with the 'light' both of the Christian Scripture and the Enlightenment project as a whole, in such hymns as:

> Thou whose Almighty Word
> Chaos and Darkness heard
> And took their flight.
> (John Marriott, in *Hymns Ancient and Modern*, 1983, p. 395)

Here we see the images of order, light and truth inextricably linked. Feminist theology has problematized such thinking (cf. Ward and Wild, 1995), while liberation theologians have also been taken up with how this view perpetuated the more violent aspects of social policy and imperialism. And so we see tolerance and normalization in tension rather than flow. The end of the binary split is Fascism, which is a perfectly unified society, obliterating diversity sometimes by means of destroying diversity. The risk of the supremely tolerant society is that it will slip into anarchy. The free flowing between these polarities produces a creative and innovative society.

The tolerance of diversity is an important element in the way a community defines itself. The tightness of the boundaries established by a particular society is a product of the degree of threat that is seen either from without or, more significantly, from within. And yet it is by the admitting of diversity that new societies and new ways of conceiving society have emerged. When the two poles of unity and diversity are balanced in a society, a society can grow and change creatively. The process of readjusting this balance can be seen in a post-apartheid South Africa, where musicians have played a part in this process. For example, in 1992, West Nkosi released a CD entitled *The Rhythm of Healing* that brings together a variety of different musical traditions from all over the country. Many other musicians have engaged in peace-making projects to contain diverse elements respectfully within musical structures. For example, Yair Dalal in Israel, and my own pieces, *The Healing of the Earth* (2001-b) and *Peacesong* (2006). These contain spaces where people can include their own music or performance, either made up or developed from their own cultural traditions.

The notion of the integrated self underpinned Jungian psychotherapy. Yet there is a rhythm of integration and deintegration. Psychologists like Thomas Fordham have challenged this, suggesting that the process of living is one of deintegration and reintegration (Jennings, 1999, p. 45). In a society that had a different value system there might be better-constructed systems for understanding and handling this diversity, as in spirit possession cults. Here diversity is applauded and regarded as a 'special' sign. The acceptance of neo-shamanism within the New Age reflects an increasing ability to accept differing frames of reference for states once considered 'sick'. What is interesting in the descriptions of the shamanic crisis is that death and rebirth are central. In traditional societies this was regarded as very real. It was experienced as part of a journey within the context of a society with established practices and procedures for handling this process of transformation. On the other side of this process, the shaman is a 'new' person. It is interesting to reflect on how this 'crisis' is viewed in Western medicine. Here there is a notion of preventing the crisis happening, as there is no established notion of a spiritual dimension to the 'sickness'. But the characteristics of such crises in the mentally sick are often suicidal thoughts and attempts. It is interesting to reflect that such thoughts and desires for death may be transformative desires that could be dealt with by a ritual or symbolic death. In the absence of a shared religious framework it is possible to construct rituals involving music that is transformative.

But in Western societies at a personal level, the pursuit of the integrated self and the perception of the journey as being a straight and steady progress have resulted in a certain internal Fascism, which we may describe as rigidity or, indeed, obsession. The pattern of the self is a cyclical exploration of deintegration and reintegration. Because of the high premium placed on integration, deintegration is frequently pathologized. A classic example is the grieving process. When a loved person, animal or object disappears, the integration of the self is that which has integrated with that person, animal or object in a particular place. When they disappear, the self has to deintegrate in order to reintegrate with a previous part missing. In former times days were given for this process to happen, and people were protected from the demands of ordinary life to give them time to grieve, which is the process of deintegration. Now the requirement that life go on as normal (when it clearly is not) means that when the self cannot stay integrated the process is pathologized, with the result that the person is now sick for a longer time and the self has huge problems in reintegrating – which it would do quite naturally given time and support. I have found in my workshops that the acceptance of multiplicity within the self can be an experience of great freedom. The work of the philosopher Gillian Rose looks at it from a slightly different angle and includes the notion of working in what she calls 'the broken middle', which has within it the necessity of living with the contradictions:

> In the middle of imposed and negated identities and truths, in the uncertainty about who we are and what we should do. . . . She [Gillian Rose] commends us to work with these contradictions, with the roaring and the roasting of the broken middle, and to know that it is 'I'. (Tubbs, 1998, p. 34)

This process of working with the broken middle can be facilitated by music. Most musical forms allow for juxtaposition and simultaneous combination; it therefore can accommodate difference and differing degrees of unity. These can even be sung or played simultaneously and can be part of the process of reforming the person; the acceptance of the more hidden aspects of the personality leads to a 're-membering' of the person. It is in this area, par excellence, that people can transform negativity into a creation of worth and value, both for themselves and for others. (In Beethoven's sketchbooks, for example, we have a record of Beethoven wrestling with the process of 're-membering' himself.)

These processes importantly involve a descent into the personal unconscious or subconscious with a somewhat chaotic nature – a personal underworld. This is part of the process of deintegration. This process is used in music therapy in its use of improvisatory techniques. This enables people without musical training safely to enter into this process of self-transformation. The ability to enter that chaos, with tools for handling it, would seem to be what differentiates the experienced composer or music therapist from the less experienced musician or music therapy client.

> What we need is to fumble around in the darkness because that's where our lives (not necessarily all the time, but at least some of the time, and particularly when life gets problematical for us) take place; in the darkness, or, as we say in Christianity, 'the dark night of the soul'. It is in these situations that Art must act and then it won't be judged Art but will be useful to our lives. (John Cage, cited Ross, 1978, p. 10)

The process of listening can enable the listener to participate in this process as listeners are called to enter into the processes of the performer and composer. The listener shares the journey and is reassured by the fact that another person has been into that chaotic place that they are experiencing. In listening we can be taken into a different world by a composer/guide who guides us through it musically. When we listen, for example, to the slow movement of Beethoven's fourth piano concerto with its bringing together of two very contrasted elements within his self, we enter into Beethoven's experience; in so far as his journey is akin to ours we can share it and use it for our own transformation. The composer together with performer becomes a therapist, who like the ancient shamans has entered the underworld on behalf of the wider community. This is illustrated in the therapy called Guided Visualization to Music, which uses pieces of classical music to guide clients through their own underworld.

The process of creation is a process of transformation. Within this process lies the possibility of redeeming the damaging experiences of the past into objects of beauty and making them new.

2 Into Acceptance – Public/Private

'You are called by my name you are mine' says God (Isaiah 43.1), and this process of acceptance is a crucial part of the healing process. At present, in the West we are in a situation where certain people – so-called celebrities – are always public (even the most intimate parts of their lives), while certain people are completely private – the homeless, the differently abled, the criminals, to name but a few. Those 'in the public eye' will be valued by means of high salaries; the others may receive nothing. And yet for each person there needs to be a balance between public and private and the knowledge of when to speak and when to be silent is a sign of maturity.

So we have a society where in some situations, like therapeutic ones, confidentiality is absolute. In situations that are abusive or inappropriately coercive in some way, this becomes twisted into an enforced secrecy, and people are deliberately silenced. Free expression is often prized as an important value system of the West, but out of balance with an appropriate privacy it leads to enforced or indecent exposure. The stress on calmness and order in Western society has not encouraged public expressions of grief, and traditions like keening and wailing were suppressed by the Church early in Western culture. These used a wide range of human vocalizations in a ritual manner to express the grief of a community.

Within the self there are introvert and extravert tendencies, even if one may appear dominant. A knowledge of when it is appropriate to speak and when to be silent is a sign, as I have said, of maturity. The introvert who fails to keep in touch with his/her extravert self becomes phobic; while the continual extravert can lose all touch with the more hidden part of his/her self.

The Western literature on music and creativity stresses the area of self-expression. This can be seen as the making of the private public, and so represents the establishing of a mature flow between the polarities. It is often linked with human emotion. Traditions of word-based psychotherapy have developed ways of accessing deep areas of feeling and painfully traumatic experiences, but they can leave people with difficult memories allied to powerful feelings, such as anger and despair, without much guidance as to what to do with them. Not only does music offer the possibility of expressing these but also of remaking them into an aesthetically satisfying object. Ray Charles confirms this in his own use of song; 'I'd like to think that when I sing a song, I can let you all know about the heartbreak, struggle, lies and kicks in the ass I've gotten over the years for being black and everything else, without actually saying a word about it' (cited Moore, 1986/1992, p. 123). The process of acceptance by a group creates a growth in maturity and this can be expressed in a variety of ways. Applause is one, and supportive discussion another. So music becomes a mature way of expressing private trauma publicly.

There is considerable debate about the precise meaning of music, where this is situated and how it is communicated. There is clearly an element of cultural and personal interpretation in the process of decoding music. Within a piece of music there is not only the meaning encoded by the creator – implicit meaning – but also meaning that has been locked on to a piece by particular circumstances in our lives – explicit meaning. An example of the latter is the phenomenon of 'they're playing our tune' – a melody that has been associated with a particularly emotional moment. This makes it, by definition, a confidential medium as well as being expressive. It is a 'veiled' medium. Particularly in instrumental music the meaning is not specific, the original events/emotions are veiled with a diaphanous cloak of unclear meaning that both reveals them and hides them simultaneously. As Lévi-Strauss writes, 'music is the only language with the contradictory attributes of being at once intelligible and untranslatable' (Lévi-Strauss, 1970, p. 18).

Because of the phenomenon of explicit meaning, music can also be used to unlock painful and pleasant areas of memory. I was using Baroque music to calm a person who loved Bach. As I played her Bach's so-called *Air on a G String* she screamed.

It was the piece of music that had been playing when she was abused. This overrode the implicit meaning in the music. No other person can know what memories are locked onto a piece by another. Sometimes the person themselves is not aware. However, because of the personal aspect of meaning, it requires more than a degree of sensitive tuning on the part of the participants and a more careful choice of material by the leader. Both leader and participants need to play a part in the choice of pieces, which will have different meanings for different people in any given group.

Music has huge potential for making the private public in a way that still remains confidential, so joining the polarities of public and private and enabling people to find acceptance for the most difficult emotions. The process of public acceptance is potentially transformative and reflects Jesus' acceptance of a wide variety of people within his ministry.

3 Gaining empowerment – Challenge/Nurture

'The glory of God is all human beings fully alive', says Irenaeus.[3] Western society is challenging. The greatest financial rewards are given to those able to meet and set the challenges for those who will fall at the hurdles without some degree of nurture. The standard attainment targets of our school systems in the UK are a case in point. The challenge of competition has now eaten into every sector of Western culture. The capitalistic market is based on a philosophy that competition necessarily produces the best solution. And yet when the two are in balance there is a sense of growth, development and empowerment.

Unfortunately, separated from nurture, challenge produces destruction as all sense of connectedness is systematically destroyed. Care separated from competition produces atrophy and the separation of those who need care from those who can withstand competition has left many of the elders of our society atrophying in old people's homes without the challenges posed by association with other generations or the wider society.

However, when well balanced, challenge and nurture together lead to empowerment and the two work in tandem, especially in person-centred models of learning. The learning of musical skills is often part of the challenge. There are many areas where

241

singing can be seen as empowerment, sometimes linked with the immune system. Estelle Jorgensen (1996), in a powerful article bringing together Paolo Freire's 'Pedagogy of Hope' with the role of the artist in society and education in the arts, high-lights the role of the itinerant singing masters in empowering the poor and the women in eighteenth-century society (an early example of liberation theology). These delivered the only formal education open to people from otherwise disenfranchised groups, especially women and girls who were excluded from much music-making in the churches and communities. She claims that the nineteenth-century political movements, which encouraged the inclusion of music in the school curriculum of the emerging state-supported schools, were inspired by the work of these singing schools.

However, in the name of music education in a normalizing curriculum we have sometimes cheated people out of their birthright to sing by the use of false challenges. The map of singing as presented in the average school is one of a restricted range of pitches and tone colours. We all have our own note, the note that is easiest for us to sing at any time. And this is variable. It changes at different times of the day. Our voices are often low in the morning, rise to the middle of the day and then sink as we get more tired. Some would also say that there is a seasonal component (a yearly cycle) as well. There are also certain staging points in our lives, points that once would have been marked by rites of passage. The male voice changes at puberty, but so does a girl's, and a woman's changes again at the menopause. Also, a trauma of some kind can be reflected in the pitch that is related to our sense of identity. In school in the UK, if you had a choirboy-type sound and a fairly high pitch, you succeeded in singing classes. If your tone-colour was dark and your pitch low, it was, in general, unacceptable (Boyce-Tillman, 1996, p. 215). What you needed was someone to accept your note and then you could develop other notes from it. If this did not happen, you might, when you left school, have been singing your note for some eleven years but it would never have appeared on the map presented by your teachers. You could be forgiven for saying that you could not sing, and even worse, that you were not musical; the truth was that the map of singing that was presented to you was too small. The task of the leader of singing is to find a pitch acceptable to a group, not choose one from pitched instruments like the piano.

When people have found their singing power they can use it in their darkest moments. From the El Mozote massacre in El Salvador in 1981 comes the remarkable story of a young girl, an evangelical Christian who was raped several times in one afternoon. Through it all she sang:

> She had kept on singing, too, even after they had done what had to be done, and shot her in the chest. She had lain there on La Cruz [the hill on which the soldiers carried out their killings] – with the blood flowing from her chest and had kept on singing – a bit weaker than before, but still singing. And the soldiers, stupefied, had watched, and pointed. Then they had grown tired of the game and shot her again, and she sang still, and their wonder turned to fear, until they had unsheathed their machetes, and hacked her through the neck, and at last the singing stopped. (Danner, 1994, pp. 78–9)

I met a nun who felt overwhelmed by her work in a community that concerned itself with violations of human rights. After the course in which she had sung some of her songs she said to me, 'I know what I had forgotten; I had forgotten to sing. If I remember to sing I can survive the stories that our community is receiving and even transform them in some way.' There are many accounts of the relation of music, healing and spirituality. This one from a woman in 1970 shows a healing miracle during a hymn: 'After the address came the hymn "All hail the power of Jesus' name". During the singing of it I felt the power of God falling upon me. My sister felt it too, and said "Floie, you're going to walk". The Lord gave me faith then' (RERC Accounts of Religious Experience, 0001301).

The polarity of nurture is connected with the handling of vulnerability. Referring back to the process of deintegration described above, the skill of the therapist is in knowing how to hold the deintegrated parts until they are ready to re-form. Music is a way of holding. (I was able to hold a man telling his story of childhood abuse by means of a steady drumbeat. I also used a repeated drumbeat very softly under a heated discussion that threatened to break up. The attitude of confrontation changed and the group was able to function again.)

243

The lullaby is an area where traditionally children have been held musically. In child rearing there have been indications of the possibility of children taking on the songs sung to them by their parents as comforters, rather like teddy bears and comfort blankets. On a visit to Gugulethu, South Africa, I was present at a service where people could come forward for healing. They told the pastor their problem. He relayed this to the congregation. The congregation then sang to support the healing. What was interesting here was that the songs were not the soft gentle sounds that we associate with the nurturing of the New Age, but strong louder pieces accompanied by drumming patterns made on hymnbooks. The greater the need, the greater the strength of the singing of the thousand people present. The song transmits loving holding through its power.

Giving musical skills through music education of some kind can improve people's independence. I arranged music lessons for four children diagnosed with chronic anxiety as part of a treatment programme in conjunction with Winchester Child Guidance Unit. The acquisition of drumming skills by one participant enabled him to become a 'normal' teenager playing in a band and at ease with his peers who had previously bullied him (Walker and Boyce-Tillman, 2002).

To summarize, through the right balance of challenge and nurture music can contribute to personal growth and allow people both individually and corporately to claim their power. However, in a society based on challenge there may need to be some stress of the nurturing role to enable people to overcome past negative musical experiences.

4 Transforming relationships – Community/ Individualism

The need of human beings for community in Western society is to be found in many sources today – political, psychological, religious, to name but a few. The relationship between the individual and the community has been expressed in different ways in different cultures. If the role of the community is paramount there will often be a certain conservatism in the society, often maintained by the elders, and a less clearly defined

Star

24 HOUR PRIVATE HIRE
CAR & MINIBUS SERVICE

0800 622 6611
0121 373 1111

718 CHESTER ROAD B23 5TE

| Customer's Name | Date | Time |
| SAPPHIRE | 13.9.17 | 15:00 |

| PICK UP |
| MARYVALE HOUSE |
| GREAT BARR |

DESTINATION	TOTAL FARE
BIRM NEOS ST	£10.00
STATION	

| Driver's Code | Signature |
| 323 | J. Hollis |

f LIKE US Star Cars & Coaches Ltd

🐦 FOLLOW US @StarCarsCoaches

Manage your bookings online at
www.starcarsbirmingham.com

Next time,
why not book
via our app
and have
your receipt
emailed to
you?

Search "Star Cars"
in your app store or
scan the QR code
below to install the app.

view of the individual self (Floyd, 1993). In societies with individualism prominent there will be a greater stress on freedom and innovation. And yet when we know who we are and where we belong in relationship we achieve an identity.

The legacy in the UK of the Thatcher years is one of fragmentation and an excessive emphasis on the individual. But it is a process that started with the Enlightenment and its rediscovery of the epic of the heroic journey. The male hero narrative (based on the *Odyssey* and *Aeneid*) is of one who asserts his individuality and 'finds himself' through the undertaking of a journey. The heroic journey was not open to larger numbers even of Western civilization – the poor and women, to name but two groups. In a society where the polarity is splitting apart, responsibility will start to lose contact with personal freedom. It may be that certain groups of people will be scapegoated for the ills of society or certain people will take on the roles of being responsible. It is often women in the West who suffer from a sense of over-responsibility. When the polarity is finally split, community can only be maintained by the coercive forces of law enforcement, and the state and its authorities will be regarded as oppressive of personal liberty. This will correspondingly be maintained by personal rights litigation. So the relationship between the two will be maintained by external forces rather than by the internal maturity of the individuals.

The individual experiences the pressures of the dominant culture in different ways. The dominant knowers in Western society will see personal liberty as of supreme importance and abrogate responsibility or see it as not part of their role. The subjugated knowers will be burdened by a sense of over-responsibility and its contiguous guilt, often feeling trapped in situations that they feel they are unable to escape. When the split of the polarity finally occurs, the dominant knower will become isolated and aggressive, sensing a complete loss of any connection with the wider community that deep down s/he knows is necessary for his/her well-being. We see this phenomenon in young people turning weapons on their peers in school. The subjugated knower will lose any sense of boundaries and be overwhelmed by the burden of guilt and anxiety. The result will be pathologized anxiety, leading to self-harm.

In the establishment of humanism at the Enlightenment, human beings became alienated from the natural world – or indeed superior to it. This resulted at best in a patronizing stewardship and at worst domination and outright rape. Many people are seeing the possibilities of including connection with environment as a therapeutic tool for people trapped in the splitting of this polarity. All music-making using instruments involves human beings in contact with the natural world. It is one of the most intimate relationships human beings have with the environment other than eating it. In traditional societies a drummer would reverence the tree and the animal that gave the material for his/her drum. We need to re-establish this reverence in relation to instruments in our Western fragmented culture.

The balancing of these poles and the ability to move with ease between them results in an identity rooted in membership of various communities. Words divide but sounds unite. The task of words is to distinguish one group of objects or people from another, to further divide them into subsets and then into individual objects or persons by detailed descriptions of individual names. When a group of people makes music together their unity is restored. The chief loss resulting from the decline of Western Judaeo-Christian theology in our culture may not be the theology but the whole community coming together once a week to make music. No Sunday morning DIY activity done often by a single person in an individualized dwelling can replace the community-building power of the hymn or worship song.

The Western classical tradition had a notion of community that included the cosmos and, in particular, God or gods up to the Renaissance. During this period, notions of healing through the creation of community were widely found. Post-Enlightenment, the heroic journey model gained prominence with the individual composer set over and perhaps against the community. The individual performer has often suffered from a hot-housing process (Kemp, 1996, p. 248), and we have lost the value of community music-making. Sonia Gergis, a North London music teacher, ran a 'Music in Harmony' festival. For this, the youngsters (and they were mostly young and included the so-called recalcitrant teenagers) could only enter in a group. There were no soloists. The result was a tremendous quality of co-operation. It was good to see piano duet teams and accompanying pianists developing their skills in sensitivity. They were learning to tune their music to other people, learning how to get their rhythms together, to blend their tone-colours, to tune their notes to one another, to support others in difficulty rather than compete with them. Such an initiative and rise of community-making offers significant ways for people to find an identity, with membership of a community a significant part of it. People are now forming musically a variety of networks that serve to give them cultural roots, and there are many stories of groups like the Jews and the black slaves that have survived unbelievable hardships by means of a sense of community created by song. One of the significant challenges for contemporary society is the establishment of an identity that includes community, and this can be achieved through music.

Summary

This chapter has set out a model of how to rebalance the system using music as healing. The music produced is a record of the process of healing – it is part of the process of redemption of the cosmos. Music offers the possibility of transformed and strengthened living. There is a beautiful Jewish story:

> A ruler had a fine diamond. It became seriously damaged. All the best jewellers were consulted to see if they could restore it to its former glory. None could do it. Eventually a jeweller came along who claimed that it could be made better than it was before. The court were astonished. After weeks of work, it was found that the jeweller had engraved around the flaw the most beautiful rose; and the place of the damage was now the place of the greatest beauty. (Source unknown)

Music is the sounding form of the rose.

> From the struggle of the individual to retain their own identity and yet belong to the community for whom connection is the lifeblood,
> from the broken middle of contradictions in the midst of the self and society,
> from the desire to rest from challenge and to free oneself from a stifling nurture,

from the reconciliation of the ineffability of the mystic experience
with the human body in its strength and weakness,
comes the music, as wounded selves in a wounded culture seek to
right their wrongs and turn them into objects of beauty.

These are indeed:
the wounds that sing.

Notes

1 Tatman links contemporary women's attempts at self-mutilation
with a desire for wholeness and at-one-ment. She looks at the
disconnection of the 'self' from the body as a result of abuse and
the person's need to feel something rather than nothing, which is
resolved by self-inflicted pain. Although she is anxious to distance
herself from notions of a transcendent deity and a separate identi-
fiable self, nonetheless she develops a concept of 'whole enough' in
relation to this alienation of the body (Tatman, 1998).
2 Unpublished conversation with an undergraduate at King Alfred's
College, 1992.
3 *'Gloria Dei vivens homo'* (Adv. Haer. IV, 20, 7)
<www.cin.org/jp2/jp961130.html> (accessed 12 June 2006).

References

Argyle, M., *Psychology and Religion*. Routledge, London and New York,
2000.
Boyce-Tillman, J., (1996) 'Getting our Acts Together: Conflict resolu-
tion through Music', in Liebmann, M. (ed.), *Arts Approaches to Conflict*.
Jessica Kingsley, London, 1996.
Boyce-Tillman, J., *Constructing Musical Healing: The Wounds that Sing*.
Jessica Kingsley, London, 2000-a.
Boyce-Tillman, J., *The Creative Spirit: Harmonious Living with Hildegard
of Bingen*. Canterbury Press, Norwich, 2000-b.
Boyce-Tillman, J., 'Sounding the Sacred: Music as Sacred Site', in
Ralls-MacLeod, K. and Harvey, G. (eds), *Indigenous Religious Musics*.
Scolar, Farnborough, 2001-a, pp. 136–66.
Boyce-Tillman, J., *The Healing of the Earth*. The Hildegard Press,
London, 2001-b.
Boyce-Tillman, J., *Peacesong*. Hildegard Press, London, 2006.
Clarke, C., *Living in Connection: Theory and Practice of the new world-view*.
Creation Spirituality Books, Warminster, 2002.
Danner, M., *The Massacre at El Mozote*. Vintage, New York, 1994.

Doyle, B., 'Introduction to the Songs', in Fox, M. (ed.), *Hildegard of Bingen's Book of Divine Works, with Letters and Songs.* Bear and Co., Santa Fe, 1987, pp. 364–5.

Exley, H. (ed.), *Music Lovers Quotations.* Exley, Watford, 1991.

Floyd, M., 'The Trouble with Old Men', paper given at a research seminar at King Alfred's College, 1993.

Foucault, M. with Gordon, C. (ed.), *Power/Knowledge: Selected Interviews and Other Writings 1972–77.* Harvester Wheatsheaf, Hemel Hempstead, 1980.

Gooch, S., *Total man: Towards an Evolutionary Theory of Personality.* Allen Lane, Penguin Press, London, 1972.

Haraway, D., 'The Promises of Monsters: A Regenerative Politics for Inappropriate/d Others', in Grossberg, L., Nelson, C., Treichler, P. A. (eds), *Cultural Studies.* Routledge, New York, 1992, pp. 295–337.

Hay, D., *Exploring Inner Space.* Penguin, Harmondsworth, 1982.

Heyward, C., *Speaking of Christ: A Lesbian Feminist Voice.* Pilgrim Press, New York, 1989.

Hymns Ancient and Modern. New Standard, Full Music Edition. Canterbury Press, Norwich, 1983.

Jantzen, G. M., *Power, Gender and Christian Mysticism.* Cambridge University Press, Cambridge, 1995.

Jennings, S., *Introduction to Developmental Play Therapy: Playing and Health.* Jessica Kingsley, London, 1999.

Jorgensen E., 'The Artist and the Pedagogy of Hope', *International Journal for Music Education.* No. 27, 1996, pp. 36–50.

Kemp, A. E., *The Musical Temperament.* Oxford University Press, Oxford, 1996.

Lévi-Strauss, C., *The Raw and the Cooked.* Weightman, D. and J. (tr.), Cape, London, 1970.

Moore, D., *Off beat; Dudley Moore's Musical Anecdotes.* Robson Books, London, 1986/1992.

Myers, I. B., *Gifts differing: understanding personality type.* Consulting Psychologists Press, Palo Alto, California, 1980/1993.

Myers, I. B. and McCaulley, M. H., *Manual: a guide to the development and use of the Myers-Briggs Type Indicator.* (2nd edn), Consulting Psychologists Press, Palo Alto, California, 1985.

Nkosi, W., *The Rhythm of Healing.* National Sound Archive 1CD004251, 1992.

RERC Accounts of Religious Experience, held at the Religious Experience Research Centre, Lampeter University, Wales.

Ross, M., *The Creative Arts.* Heinemann, London, 1978.

Sandoval, C., *Methodology of the Oppressed.* University of Minnesota Press, Minnesota, 2000.

Tatman, L., 'The Yearning to be Whole-Enough or to Feel Something Not Nothing: A Feminist Theological Consideration of Self-Mutilation as an Act of Atonement', *Feminist Theology*. Vol. 17, 1998, pp. 25–38.

Tubbs, N., 'What is Love's Work?', in *Women: A Cultural Review*. Vol. 9, No.1, October 1998, pp. 34–46.

Walker, J. and Boyce-Tillman , J., 'Music Lessons on prescription? The impact of music lessons for children with chronic anxiety problems', *Health Education – The Arts and Health*. Vol. 102, No. 4, 2002, pp. 172–9.

Wallas, C., 'The art of thought' (1927), in Vernon, P. (ed.), *Creativity*. Penguin, Harmondsworth, 1970, pp. 91–7.

Ward, H. and Wild, J., *Guard the Chaos: Finding Meaning in Change*. Darton, Longman & Todd, London, 1995.

13

Dramatherapy at Holy Rood House: telling a new story

ROGER GRAINGER

It is commonly accepted, although often neglected, that the arts enrich human life in an unparalleled way. However, as Roger Grainger points out, the arts are not merely an enriching experience. Rather, they are essential to the well-being of personal and cultural identity. This is particularly the case with theatre and dramatherapy, where both individuals and communities learn to face the truth of their predicament, their strengths and vulnerabilities, in a safe, because boundaried, way. Here Grainger describes that process as a sort of 'spiritual "pilgrims progress"', as a healing journey towards transformation and hope.

* * *

I would like in this chapter to try to explain why my contribution to the life of Holy Rood House centres around dramatherapy. I think it needs explanation, because drama is associated with some very negative feelings in people's minds, and the people who come to Holy Rood are often very sensitive. Dramas taking place in one's own life are inherently frightening, as are those witnessed in theatres, although in a rather different way; and the business of playing an active role in this second kind of drama may be downright terrifying.

So – why dramatherapy at Holy Rood House? Or even, why drama*therapy* anywhere at all? The answer is, because drama and theatre specialize in saying things that are both hard to say, and benefit from being said. They help us create a new story about ourselves, one that is both more honest and more faithful.

Theatre is founded upon the human truth, that people are nervous about, and *of*, one another. The corollary to this, of course, is that the more vulnerable we ourselves are, the more vividly we experience others as *less* vulnerable than ourselves. Theatre is intended to be a place where nervousness of this kind – what we are accustomed to call 'anxiety' – can somehow be put on hold. Theatre uses the 'suspension of disbelief' in order to achieve the suspension of nervousness. Someone has to break the ice for this to happen, of course. Someone has to go on stage themselves, and by saying 'Let's all pretend, shall we?' (in one way or another), has to set about the business of revealing true things about being human while managing at the same time not to be blamed for it; not having to carry the can for their own humanness.

'Keep me as the apple of an eye, hide me under the shadow of your wings' (Psalm 17.8); however expressed or embodied, the need for security remains intrinsic to being human. Holy Rood House is a living icon of this fundamental truth. In every bedroom here, there is a notebook for people to write things down about their stay, if they should feel like doing so: 'I was lost and frightened – you have helped me find myself again'; 'Peace here, when I never expected to find it anywhere'; or simply, 'Thank you, Holy Rood!'

To get back to theatre and dramatherapy. Theatre itself is best described in terms of a kind of game that people make arrangements to play together (Scheff, 1979; Grainger, 2006). In dramatherapy, any distinction between theatre and playing games is reduced to a minimum. To develop this idea a bit further – theatre is a game that knows it is one and celebrates the knowledge among its participants as something consciously shared, as distinct from the kind of interpersonal situational manoeuvring described by Erving Goffman as 'the presentation of self in everyday life' (Goffman, 1971), where the game has usually to be played whether or not we happen to like playing it. This is not to say that this game need not be taken seriously. It is a serious statement of what life is like, a way of using life to speak about itself. 'Take this as fiction, and you miss the point', says a character in the seventeenth-century Classical French tragedy, *Le Véritable Saint Genest* (Jean de Rotrou, 1646). In the same way, dramatherapy is basically serious; as serious as the children's games it sometimes resembles. Like them it is committed to the purpose of using imagination in the service of truth and of enjoying doing so.

Serious joy and serious pain – in theatre as in life the two go together. At Holy Rood House, when we do dramatherapy, we make up our own plays. To give an example, here is a short drama about the coming of spring, which a group of us put together (once we felt we had got to know one another a little better through playing a game involving an imaginary balloon that each of us had to keep aloft without letting anyone else steal it from us):

ACT 1 – all seven of us huddled together under a table, wearing as many pieces of clothing as we could lay hands on – heavy sweaters, baggy trousers, multiple pairs of gloves, scarves over our faces, woolly hats etc. Lack of space to move kept us almost motionless apart from the occasional twitch.

ACT 2 – then one by one we clambered out and sat round the table that had been imprisoning us, hugging ourselves to keep warm. Someone offered someone else something to eat. People rubbed hands and feet, their own and each other's, because it was colder out here than it had been huddled together under the table. Most of the time, however, we just sat like statues; then somebody got up from the table and went across to stare out of the window. To everyone's alarm, she started to open it.

ACT 3 – in the fresh spring air that was rushing into the room, we found ourselves starting to revive. It was a real window she had opened not an imaginary one, and the impact on the group was amazing: people got up from the table and began unwrapping themselves and moving their arms and legs to get them going again. Shouting with delight, we ran out into the space where the audience would have been sitting.

The play ended with all of us joining hands and dancing round the table. When we talked about what we had created together, and had quietened down somewhat – there was a good deal of laughing and congratulating – we reflected on whether our play might perhaps have been about more than just changes in the weather conditions. Perhaps it had something to do with the things that had come up for us at the very beginning of the dramatherapy session, when people in the group had been sharing together some of their personal problems, difficulties and sorrows – the things that had brought them to Holy Rood House in the first place. Our drama had been both an experience of present distress and future hope, and a commentary on the particular circumstances obtaining at Holy Rood House, where people with their own private grief are brought together into very close contact with one another and find that somehow they can share their privacy and lessen its hold on them in a way they would normally never have dreamt of doing. After all, doing drama like this isn't 'normal'. People consider acting to be a very specialized skill, a particular talent not given to everybody. We may spend a good deal of our time 'putting on an act', both for ourselves and other people (and that is normal!), but we don't do it publicly in the sense of admitting that we're doing it. For one thing, most of us don't think we have the skill to be performers of this kind, and even if we had, it isn't something we feel we can do under such circumstances, when our *real* role is to be guests in a 'house of healing' – somewhere we have come in order to be looked after rather than challenged! If emotionally vulnerable people are going to be somehow helped 'to feel stronger', then Holy Rood House is certainly an ideal setting because of its atmosphere of acceptance and understanding; it does feel like somewhere you can at least try to relax.

So it is not very surprising that when a session of drama-therapy is announced over lunch at Holy Rood House, people say that they are interested in attending, but actually need quite a bit of persuading; even then, they often say, 'Well, I'll come, but I'll just watch if you don't mind. I'm not an actor, you see.' 'Of course you can come and observe', I say; and they do, and before long they are joining in with everyone else, drawn into whatever is going on by things that they recognize – 'Yes, that's happened to me too' – opportunities to express themselves they didn't know they wanted. In this approach to psychological healing the drama emerges *almost by itself*, from the sharing of thoughts and feelings, ideas and images, which happens when people are encouraged to feel at ease with one another so that they begin to relax and play games; and when it comes, it isn't directly 'about me,' but 'about what we were all talking about'. Certainly 'I myself' does figure in the action, either as actor or spectator, but it is by implication and not by direct exposure; and, as everyone knows who has ever been to see a play, there's an important difference.

The arts therapies – art, music, dance/movement and drama – use the language of art in order to speak indirectly about life.

Because their approach is poetic rather than direct, they can say things that are not otherwise easy to listen to, things filtered out by our native defensiveness. This means that they are capable of a directness that goes beyond plain speaking. As Aristotle says, playing with life in the way that drama plays with it is very far from trying to avoid it (Butcher, 1951). Theatre was never intended as an alternative to engagement with other people, but as a way of making contact with aspects of our shared experience that we would rather steer completely clear of, but that nevertheless require to be taken very personally – not least, the sheer reality of other people experienced as both a comfort and a threat to the self. For those who find other people potentially oppressive (and for all of us, to the extent that we are capable of finding them so), dramatherapy holds out a very specific promise of relief.

Somehow, art manages to be real and imaginary at the same time (Courtney, 1981). Glancing at some notes I made after a recent dramatherapy session at Holy Rood House I came across the following: Freud describes a small boy who manages to cope with the absence of his mother by continually throwing away a wooden reel he has tied to the end of a piece of string so that he can no longer see it, and then tugging it back to make it reappear (Freud, 1923, p. 56). In this way internal dangers – abandonment, frustration and loss – are projected onto the external world and 'practised' there, in order to be reintegrated within awareness in a way that permits a degree of control by the subject. The anxiety itself is a mixture of fantasy and reality; in other words, it resembles theatre. In playing, anxiety is aroused specifically in order to be mastered. Play, like dreaming, 'develops the anxiety whose omission was the cause of a traumatic neurosis' (Freud, 1923, p. 236) – in other words a realistic, and therefore necessary fearfulness.

Ideas about distance and safety play a crucial role in psychotherapy. Distance (as distinct from mere space) always involves structure; we are always distant from something or someone, and if we are to make contact then this must be overcome: no distance, no contact. Although this is so obvious – *because* it is so obvious – it tends to be overlooked. The relationship between distance and proximity becomes one-sided because of our eagerness to evolve structures for establishing

255

some kind of psychological continuity within our shared experiences. Our aim is to ignore or even cancel out 'between'.

And yet, as Erikson points out, our identity depends on 'a mutuality of recognition', of 'separateness transcended' and 'distinctiveness confirmed' by the presence of the 'primary Other' as this is expressed in interpersonal rituals (Erikson, 1985, pp. 43–5). In his early work Martin Buber – the writer associated most closely with the notion of betweenness in personal relationships – wrote vividly about theatre. He stressed the fact that the way to involve the audience in the world of the play was by preserving theatrical distance, the 'over against of I and Thou' (Buber, 1957, p. 66). The 'I–Thou' or 'I–You' relationship is one in which I allow you to be your own subject, the subject of your world rather than an object within mine. This involves me in a personal gesture, a definite action of moving 'out and away' from myself in order to meet you as someone who is *not* myself, so bridging the gap between us by recognizing its existence; something I must do in order to permit you to be really *you*. As Rollo May points out, this way of perceiving other people involves a whole attitude of mind towards them; it is something belonging to the very nature of human consciousness: 'Consciousness is defined by the fact that it intends something, points towards something not itself – specifically, that it *intends the object*' (May, 1972, p. 226).

All this has great significance for dramatherapy. The awareness associated with I–Thou is essentially reflexive: it is my awareness that I am just as much the object of your intention, the recipient of your gesture, as you are of mine. From the point of view of the actual therapeutic intervention this is obviously easier said than done; even 'person-centred' Rogerian psychotherapy remains, from Buber's point of view, an 'I–It' intervention aimed at reducing the person to something understood rather than genuinely encountered. Buber suggests that we are engaged in continually creating ourselves at the contact boundary between self and other. The health of our personality depends, he says, upon the quality of this contact, its reality as a true meeting with our environment of people and things.

Neurosis, on the other hand, involves a reaching for contact that doesn't really achieve what it sets out to do – usually because we have trained ourselves to make do with relationships

that are not genuine *encounters*, in which aspects of our awareness of our self are made to stand in for real meetings with the
reality that is not us. For example, the various defensive strata-
gems described by psychodynamic psychology are all ways of
protecting oneself against the two things that are the hallmarks
of an authentic meeting of persons – freedom and flexibility.
Thus Gestalt therapy describes how, in cognitive terms, contact
involves awareness of a perceptual foreground experienced as
possessing meaning for the self. Or, as Mackewn puts it, 'Awareness
is the holistic process of contact with and withdrawal from
others in the field' (Mackewn, 1997, p. 113).

Thus our capacity for being 'in touch with' other people
depends on our ability to withdraw from immediate psychological contact with them as well as focusing on their presence.
We need to feel safe enough to be able to do both these things;
and some forms of psychotherapy – notably Gestalt – aim at
establishing alternative opportunities for contact with reality
'outside' the self, using dramas and games to give shape and
meaning to our conscious interactions with other people.

The action of playing a game is revealing in itself: word games,
mime games, action games, games inventing things. To play a
game, 'only a game', can be the best way of establishing betweenness, because in games we have to keep our distance and to
share at the same time acceptance and enjoyment of the other
person as themselves, the actual, lived appreciation of their
otherness; being able sometimes to suspend the urge to understand others solely in terms of our own well-established ideas
and assumptions; leaving space for insight and intuition by
approaching things from a new angle; letting the way someone
plays a game (any kind of game) reveal things that we wouldn't
ordinarily allow ourselves to see, and that they perhaps have
difficulty showing us; revealing ourselves to someone else
without embarrassment; being able to talk with other people
about an experience you've all just been sharing – these are all
things we associate with games. Erik Erikson speaks of 'the life-
long power of human playfulness' (Erikson, 1985, p. 77); and
Donald Winnicott showed that the right kind of game is the most
effective antidote for fear (Winnicott, 1980).

The need for playing underlines the fact that confrontation
with pain is the fundamental reality of, and reason for, theatre.

For those who are oppressed by the burdens and failures of living, theatre can be the very best kind of playing: any kind of theatre, not just comedy. The ancient Greek actors wore masks, but these are not really necessary, for the person being played disguises the actor's own actual identity without any need for further protection. All the same, masks serve to illustrate the root principle of theatre, which is that of using fiction to reveal fact. This kind of disguise is acceptable to everyone, actors and audience; indeed, its necessity must be recognized by both parties in the agreement for it to have any chance of working at all. Thus audiences know that their business is with the personages of the play, and that any ideas expressed or emotions aroused are not to be taken as the personal responsibility of the actors playing the parts, whose job of communication is carried out on behalf of the author and producers of the play (although they may of course criticize them for agreeing to take part in it!).

In this sense, the play functions as a release from the pressure of responsibilities pressing down upon us from the world outside the theatre. First of all we make a bond with everyone involved to 'suspend our disbelief' in whatever it is that will be taking place among us in this particular place for this particular period of time. Having done this, we – actors and audience – agree to take seriously the personages of the play, in the sense of becoming imaginatively involved in their experience as if it were our own. By doing this we are relieved of some of the emotional pressure of which we are normally conscious by virtue of being alive under the conditions of the world apart from these special circumstances. The fundamental task of theatre, then, is to set current reality at a distance and to offer us an alternative one that we may feel free to accept or reject. If we find that we would like to accept it, and still feel the same way on leaving the protected area of the theatre, then we can allow our ongoing lives to be influenced by our experiences within the play. This applies to audience and cast alike.

It is not only in theatres that people wear masks. It is only in the theatre – and in theatre-like situations – that the need for them may be publicly admitted, and their essential purpose of reducing ontological anxiety recognized for the blessing it is. Their action is not only to protect, however, but also to liberate. Once assumed, disguises may be *exchanged*. When this happens the mask's symbolic nature changes; it becomes a token of relationship, a pledge of the gift of self to other.

In the drama described earlier, the actors muffled themselves up in heavy clothing that both protected them and also expressed their painful nakedness and vulnerability; the result was a powerful statement about 'matters too deep for words'. But dramatherapy is not always so dramatic. Like other forms of therapy it works at different levels. Here at Holy Rood House the approach is mostly gentle, almost tentative, as befits somewhere that the wounded take refuge. Sessions begin reassuringly and end reflectively. Only in the middle is there any kind of challenge to participants' emotional status quo. This is the usual course of events with regard to dramatherapy. The session itself has a definite shape, so that those involved can register it as an event in itself, complete with a beginning, a middle, and an end – identified as a happening by whatever it is that takes place at its heart, the action to which both beginning and end refer, and from which the whole derives its meaning.

The central part of a dramatherapy session establishes it as an existential exploration of a specially embodied kind. Anxiety and self-consciousness characterize the first stage, but the therapist's main attention is concentrated on this middle movement, when things associated with our pain are played out among us – something that can only happen once the game-like nature of the proceedings has been established. Then, in the last part, things move into gentler waters, and there is a sort of homecoming – a feeling of peace. Things people have said stick in my mind:

- I only came to the session because my friend persuaded me. When I arrived I almost walked out, but then I felt drawn in somehow.
- I started to follow the others. Some of the things we did struck a chord, although I didn't know why. As a matter of fact I still don't.
- It was worth coming. If I come again I may find out what it was all about. Oh yes, I do have a kind of inkling!

Holy Rood provides opportunities for a great deal of this kind of shared experience of self-and-other discovery. Dramatherapy – of various kinds – is going on here all the time, without people knowing it. My job is to make it more self-aware;

not *self-conscious*, but more like what happens in theatre. The connection with actual theatre is not usually as obvious as it was in the example described at the beginning of this chapter, however. Most of the time we concentrate on devising the right kind of game, the kind that has the potential for development within the life of the house, tapping into a deeper and more personal significance within the ongoing life of those involved. At what point does the event lose its game-like nature and the drama move into therapy? This is not easy to determine. For my part, it is when the features of a game that distinguish the way I'm playing it from my experience of life outside its limits – characteristics of control over outcomes and skill in performance, dimensions I myself contain as distinct from the ungraspable totality that contains us – begin to become less restrictive and inclusive than they were before, and I find myself able to bring wounded parts of myself (or parts I discover to be wounded) into the space where the game allows real contact to happen. As someone who had experienced dramatherapy at Holy Rood House once said, 'Suddenly it wasn't the same at all. Suddenly it wasn't just a game, only a bit of fun, a way of filling in time. Suddenly it was *really about me* – who I was, who I am. More to the point, and perhaps because of this, it gave me something I think I can use when I leave here, something I'll be able to return to when I need it, as I know very well I probably shall do. An active feeling of peace.'

Everything I have been saying up to now adds up to this: dramatherapy is an experience, not an argument; a life-enhancing event, not an idea. It is an event embodying an idea, realizing it in a story that becomes part of our own ongoing life story, where it subtly and powerfully affects the way we see ourselves and our world; the way we tell ourselves to ourselves. This is why it takes place in three stages, with a beginning, middle and end, so that it may symbolize something achieved, projecting our life experience as a real event, an authentic story about reality.

Dramatherapy – like liturgy itself – involves us in a spiritual 'pilgrim's progress', in which we pass *through* experiences of change and renewal instead of merely thinking *around* them. Even when things get in our way, it retains its identity as the metaphor of spiritual journeying, the threefold shape of the rite of passage in which divine perfection is expressed in the language of place and time spoken – inhabited rather – by human beings. Even to set out in this direction, to glimpse the vision far off, is life-enhancing, because it expresses willingness to participate in the living iconography of spiritual transformations and to receive validation through sharing in the affirmation of a transcending hopefulness (cf. Grainger, 1995).

The nature of Holy Rood House itself, a place dedicated to healing whole persons, makes it a particularly privileged setting for this kind of psychotherapy.

References

Buber, M., *Pointing the Way*. Routledge, London, 1957.

Butcher, S. H., *Aristotle's Theory of Poetry and Fine Art*. Dover, New York, 1951.

Courtney, R., 'Aristotle's Legacy', *Indiana Bulletin*, 2, 3, 1981.

Erikson, E., *The Life Cycle Completed*. Norton, New York, 1985.

Freud, S., *The Ego and the Id*. Hogarth Press and the Institute of Psychoanalysis, London, 1923.

Goffman, E., *The Presentation of Self in Everyday Life*. Penguin, Harmondsworth, 1971.

Grainger, R., *The Glass of Heaven*. Jessica Kingsley, London, 1995.

Grainger, R., *Healing Theatre: How Plays Change Lives*. Trafford, Victoria, 2006.

Mackewn, J., *Developing Gestalt Counselling*. Sage, London, 1987.

May, R., *Love and Will*. Collins, London, 1972.

Scheff, T. J., *Catharsis in Healing, Ritual and Drama*. University of California Press, Berkeley, 1979.

Winnicott, D. W., *The Piggle*. Penguin, Harmondsworth, 1980.

14

An invocation of healing: Hölderlin's 'Patmos'

ANDREW SHANKS

Of the threefold task of Christian ministry – the proclamation of the Word, the administering of sacraments and the delivery of pastoral care – it is perhaps the proclamation of the Word, what Walter Brueggemann calls the 'daring speech of proclamation', that is most in need of renewal. After all, without the Word, that imaginative transformation of language into flesh, both the sacraments and pastoral care can be reduced to pragmatic meanings. Taking up this challenge, Andrew Shanks introduces and translates the poem 'Patmos' by Friedrich Hölderlin, arguing that here we find 'a direct therapeutic antithesis to the usual clichés' of Christian hymnody when it comes to expressing the sickness, danger and sacredness of life. By arguing thus, Shanks' chapter serves as a final flourish to this book, encouraging us to face the sickness of both our culture and ourselves with renewed verve and imagination.

* * *

'What's the use, in lean years, of a poet?' So Hölderlin asks in his great elegy 'Bread and Wine' of 1800.[1] He means 'lean years' in a spiritual sense: a period of history in which what one might call the spirit of prophecy is culturally stifled. That is to say, when the prevailing forms of religious life have become imaginatively impoverished, and no longer foster any very inspiring creativity. Or when real artistic creativity appears to be largely confined to the secular sphere alone.

This was how he saw his own age. He considered it to be an age of catastrophic cultural sickness, in this sense. And no doubt he would pass the same verdict on our twenty-first century world as well.

Of what use are poets, in such a context? First and foremost, it would seem, for Hölderlin their prophetic calling is just to *register* the sickness here, as the sickness that it. truly is. In the Hölderlinian ideal poet, so to speak, the objective sickness of the culture as a whole is to become a subjective personal sickness; so generating a therapeutic, sheer intensity of yearning to be healed.

His own great poetry is very much a product of extreme mental disturbance. It was all produced in a brief period of six years, between 1797 and 1803; after which the pressure simply became too great. Three years later, at the age of 36, he was forcibly interned in the pioneering Autenrieth psychiatric clinic in Tübingen, where they believed in cages, forcible immersions in cold water, the straitjacket and a specially designed mask to prevent screaming; after a year of which, he was discharged as 'incurable', to drag out the remaining 36 years of his life as a docile broken man. In so sick a world, it seems, so oversensitive a soul could not for long retain sufficient sense of his own 'usefulness' to be sane.

'What's the use, in lean years, of a poet?' Hölderlin himself essentially dedicated his poetry to a prophetic lament, over the 'leanness' of the 'lean years'. He does so by constructing a myth. His myth speaks of a lost golden age, it is a mythic idealization of Ancient Greece. The Ancient Greeks, he suggests, had a religious culture that essentially celebrated the most free-spirited artistic creativity. Here were sacred practices that engaged the imagination of a whole people, all equally, in the most vivid way; but in which, also, the true poet could feel altogether at home. And so, back then, the earth was – as it were – openly inhabited by gods. The whole point of this myth, however, lies in the contrast with the Christian present-day, the sickness with which Hölderlin is preoccupied; both the sickness of the culture as a whole and his own personal sickness, he articulates precisely as god-forsakenness, in these terms.

And yet, he is not just a poet of cultural nostalgia. At the age of 18 he had been sent to train as a prospective Lutheran minister at the seminary in Tübingen. The following year saw the outbreak of the French Revolution, and he was one of those onlookers who were seized with a tremendous enthusiasm for what was unfolding in Paris. This enthusiasm mixed with his growing revulsion against what he felt to be the sheer staleness of the establishment-church culture within which he was being trained. But then came the Jacobin Terror. At the same time, the Revolutionary regime launched its own post-Christian civil religion. Hölderlin himself started to write neo-classical hymns that might be used in the liturgy of such a cult – until, at length, he was overcome by dismay at the accompanying violence. Recoiling from the Terror, he was in a certain fashion reconverted to Christian faith. The lesson he drew from the events in France was that after all, no matter how stale an established religious culture may have become, in so far as it still has genuine roots in a people it needs to be cherished; not impatiently rejected, as the Jacobins rejected church-Christianity, but revived. And therefore he sought to integrate the worship of Christ into his myth of the gods' departure. He speaks of Christ as the last of the gods to go; and the first, hopefully, one day to return.

This somewhat eccentric poetic Christology is set out, above all, in his poem 'Patmos', the first version of which, translated below, was completed by January 1803. It was then presented to the Landgrave Friedrich of Hessen-Homburg, one of Germany's smaller principalities, on the occasion of the Landgrave's fifty-fifth birthday.

The Landgrave was Hölderlin's patron, a conventionally devout Lutheran, author of several pamphlets denouncing Enlightenment irreligion and its Jacobin consequences, who had asked for a poem in that general spirit. (In fact, he had originally tried to commission the venerable poet Klopstock for the purpose; Hölderlin was only a substitute after Klopstock declined.) It is the Landgrave who is respectfully addressed in the penultimate strophe. But notwithstanding this flattery, one may well wonder just how he will have felt about the resultant work!

Hölderlin's poetry, one might say, is essentially a systematic protest against devout cliché, as such. And so the problem he sets himself is this: how still to remain absolutely devout, even while abandoning all the usual assistance of cliché? The poem begins with the famous lines: 'So near / The god is, so elusive. / But yet beside danger grows / That which saves.' The antique Greek phrase, 'the god', immediately establishes a certain distance from the clichés of conventional Lutheran piety. As for the 'danger' in question, it soon becomes clear that this is what derives from the acute inner isolation of the prophetic poet, in a largely god-forsaken culture where the sacred is concealed by cliché. The prophetic poet is isolated as one to whom 'the god' has, by way of exception, drawn near, beyond all cliché. But this presence remains 'elusive': the culture provides no adequate support in comprehending it, learning to live with it, coping with its exorbitant demands. Hence the 'danger' of being overwhelmed, as a result.

Nevertheless, this is also the source of salvation. And there follows a prayer, couched in Alpine imagery, for solidarity among kindred free spirits, as in a shared baptism. 'Wings' are mentioned – and suddenly the poet is swept up, away into the air, on a dream-like cartoon journey. Hölderlin was from Swabia, in southern Germany. But here he is carried, in the spirit, away from Swabia to what was once Greek Asia Minor; where we glimpse the river Pactolus, famous for its gold, and the mountains Tmolus, Taurus and Messogis. Then, the next thing we know, he is in a boat crossing the Aegean to the island of Patmos.

Patmos was of course the island on which John the author of the Revelation was granted his great vision of the coming end of time. However, in Hölderlin's day it was simply assumed that there was only one significant New Testament John; that the author of the Revelation was the same John who also wrote the fourth Gospel and its two accompanying Epistles; and that this was the apostle John, the 'beloved disciple'. Hölderlin's poem is premised on that belief. John, here, is in effect an ideal symbolic representative of truthful Christian poetry in general; the island landscape of Patmos is a symbol for the special atmosphere of Christian poetry.

But the thought of poetry, for Hölderlin, is also immediately associated with Dionysus, the wine god, and hence with 'the rites of the vine'. Thinking of John, his mind therefore turns straight away to the consecration of wine at the Last Supper, which then leads him into a meditation on the gospel as a whole. 'Patmos', above all, is the work in which Hölderlin sets out fundamentally to rethink the gospel story, in relation to his own protest-myth.

Having become as it were Ancient Greek, Christ is playfully referred to as 'the Demi-God'; and is linked, not only to Dionysus, but also to Apollo, as the sun god. There is none of the conventional polarization of conflict between Christian and non-Christian, as such, in this version of the gospel, and certainly no church-triumphalism. Everything is, on the contrary, pervaded with a quite unconventional melancholy. Hölderlin's turning to Christ was, essentially, a turning away from Jacobin rage. He is still tempted by the revolutionary anti-Christian hubris that drove the Jacobins; and at a certain point in the poem this temptation takes on human form, as a companion on the road. But he is resolute in humble resistance to the goading of this gloomy companion. Indeed, the whole poem is none other than an exercise in such resistance. Thus, Hölderlin confronts the god-forsakenness of his world, but refuses either to rage or despair. Instead, he recognizes the purgative, long-term educational value, to humanity at large, of divine withdrawal. And so resigns himself to its providential necessity, after all. 'What's the use, in lean years, of a poet?' On the one hand, in short, the poet's calling is to register the spiritual sickness of the age in all its true gravity. On the other hand, it is a calling to keep the faith in a properly chastened spirit of patience.

Translations vary, partly because of the different priorities with which translators approach the task. In producing the English version of 'Patmos' that follows, I have put an especially high priority on *incantatory flourish*. It is in fact one of a number of free-flowing poems that Hölderlin himself called 'patriotic songs', and I have tried, so far as possible, to accentuate the 'song' quality of the work. His editors have traditionally categorized these poems as 'hymns'. 'Patmos' is certainly a very odd Christian hymn – most hymns are so cliché-ridden! But here is one that is indeed, quite precisely, intended as a direct therapeutic antithesis to the usual clichés.

It goes something like this:

Patmos

For the Landgrave of Homburg

So near,
The god is, so elusive.
But yet beside danger grows

That which saves.
In the dark dwell
The eagles and fearless,
On flimsy bridges, the sons of the Alps
Cross the torrential abyss.
There, heaped up all around, stand
The summits of time, and friends dearly loved
Are in trouble, close by. But
On quite separate slopes.
So, now, give us chaste water.
And wings – O, give us wings – for the high soaring
Loyalty needed to traverse the chasms.

So I was praying – when,
With astonishing speed,
A genius swept me
Up and away, further from home than I'd
Ever before thought to go! In the twilight,
As I shot past, there glimmered
The shadowy woods
And the fierce yearning streams
Of my childhood; places I no longer knew.
Soon, though, fresh and radiant,
In the mysterious
Aureate haze,
With stride after stride of
The sun, suddenly looming, land
Of a thousand sweet-scented peaks,

There, dazzling, before me, bloomed Asia.
And I – as a stranger, and mapless,
Amidst those great roadways
Where golden-flecked Pactolus flows
Down from Tmolus,
And Taurus stands, and Messogis, and,
A quiet cauldron of flowers, the garden –
Sought for landmarks; and saw shining,
In the thin air, silver snow;
And, witness to life everlasting,
On lost crag-top walls
Primeval ivy; and cedars and laurels,
Live pillars, upholding
The festive,
God-designed palaces.

And many, indeed, are the murmuring roads
At Asia's gates,
Criss-crossing vast tracts,
Here and there, of shadowless sea.
Not that the boatman is lost; he knows his islands.
But when I heard
That amongst them, near at hand, one
Was Patmos,
I instantly wished,
As a pilgrim, to land there
And see the dark grotto.
For, lacking sweet springs
Such as Cyprus, say, has,
Patmos, alas, is
Arid and poor,

Yet is a place
Of open-doored
homeliness.
And when a stranger appears,
Shipwrecked perhaps, or exiled,
Or, maybe, newly
Bereaved,
She's glad, and her children – the voices
That fill the shimmering grove,
And, where the sand falls, where the soil
Cracks apart, those sounds –
The spirits, they hear him, and tenderly
Add their lament. And so, once, she bade welcome
That seer, the belovéd
Disciple, who in his youth

Had walked arm in arm
With the thunderous Son of the Most High.
Chosen because he was guileless,
And sharp-eyed; he who, not least, had so closely
Observed that look on the face of the God
When, sat together at dinner, they shared
In the rites of the vine, and, serenely aware
Of what was to come, the ever magnanimous Lord
Spoke of death, in fulfilment of love. Always in search,
As He was, of fresh means
To communicate kindness, and to soothe, where
He saw it, the rage of the world.

For all shall be well. And then – then He had died. Much
Might be said about this. And, at the end, the friends saw Him
Gazing, jubilant, upwards in triumph,

Yet they were sad, now that
Dusk was upon them, and greatly
Perturbed, for, though their callings were weighty indeed,
Yet, under the sun, these men were lovers of life.
Nor could they bear to be wrenched from
The Lord's earthly countenance,
And from their homeland. Their souls
Were a passage of fire into iron; they walked
With His shadow always beside them.
And therefore He sent them
The Spirit. Whereupon, the house shook –
As, with a menacing flourish, God's weather
Rolled in, and, deep in thought,
With heads bowed, they gathered together,
The heroes, in anticipation

Of death; whilst He,
Now, having made his final
Post-mortem farewells – now, He
Majestically put out the sun. And
Snapped asunder the straight beam.
The sceptre. Sovereign, yet sorrowful;
Biding His time, before
All is renewed. For it would have been wrong
To delay, but unjust, at a stroke, to cut short
The work of the church; yet, what a joy,
From now on,
To dwell in love's darkness, and to grant, glinting, those
Deep-delving insights, in the contemplative's
Disciplined eyes. And there is plenty,
Even low down on the mountain, to gladden the soul.

But, still, it is dreadful, this
Habit of God's, to scatter us creatures apart.
For they'd made double sure
Of the heavenly Spirit's
Decree, they well knew that they each had their own
Lonely roads they must go,
Out there in the world,
They were ready for that; but, truly, it shocked them,
For a moment their hair stood on end, when,

As He hastened away, the God – of a sudden –
Glanced back, one last time.
And they, yearning
To keep Him, now that they knew what real loss was,
Reached out their hands to each other,
And vowed golden vows, like so many rope-knots –

Yet, when He goes and dies,
He, round Whose beauty,
Beyond all compare, the angels
Had gleefully spun; when those once united
By what they remembered
Now shrink back apart, forgetting
For ever, it seems, how, truly, to love
One another; when it's not the sand
Only, not only the willows, the wind whips away,
But also the temples are going;
When the Demi-God's honour dissolves,
And that of His friends; when the Highest
Himself turns aside
From a world in which
No immortal appears, any more, either up in the skies
Or down on the fertile earth: what is this?

It is the Winnower's cast, when he scoops up
The wheat with His shovel
And flings it out, clear, swinging it over the floor.
The husk falls at His feet, but the grain
Is released and flies free.
And if in the process some should be lost,
Or if the live sound of eloquent speech
Should possibly fade – well, never mind;
For God's work, just like ours, must advance
By degrees. And meanwhile
The pit bears its iron,
And Etna its red-hot resins,
So I should have plenty
To work with, to make me an image
Of Christ, as he was, here on earth.

Yet – just in case, now, a tempter should come
And catch me off guard, as we walked on the road,
    with sorrowful words,
So that, slave as I am, I was in this
Goaded to blasphemous folly –

An invocation of healing: Hölderlin's 'Patmos'

Let me confess: all I, with these eyes, ever saw
Was a vision of wrath. I have nothing to boast of. But have
Simply been warned. They wish us well, up above, but,
As rulers, what they abhor is pretension. And then
The consequent loss, amongst human kind, of true
   human-kindness.
For it's not we, not we mortals, who rule,
But we're subject to fate. Whereas, what they decree
Moves of its own accord, swift to its end.
Yes, and when, through the clouds, the Saviour ascends
In triumphal procession, rejoicing,
Then they'll acclaim Him, the strong ones, name Him

The Sun-God. Oh, and see here the sign:
The conductor's wand, waving him down!
For nothing's too mean. So He wakens the dead;
All whom corruption will spare,
He liberates them. And there's no lack
Of eyes waiting, craving
His gentle light. Petals curled up,
Out of the glare, now.
Like mettlesome steeds, God holds them in check.
But when (as it were) their gaze
Becomes shadowed in thought,
And undistracted,
Graced by, and reflecting, the scriptures' luminous peace,
They may be glad of the chance,
Thereby given, to thrive.

And if, as I hope, Heaven
Looks with some favour on me,
How much more favoured,
Surely, are *you*! For are you not known
As one who fears God?
Even now – these drab days.
Yet, though the skies are tight shut, still the watchman
Remains. Christ sticks to His post.
He has inspired – His children have done – so much
That's heroic; so many books have been written about Him;
Such events we have seen in the world –
Lightning bolts all around us,
An unstoppable tumult. But, still, He is there. For, from the
   beginning
He knew what His chosen course meant.

271

And we've waited too long. For far too long now
The heavenly glory's been veiled.
And our fingers so clumsy, they have to be
Guided. And our hearts
Ignominiously pawned.
Every aspect of truth demands to be
Honoured; if any's neglected,
It's always a mischief.
Mother Earth we have served,
And, lately, Enlightenment also.
Albeit, naively. But what above all
The sovereign Highest requires
Is, simply, a love for solid tradition. Plus
Proper care in reading the signs of the times.
German poets – let's stick to the task!

Note

1 'Brot und Wein', strophe 7: 'wozu Dichter in dürftiger Zeit?'

References

For the German text, see:
Adler, J., (ed.), *Friedrich Hölderlin: Selected Poems and Fragments*. Penguin, Harmondsworth, 1998; also contains a translation by Michael Hamburger.

Other translations are to be found in:
Constantine, D., *Friedrich Hölderlin: Selected Poems*. (2nd edn), Bloodaxe, Newcastle, 1996.
Sieburth, R., *Hymns and Fragments by Friedrich Hölderlin*. Princeton University Press, Princeton, NJ, 1984.

CPSIA information can be obtained at www.ICGtesting.com
Printed in the USA
BVOW011130180313

315797BV00022B/924/P